*Economic Management and the
Division of Powers*

This is Volume 67 in the series of studies commissioned as part of the research program of the Royal Commission on the Economic Union and Development Prospects for Canada.

This volume reflects the views of its author and does not imply endorsement by the Chairman or Commissioners.

Economic Management and the Division of Powers

Thomas J. Courchene

Published by the University of Toronto Press in cooperation with the Royal Commission on the Economic Union and Development Prospects for Canada and the Canadian Government Publishing Centre, Supply and Services Canada

University of Toronto Press
Toronto   Buffalo   London

Grateful acknowledgment is made to the following for permission to reprint previously published and unpublished material: Australian National University; *Bank of Canada Review*; Ian Bushnell; *Canadian Banker*; *Canadian Public Policy / Analyse de politiques*; Dataline Inc.; Holt, Rinehart and Winston of Canada Ltd.; Macmillan Publishing Co., Inc.; Minister of Supply and Services Canada; Professor Robert Mundell, University of Waterloo; Wallace Oates; Ontario Economic Council; Jacques Parizeau; Queen's University, Institute of Intergovernmental Relations; Louis Rasminsky; Strategic Planning Group; University of Manitoba, Institute for Social and Economic Research.

©Minister of Supply and Services Canada 1986

Printed in Canada
ISBN 0-8020-7315-8
ISSN 0829-2396
Cat. No. Z1-1983/1-41-67E

CANADIAN CATALOGUING IN PUBLICATION DATA

Courchene, Thomas J., 1940 –
Economic management and the division of powers

(*The Collected research studies / Royal Commission on the Economic Union and Development Prospects for Canada,*
ISSN 0829-2396 ; 67)
Includes bibliographical references.
ISBN 0-8020-7315-8

1. Canada — Economic policy. 2. Federal government — Canada. 3. Canada — Constitutional history. I. Royal Commission on the Economic Union and Development Prospects for Canada. II. Title. III. Series: The Collected research studies (Royal Commission on the Economic Union and Development Prospects for Canada) ; 67.

HC113.C68 1985   338.971   C85-099637-6

PUBLISHING COORDINATION: Ampersand Communications Services Inc.
COVER DESIGN: Will Rueter
INTERIOR DESIGN: Brant Cowie/Artplus Limited

CONTENTS

HC
113
.C68
1986

When the members of the Rowell-Sirois Commission began their collective task in 1937, very little was known about the evolution of the Canadian economy. What was known, moreover, had not been extensively analyzed by the slender cadre of social scientists of the day.

When we set out upon our task nearly 50 years later, we enjoyed a substantial advantage over our predecessors; we had a wealth of information. We inherited the work of scholars at universities across Canada and we had the benefit of the work of experts from private research institutes and publicly sponsored organizations such as the Ontario Economic Council and the Economic Council of Canada. Although there were still important gaps, our problem was not a shortage of information; it was to interrelate and integrate — to synthesize — the results of much of the information we already had.

The mandate of this Commission is unusually broad. It encompasses many of the fundamental policy issues expected to confront the people of Canada and their governments for the next several decades. The nature of the mandate also identified, in advance, the subject matter for much of the research and suggested the scope of enquiry and the need for vigorous efforts to interrelate and integrate the research disciplines. The resulting research program, therefore, is particularly noteworthy in three respects: along with original research studies, it includes survey papers which synthesize work already done in specialized fields; it avoids duplication of work which, in the judgment of the Canadian research community, has already been well done; and, considered as a whole, it is the most thorough examination of the Canadian economic, political and legal systems ever undertaken by an independent agency.

The Commission's research program was carried out under the joint direction of three prominent and highly respected Canadian scholars: Dr. Ivan Bernier (*Law and Constitutional Issues*), Dr. Alan Cairns (*Politics and Institutions of Government*) and Dr. David C. Smith (*Economics*).

Dr. Ivan Bernier is Dean of the Faculty of Law at Laval University. Dr. Alan Cairns is former Head of the Department of Political Science at the University of British Columbia and, prior to joining the Commission, was William Lyon Mackenzie King Visiting Professor of Canadian Studies at Harvard University. Dr. David C. Smith, former Head of the Department of Economics at Queen's University in Kingston, is now Principal of that University. When Dr. Smith assumed his new responsibilities at Queen's in September 1984, he was succeeded by Dr. Kenneth Norrie of the University of Alberta and John Sargent of the federal Department of Finance, who together acted as Co-directors of Research for the concluding phase of the Economics research program.

I am confident that the efforts of the Research Directors, research coordinators and authors whose work appears in this and other volumes, have provided the community of Canadian scholars and policy makers with a series of publications that will continue to be of value for many years to come. And I hope that the value of the research program to Canadian scholarship will be enhanced by the fact that Commission research is being made available to interested readers in both English and French.

I extend my personal thanks, and that of my fellow Commissioners, to the Research Directors and those immediately associated with them in the Commission's research program. I also want to thank the members of the many research advisory groups whose counsel contributed so substantially to this undertaking.

DONALD S. MACDONALD

At its most general level, the Royal Commission's research program has examined how the Canadian political economy can better adapt to change. As a basis of enquiry, this question reflects our belief that the future will always take us partly by surprise. Our political, legal and economic institutions should therefore be flexible enough to accommodate surprises and yet solid enough to ensure that they help us meet our future goals. This theme of an adaptive political economy led us to explore the interdependencies between political, legal and economic systems and drew our research efforts in an interdisciplinary direction.

The sheer magnitude of the research output (more than 280 separate studies in 70+ volumes) as well as its disciplinary and ideological diversity have, however, made complete integration impossible and, we have concluded, undesirable. The research output as a whole brings varying perspectives and methodologies to the study of common problems and we therefore urge readers to look beyond their particular field of interest and to explore topics across disciplines.

The three research areas, — *Law and Constitutional Issues*, under Ivan Bernier; *Politics and Institutions of Government*, under Alan Cairns; and *Economics*, under David C. Smith (co-directed with Kenneth Norrie and John Sargent for the concluding phase of the research program) — were further divided into 19 sections headed by research coordinators.

The area *Law and Constitutional Issues* has been organized into five major sections headed by the research coordinators identified below.

- Law, Society and the Economy — *Ivan Bernier and Andrée Lajoie*
- The International Legal Environment — *John J. Quinn*
- The Canadian Economic Union — *Mark Krasnick*

- Harmonization of Laws in Canada — *Ronald C.C. Cuming*
- Institutional and Constitutional Arrangements — *Clare F. Beckton and A. Wayne MacKay*

Since law in its numerous manifestations is the most fundamental means of implementing state policy, it was necessary to investigate how and when law could be mobilized most effectively to address the problems raised by the Commission's mandate. Adopting a broad perspective, researchers examined Canada's legal system from the standpoint of how law evolves as a result of social, economic and political changes and how, in turn, law brings about changes in our social, economic and political conduct.

Within *Politics and Institutions of Government*, research has been organized into seven major sections.

- Canada and the International Political Economy — *Denis Stairs and Gilbert Winham*
- State and Society in the Modern Era — *Keith Banting*
- Constitutionalism, Citizenship and Society — *Alan Cairns and Cynthia Williams*
- The Politics of Canadian Federalism — *Richard Simeon*
- Representative Institutions — *Peter Aucoin*
- The Politics of Economic Policy — *G. Bruce Doern*
- Industrial Policy — *André Blais*

This area examines a number of developments which have led Canadians to question their ability to govern themselves wisely and effectively. Many of these developments are not unique to Canada and a number of comparative studies canvass and assess how others have coped with similar problems. Within the context of the Canadian heritage of parliamentary government, federalism, a mixed economy, and a bilingual and multicultural society, the research also explores ways of rearranging the relationships of power and influence among institutions to restore and enhance the fundamental democratic principles of representativeness, responsiveness and accountability.

Economics research was organized into seven major sections.

- Macroeconomics — *John Sargent*
- Federalism and the Economic Union — *Kenneth Norrie*
- Industrial Structure — *Donald G. McFetridge*
- International Trade — *John Whalley*
- Income Distribution and Economic Security — *François Vaillancourt*
- Labour Markets and Labour Relations — *Craig Riddell*
- Economic Ideas and Social Issues — *David Laidler*

Economics research examines the allocation of Canada's human and other resources, the ways in which institutions and policies affect this allocation, and the distribution of the gains from their use. It also considers the nature of economic development, the forces that shape our regional and industrial structure, and our economic interdependence with other countries. The thrust of the research in economics is to increase our comprehension of what determines our economic potential and how instruments of economic policy may move us closer to our future goals.

One section from each of the three research areas — The Canadian Economic Union, The Politics of Canadian Federalism, and Federalism and the Economic Union — have been blended into one unified research effort. Consequently, the volumes on Federalism and the Economic Union as well as the volume on The North are the results of an inter-disciplinary research effort.

We owe a special debt to the research coordinators. Not only did they organize, assemble and analyze the many research studies and combine their major findings in overviews, but they also made substantial contributions to the Final Report. We wish to thank them for their performance, often under heavy pressure.

Unfortunately, space does not permit us to thank all members of the Commission staff individually. However, we are particularly grateful to the Chairman, The Hon. Donald S. Macdonald; the Commission's Executive Director, J. Gerald Godsoe; and the Director of Policy, Alan Nymark, all of whom were closely involved with the Research Program and played key roles in the contribution of Research to the Final Report. We wish to express our appreciation to the Commission's Administrative Advisor, Harry Stewart, for his guidance and advice, and to the Director of Publishing, Ed Matheson, who managed the research publication process. A special thanks to Jamie Benidickson, Policy Coordinator and Special Assistant to the Chairman, who played a valuable liaison role between Research and the Chairman and Commissioners. We are also grateful to our office administrator, Donna Stebbing, and to our secretarial staff, Monique Carpentier, Barbara Cowtan, Tina DeLuca, Françoise Guilbault and Marilyn Sheldon.

Finally, a well deserved thank you to our closest assistants: Jacques J.M. Shore, *Law and Constitutional Issues*; Cynthia Williams and her successor Karen Jackson, *Politics and Institutions of Government*; and I. Lilla Connidis, *Economics*. We appreciate not only their individual contribution to each research area, but also their cooperative contribution to the research program and the Commission.

IVAN BERNIER
ALAN CAIRNS
DAVID C. SMITH

Economic management is an essential criterion in any analysis of federalism. Does the division of taxation and spending authority, for example, allow governments to carry out their economic responsibilities effectively? Is the process whereby powers are reallocated sufficiently flexible to be able to adapt to new economic and political circumstances?

Canadian federalism has been both roundly condemned and unstintingly praised on these scores. Critics have seen federalism as the root cause of many of our economic problems, although often for quite different reasons. To some, the fragmentation of political authority has hamstrung efforts to develop effective national policies on everything from labour relations to foreign ownership, at great cost to the country. To others, however, the considerable leeway the federal government enjoys in the economic sphere has allowed it to distort local social and economic development priorities, and has generated an undue amount of regional alienation.

Other analyses have been kinder. They point out that expectations of government are very different today from 1867, when the Constitution Act was written. Not all new demands upon government are compatible with the existing divisions of power and authority, but constitutional reassignments, however pursued, are seldom achieved. The genius of the Canadian federal system, it is argued, lies in its ability to substitute de facto constitutional changes for actual ones, generally through the medium of federal-provincial fiscal arrangements but in other ways as well. Thus, federalism has enhanced rather than detracted from the task of economic management. We have usually managed to have the proper level or levels of government involved.

This monograph by Thomas J. Courchene focusses directly on the issue of federalism and economic management. It asks whether our ability to manage our economic affairs would be enhanced by a division of powers different from what we have today. Courchene first sets out a conceptual framework to address the question. He then looks at six particular areas of policy concern: equalization, social policy, monetary policy, fiscal policy, capital markets, and the internal economic union. In each case the object is to ascertain whether problems, where they exist, stem from constitutional design faults or simply unwise policy selections.

His conclusion leans toward policy selection. He finds some fault with the Constitution, and some instances where redesign could play a role. In general, though, Canadian federalism receives good grades. We have been able to adapt the Constitution to the times, in practice if not always in strict legal terms. The credit in this respect goes largely to the constantly evolving system of intergovernmental fiscal arrangements.

KENNETH NORRIE

ACKNOWLEDGMENTS

It is a pleasure to acknowledge the encouragement and guidance that I received in writing this monograph. My greatest debt is of course to those whose role it was to oversee this project — initially David Smith and later Ken Norrie. Other commission staff, particularly Richard Simeon and Mark Krasnick, also played an important role in terms of project design and comments on the material. The list of persons who have commented on various parts of the monograph or provided valuable insight would include Gérard Bélanger, Richard Bird, Keith Banting, Rodrigue Tremblay, François Vaillancourt, John White, Ivan Bernier and Albert Breton. Daniel Liebman and Rosemary Shipton turned the style editing of the manuscript into a pleasurable experience. At the Western Ontario end, I want to thank my colleagues John Whalley, John McDougall and Bob Young, with special thanks to Barb Ross for her word-processing skills. Finally, I must express my sincerest thanks to Robin Boadway and Peter Leslie for their very thorough review and evaluation of the penultimate draft. There are probably major sections of the manuscript with which they will still not be in sympathy, but the final product is much improved because of their thorough comments.

As is typically the case, and even more so given the subjective nature of the material, responsibility for what follows rests with the author.

THOMAS J. COURCHENE

Chapter 1

Introduction and Overview

There are many more ways to structure a federation than there are federations. Hence, there are no definitive answers to the range of issues that are the subject matter of this monograph: the implications of alternative divisions of powers for the economic management of the Canadian federation. Indeed, the entire question is not well defined since, for example, there is no unique way to specify what is meant by greater decentralization. Does greater decentralization mean that the provinces would be granted more policy areas where they alone (on a constitutional basis) are allowed to legislate? Or does it mean that there would be a greater number of policy areas with respect to which the provinces could act jointly with Ottawa? Or does it mean that there would be more areas where the provinces could exert a veto over federal policy design? And so on.

Even if we could sort out these issues in a satisfactory manner, there is a further general set of concerns that would still remain. Assessing whether economic management will be enhanced probably requires taking into account a range of issues extending well beyond the realm of economics. One of the lasting contributions of the research effort of the Royal Commission on the Economic Union and Development Prospects for Canada will be the integration of economic, political, and legal perspectives on the range of issues under consideration. However, this monograph is written largely from the perspective of an economist. No doubt this has some advantages but, equally, it also has some drawbacks.

At the outset, we might ask the question whether or not the formal division of powers as laid down in the BNA Act (Constitution Act, 1867) matters very much to the way the Canadian federation functions today.

Perhaps this issue is better phrased as follows: Suppose that the United States had Canada's Constitution and we had theirs, would the American federation today be the more decentralized? Or are there other underlying factors (e.g., the melting-pot approach of the United States versus the language and regional differentiation of Canada, or the dominant position of Ontario and Quebec in the Canadian federation and the lack of any such dominant states south of the border) that would ensure that Canada would end up as the more decentralized federation, in terms of the range of powers associated with the second tier of government? While I find the question to be very intriguing I do not know the answer (though, for what it's worth, my hunch is that we would still be more decentralized). The point is that a singular focus on economic principles may lead us astray if in the process we ignore cultural, historical, institutional, and regional factors. In large measure this is why the analysis that follows will focus to some degree on history and institutions as well as on economics.

In order to make the analysis more manageable we must outline the various ways in which the subject matter can be narrowed. This description will occupy the first part of the introduction, followed by a chapter-by-chapter outline of the monograph. The final section of the introduction will focus on the economists' "traditional" approach to the division of powers in a federation.

Approaches to Federalism and the Division of Powers

Although there are as many varieties of federalism as there are federations, all federations engage the two levels of government in a "self-rule, shared-rule" relationship, as Daniel Elazar has frequently noted. But beyond this general observation, cross-federation comparisons become difficult. Not only do the allocations of powers between the two levels of government vary widely but so do the ways by which decisions are made with respect to any shared powers. As a further complication, the omnipresence of the modern state implies that actions by one level of government will necessarily impinge on the actions and policies of the other level, even in those spheres that fall under self-rule. This increasing degree of interdependence places a corresponding emphasis on the co-ordination of policies. As a result, some observers have concluded that "federalism is not merely a *structure* of government but also a *process*" (Bastien, 1981, p. 48).

In order to relate some of these concepts to the Canadian situation, it is instructive to focus briefly on two quite different approaches to the workings of federalism: interstate federalism and intrastate federalism.

Interstate Federalism

Interstate federalism is characterized by a structure within which there is a clear institutional separation between provincial (state) and national governments and in which interaction on policy matters occurs via "diplomatic" relations between these two levels of government. In other words, there is no direct provincial representation in federal decision-making bodies. The Canadian federation is probably the classic example of this structure. The upper chamber in many federations provides the avenue for provincial (or state) participation in federal policy-making, but in Canada the Senate is, despite its geographical composition, unimportant, unelected, and composed of federal (not provincial) appointees. Moreover, the provinces have no formal say in the appointments to the Supreme Court or to other national bodies. Therefore, provincial concerns tend to be reflected through, and promulgated by, provincial governments. Indeed, given the regional nature of the national parties in recent years, the provinces have on many occasions become the (un)official opposition to the government of Canada. With this lack of direct provincial participation at the centre, some other avenues have had to be developed to satisfy the joint needs of policy coordination and provincial input. The principal solution was, and is, "executive federalism" — the interchange among the executives of the federal and provincial governments. These federal-provincial dealings run the gamut from informal interchanges among lower-level bureaucrats through to more formal meetings of senior executives and ministers culminating with first ministers' conferences. Numbering in the hundreds, these federal-provincial interchanges and the concept of executive federalism which they reflect may well represent Canada's "contribution to the art of federalism" (Safarian, 1980, p. 18).

Intrastate Federalism

The alternative approach is to have institutions structured so as to bring the constituent units (provinces, states, or whatever) directly into the operations of the central government. This system is referred to as intrastate federalism. As Dunn and Simeon note:

> Germany, the United States, and Switzerland approach the intrastate model, with highly institutionized interaction between the two levels of government. In the United States that interaction currently takes the form of a highly localized and powerful Congress with weak party discipline, and in which local, state and regional coalitions play an important role in negotiations with the executive branch. In Germany, intrastate mechanisms are focussed on the representation of the governments of the states within the national government, through the Bundesrat whose members are direct delegates of the states. Intrastate federalism in Germany is also reflected in the division between law-making and implementation by which the national government with state participation passes legislation, but laws are administered by the states. (chap. 5)

In Switzerland, Dunn and Simeon note that the bicameral federal assembly is also consistent with intrastate federalism. The upper chamber, the Council of States, has the same powers as the lower chamber and is composed of 44 cantonal deputies — two from each canton regardless of population. However, intrastate federalism in Switzerland is carried even further by means of the referenda process:

> Referenda can be held to initiate or approve constitutional change and also be used to approve federal legislation. Constitutional revision can be initiated by a petition with 100,000 signatures asking that a referendum be held to ascertain whether constitutional change is desired. If a favourable majority is obtained in the referendum, both chambers of the Federal Assembly are dissolved and re-elected to undertake constitutional change. The proposed amendments must be approved by a double majority — a majority of the national popular vote and a majority of cantons. (chap. 6)

These structures are radically different from those in Canada,[1] where the interaction between the two levels of government resembles more the diplomatic relationship among nation states. Indeed, one study of Canadian federalism is appropriately entitled *Federal-Provincial Diplomacy* (Simeon, 1972).

In light of these two conceptions of federalism, one approach to this study would be to assess their respective merits and then to redesign the institutional and constitutional machinery in a manner consistent with the "winning" conception. For example, the proposed "House of the Provinces" can be viewed as a step toward intrastate federalism. The analysis that follows, however, will be conducted within the parameters of the existing constitutional framework as it relates to the structure of federalism. It may well be that this framework is unduly limiting, particularly in those instances where the analysis calls not so much for a reassignment of powers but for more co-ordination in policy design and where intrastate federalism may appear to have much to offer.

Nonetheless, for most policy areas comparisons with other federations will be an important part of the analysis. In those cases where the treatment elsewhere owes more to the institutional structure than to the division of powers per se, this aspect will obviously be highlighted. Moreover, the line between interstate and intrastate federalism can be very fuzzy. For example, Canada's new amending formula brings the provinces into the process of constitutional change. Also, as will be pointed out in Chapter 6 on social policy, the arrangements for altering the Canada Pension Plan (which was constituted by an act of the Parliament of Canada) require the support of two-thirds of the provinces with two-thirds of the population. This is intrastate federalism in the sense that there exists a direct provincial role in federal (or, perhaps, national) policy formation.

Some Comments on Decentralization

If there is ambiguity associated with federalism in terms of the mechanisms through which the centre and the states interact, there is also ambiguity associated with centralization or decentralization. In this study no one definition will be used throughout: depending on the policy area under consideration, an increase in provincial powers can mean, among other developments, a transfer of additional constitutional responsibilities to the provinces, an increase in the proportion of provincial revenues that arise from own-source taxation as distinct from federal transfers, an increase in the proportion of unconditional federal transfers to the provinces, or an increase in the range of policy areas on which the provinces must be consulted.

Traditionally, the notion of decentralization was closely associated with provincial autonomy. In the Canadian context this concept was probably developed most fully in the Tremblay Report,[2] which proposed the separation and exclusive assignment of functions between the two levels of government. In Chapter 6 on social policy this decentralization is referred to as "unilateralism" — the right of a province to manage its own affairs without having to worry what other governments are doing. Fortunately or unfortunately, the pervasive nature of modern-day government implies that autonomy in this sense is giving way to interdependence. One level of government may still have the responsibility for action in a particular sphere, but given the interdependence of policies, there is now the presumption that actions of other governments will spill over into this policy sphere. For example, "disentanglement" is a popular expression in the mid-1980s, and there are no doubt many areas where duplication can and should be minimized, if not eliminated. However, there are also a great many areas where we are likely to encounter greater "entanglement" in the sense of policy integration or co-operation. Bastien addresses the implications of this greater interdependence as it relates to the division of powers and decentralization:

> [I]t can never be emphasized too strongly that the lessening of autonomy does not mean the end of decentralization. In fact there appear to be two basic ways to satisfy the requirement for consultation and co-ordination in a federal system. The first is to grant the federal order the responsibility for making major policy decisions and give to the provinces or states the role of implementing the policies. The United States and Australia seem to have adopted this centralist approach. The second approach is to grant the two orders of government the responsibility for developing *jointly* major policies of national concern and, to the greatest extent possible, ensure that the provinces have the means to implement these policies themselves. The latter decentralized method seems the one best suited to countries as heterogeneous as Canada and Switzerland. Thus decentralization does not lead to a separation of powers, as in traditional federalism, but rather to co-operation in decision-making. (Bastien, 1981, p. 47)

The difficulty inherent in attempting cross-federation comparisons is readily apparent when we recognize that Dunn and Simeon classify Switzerland and the United States in the intrastate camp and Canada and Australia (largely because the latter also makes considerable use of executive federalism) in the interstate group, whereas Bastien lumps Australia and the United States in the centralist group with Canada and Switzerland exemplifying those federations that have leaned toward decentralization. Were we to focus on other aspects, the groupings would be different again. For example, personal and corporate income tax rates are uniform within Australia but not in the other three federations with their decentralized systems of direct taxation. And so on.

These examples lend support to the earlier observation that there are many ways to structure a viable federation. As will become evident, there is a rich variety of arrangements across policy areas in the way we structure our own federation. Indeed, because of these wide variations, it may be constructive to focus selectively on various policy areas and render an assessment from an economic vantage point on whether more or less decentralization would enhance the economic management of the federation.

Inevitably, my personal biases will creep into the analysis from time to time. In economic philosophy I favour the operation of markets, and in political philosophy I lean toward decentralization. Moreover, when searching for evidence (anecdotal or factual) on particular issues I shall rely on my own experience, which probably reflects an Ontario perspective. On occasion, this will mean that the analysis is not value-free, particularly in controversial areas such as social policy and the Canadian economic union.

Outline of the Study

In broad terms, this monograph is divided into four parts, with an introductory and a concluding chapter. The first part (Chapters 2 and 3) outlines some underlying analytical concepts designed to provide a backdrop for the various policy areas. The following three parts focus in turn on selected aspects of stabilization (Chapters 4 and 5), distribution (Chapters 6 and 7), and allocation policies (Chapters 8 and 9) as they interact with the division of powers. An attempt has been made to ensure that each chapter is reasonably self-contained. On occasion, this warrants some repetition of material that appears in other chapters.

Federalism, Decentralization, and Economic Management: Some Analytical Underpinnings

Chapter 2 focusses on the centralization/decentralization spectrum as it relates to political structures. If we define federalism as the ability of subnational government units to provide public goods and services, then all political structures are "federal" in some degree. The analysis indicates how federations might compare with confederations and unitary states in terms of centralization of functions, and then attempts a loose ranking of various federations according to their degree of decentralization. Since any assessment of decentralization will probably be time-dependent, the chapter contains a brief historical overview of the fluctuations in power between Ottawa and the provinces. The chapter concludes with a focus on intergovernmental transfers and how they relate to the de facto division of powers as distinct from the de jure allocation. In effect, a major change in the magnitude and form of these transfers is equivalent to a change in the division of powers even though the formal wording of the Constitution may remain unaltered.

Chapter 3 attempts to integrate economic decision-making into this political structure. The approach is two-fold: the range of alternative goals or objectives that Canada can adopt with respect to a given policy area; and the way in which implementation of a given objective interacts with the division of powers. Economic analysis comes into play at several points. First, some of the possible objectives can be ruled out on the basis of economic principles. Second, while some means of implementing a given policy may run into constitutional constraints, there are frequently alternative approaches to policy design — what economists call the calculus of the optimal policy instrument. Third, and perhaps most important, whether or not there is a need for an altered division of powers will depend on the precise policy objective that is chosen. To illustrate these points, the analysis focusses on some aspects of Canadian regional policy. The final section of the chapter is devoted to discussion of constitutional determinism versus economic determinism as this issue relates to the division of powers. While there is no presumption that this framework is in any way general, it does provide a reference point for evaluating at least some of the policy issues dealt with in the remaining chapters.

Stabilization Policy and the Division of Powers

The two big levers of stabilization or macro policy — monetary policy and fiscal policy — are the focus of Chapters 4 and 5, respectively.

Monetary policy is centralized in all countries, federal and unitary states alike. The pleas for regionalizing monetary policy do not make economic sense. Indeed, if anything, monetary policy may undergo enhanced central control in the future. The issue here relates to the fact that not all deposit-taking institutions are subject to the monitoring provisions of the Bank of Canada. While present powers appear adequate, the rapid pace of technological change and the erosion of the "four pillars" (banking, trusts, insurance, and underwriting) may imply that Canada will move to a functional rather than an institutional approach to financial regulation. Under such a system, it is likely that primary reserve requirements would be applied to all deposits transferable by cheque regardless of the institution in which they are held. The chapter ends with a discussion of the federal powers with respect to controls — wage and price controls and exchange controls.

The fiscal side of stabilization policy is markedly different from the monetary side in that a good deal of decentralization already exists. On the expenditure side, Ottawa's power appears to be plenary so that it is hard to argue that it needs greater authority. Some analysts would probably argue that there is at present too much decentralization in terms of the taxing function. And there may well be. Chapter 5 argues, however, that Canada's tax system, while very much decentralized, is still harmonized. Hence, the task at hand is to ensure that the present system does not fragment into eleven separate personal and corporate income tax systems. It is true that this decentralization probably complicates the exercise of stabilization policy. In turn, this means that there is a premium on consultation and co-operation in the design and implementation of fiscal policy, particularly on the tax front.

Income Distribution and the Division of Powers

Chapter 6 focusses on the social programs (e.g., the established programs, the Canada Assistance Plan and pensions) and the division of powers. The first section is devoted to a brief historical review of these programs, one important aspect of which is that the existing constitutional framework has permitted dramatic shifts in federal and provincial responsibility for these programs. The second section presents a personal overview of the past, present and future of the social programs — an "economic determinist" approach, as it were. The 1960s, which gave birth to the current structure of the social programs, was a period of rapid economic growth which allowed equivalently rapid development on the social and regional policy fronts. The economy in the 1980s is in a much more difficult position. The requirements over the next decade will be for an economy that is flexible and capable of adjusting to the changing patterns of world demands. The social programs must be designed or redesigned to accommodate this needed adjustment. In my view this calls for an emphasis on efficiency, decentralization, and private-sector input into the design and financing of the social programs. In this context, the division of powers becomes important principally to the extent that some allocations are more conducive to achieving this goal than are others. The following section focusses in detail on the division of powers in the income security area. Interestingly enough we find a surprisingly wide range of arrangements, running from a complete separation (unilateralism) to co-operative federalism to a complex system of checks and balances (intrastate federalism). The degree of interaction within this area and between it and other policy areas is so pervasive that it tends to downplay the importance of a particular structure of powers and correspondingly puts greater emphasis on the policy-making process. The final section of the chapter deals with the notion of "fiscal balance" between the two levels of government and in particular on the way that this equilibrium interacts with the division of powers in the income distribution area.

The equalization program is the subject of Chapter 7. Equalization payments are the quintessential form of unconditional transfers and, as such, are intimately related to the division of powers. The first sections of the chapter focus on the various "political" rationales for equalization. Drawing from the Royal Commission on Dominion-Provincial Relations (the Rowell-Sirois Commission), I identify a "federal" and a "nationhood" rationale for a system of equalization payments. Most economists would probably prefer to identify these explanations as falling within the purview of an equity rationale. However, the thrust of the chapter is that the particular nature of Canada's equalization program has allowed our federation to decentralize on the tax side. There can also be an efficiency rationale for equalization, particularly in the presence of massive resource rents accruing to the energy rich provinces. The degree to which Canada's equalization program conforms to the dictates of efficiency is then pursued. The chapter concludes with a brief comparison of the role that equalization plays in other federations.

Allocation and the Division of Powers

The selection of chapters relating to allocative efficiency is quite arbitrary. Chapter 8 focusses on the financial system and Chapter 9 on the Canadian economic union issue. Both of these issues are currently in the policy limelight and both have important division-of-powers implications. I have shied away from dealing with regional policy because it was touched on in Chapter 3 (and it will receive some attention in Chapter 8) and is covered adequately elsewhere in the Royal Commission's research agenda.

Chapter 8, on the allocative efficiency of financial markets, is divided into three sections. The first deals with the securities industry. Unlike the United States with its federal Securities and Exchange Commission (SEC), the Canadian securities industry is regulated by the securities commissions of the various provinces, with little or no federal regulatory presence. The pros and cons of provincial versus federal regulation are evaluated. Constitutionally, the federal government could move into this area, though it is not obvious whether this transfer is desirable since the provinces have succeeded well thus far. An analysis of the "four pillars" constitutes the second section of the chapter. The regulatory environment is complex, with extensive federal and provincial overlap, and there probably is an important division-of-powers issue at stake. Once again the federal government probably has the authority to enlarge its regulatory role. However, the real issue is one of policy: should the four pillars be preserved or should the regulatory system accommodate financial integration? Once this underlying issue is resolved, the alloca-tion-of-powers issue will follow suit. The final section of the chapter deals with the pension system. Among the arguments put forward here is that pensions represent one area where the division of powers may have influenced the policy choices — i.e., there may be a "constitutional determinism" at work in this area. The chapter concludes with some observations relating to the role of pension funds in equity ownership of the economy. Specifically, the analysis focusses on the role of the caisses in Quebec and the concern that their equity investment policy is attempting to influence transportation policy, an area which falls under federal jurisdiction.

Chapter 9 is concerned with the Canadian economic union (CEU) — an integral issue in any discussion of the division of powers. The chapter begins with some economic and political arguments for a CEU. Next, the analysis identifies and classifies some of the CEU barriers and attempts to assign costs to these barriers. The chapter then traces the role that the CEU issue played in the recent constitutional debates and relates the Canadian situation with that of other federations. While it seems clear that Canada should enhance its internal common market, it is less clear that this should be done by enshrining the concept in the Constitution, particularly if, as a result, it implies a dramatic centralization of powers. Evidence suggests, after all, that it is the federal and not the provincial impediments to the domestic economic union that are the most costly. The chapter concludes with a compromise proposal for approaching the CEU issue.

Conclusions and Implications

The concluding sections draw together the many strands of the analysis. There are many ways to structure a federation, and in the Canadian federation the arrangements pertaining to the division of powers vary widely over different policy areas. Moreover, there are two other fea-tures that are characteristic of our (and probably other countries') fed-eral structure: the Constitution has proved to be a flexible and accom-modating document, and there have been dramatic shifts to and from the centre which have occurred without any change in the formal divisions of powers.

A second general theme is that, while federations are structured differently, over the years there has developed a concept of "balance" in each federation — a balance with which the various levels of govern-ment have learned to co-exist. In turn, this balance has enabled a policy-making process to develop in each federation. From an economic van-tage point, some alternative structures and processes may be preferred in the abstract. However, it is important to remember that the range of existing structures and processes are part of a federation's social and institutional capital. Such capital may not easily be transferred across federations. Hence, considerable caution is probably called for in terms of redesigning the nature and processes of a given federation simply by changing the constitution. Indeed, the analysis appears to suggest that what is at work in the Canadian federation is an economic, not a constitutional determinism. If this is the case, what is critical is not the particular structure of the Constitution or the formal allocation of powers but rather that the constitutional framework be able to accommodate the evolution of structures and processes in response to changing economic (or political) needs.

In spite of this rather conservative approach to constitutional design or redesign, the analysis does point in the direction of some needed changes in the structure and processes of Canadian federalism. These changes are summarized in the concluding section of the monograph, "Toward an Economic Constitution for Canada."

Economics, Federalism, and the Division of Powers
Allocation, Stabilization, Distribution

It is generally accepted that the role of the public sector in the economic sphere is to address itself to three primary goals: the attainment of high employment with stable prices (economic stabilization), the attainment of an equitable distribution of income (income distribution), and the establishment of efficient resource use (allocative efficiency).

Wallace Oates, in his book *Fiscal Federalism*, addresses the manner in which alternative political structures are likely to be able to achieve these goals. His initial comparison is between a unitary form of government and a set of local governments. The existence of mobile labour and the likelihood of policy spillovers[3] lead him to the conclusion that:

> [A] unitary form of government has several important advantages over its counterpart at the opposite end of the spectrum. In a system comprising only local governments, the public sector will be seriously handicapped in its capacity to meet its economic responsibilities. Local governments . . . would find it extremely difficult to stabilize their respective economies, to realize the most equitable distribution of income, and to provide efficient levels of output of those public goods that confer benefits on the members of all or several communities. (Oates, 1972, p. 11)

Nonetheless, there are economic advantages of decentralized government:

> First, it provides a means by which the levels of consumption of some public goods can be tailored to the preferences of subsets of society. . . . Second,

by promoting increased innovation over time and by providing competitive pressures to induce local governments to adopt the most efficient techniques of production, decentralization may increase both static and dynamic efficiency in the production of public goods. Third, a system of local government may provide an institutional setting that promotes better public decision-making by compelling an explicit recognition of the costs of public programs. (Ibid., p. 13)

From these observations Oates concludes that federalism may well be the optimal form of government:

[In a federal system] each level of government, rather than attempting to perform all functions of the public sector, does what it can do best. The central government presumably accepts primary responsibility for stabilizing the economy, for achieving the most equitable distribution of income, and for providing certain public goods that influence significantly the welfare of all members of society. Complementing these operations, subcentral governments can supply those public goods and services that are of primary interest only to the residents of their respective jurisdictions. In this way, a federal form of government offers the best promise of a successful resolution of the problems that constitute the economic *raison d'être* of the public sector. It is in this sense that federalism may, in economic terms, be described as the optimal form of government. (Ibid., pp. 14–15)

This perspective (which I am assuming to be broadly representative of public finance specialists) surely goes a long way toward rationalizing or understanding federations like Australia, Germany and Austria. As a prototype, however, it would appear to be somewhat off-base with respect to the Canadian and Swiss federations which are characterized by considerable decentralization of the distribution and stabilization functions. One way to rationalize the Swiss and Canadian systems is that the degree of decentralization is related to their inherent diversity (i.e., political-cultural-historical factors) and, therefore, they need not be viewed as departures from the overall proposition which is cast principally in economic terms. However, Oates's description of a "federal" system also coincides quite well with a unitary state in which municipal governments exercise control over the provision of certain local goods. This is fully consistent with his concept of federalism since, for him, the term relates not to a particular political structure but rather to a situation where there are different levels of government (including municipal governments, so that most unitary states would qualify in terms of the definition of a federal structure).

Tax Assignment in Multilevel Jurisdictions

In order to relate these general principles to real world situations it is useful to address one aspect of the assignment of powers in more detail — the optimal assignment of taxing powers. Once again, the focus will be on the views of a single economist (in this case Richard Musgrave), with the expectation that his opinions are reasonably representative of the mainstream. Musgrave approaches the tax assignment problem as follows:

> Suppose that a given set of central, state, and local jurisdictions, in the process of forming a federation, confront the issue of tax assignment. The available taxes are personal income tax, corporation profits tax, destination-type consumption tax (retail sales tax or VAT), and property tax. What is their suitability for each level? An obvious minimum requirement for each jurisdiction is to adhere to the rules of good tax manners. . . . That is to say, there should be a minimum of burden export, with each jurisdiction restrained (in the absence of benefit spillover) to tax its own bases only. The following assignment rules then seem appropriate:
>
> (1) middle and especially lower level jurisdictions should tax those bases which have low inter-jurisdictional mobility;
> (2) personal taxes with progressive rates should be used by those jurisdictions within which a global base can be implemented most efficiently;
> (3) progressive taxation, designed to secure redistributional objectives, should be primarily central;
> (4) taxes suitable for purposes of stabilization policy should be central, while lower level taxes should be cyclically stable;
> (5) tax bases which are distributed highly unequally among sub-jurisdictions should be used centrally; and
> (6) benefit taxes and user charges are appropriate at all levels. (Musgrave, 1983)

There is, of course, nothing inherently wrong with these six precepts. Indeed, most economists would subscribe to all of them. The only problem is that they typically do not play a very large role in the tax structure of federal nations. In Switzerland, West Germany and Austria, the federal level is financed primarily by commodity taxes whereas the revenues from income taxation flow largely to the state and local levels. This contradicts points 3 and 4 and, to the extent that commodity taxes relate to consumer goods, probably point 1 as well. Provincial corporate income taxes in Canada and elsewhere run afoul of point 1 since the burden of such source-based taxes can clearly be exported to other jurisdictions. The new provision in our Constitution which gives the provinces a larger say over indirect taxation of resources is counter to points 1 (because of tax exporting) and 5 as well. And the list can be expanded virtually ad infinitum.

One explanation of this divergence is that federations are political as well as economic entities. As Nowotny comments on the approach to taxation in the Swiss and West German federations:

> This pattern of tax allocation is in obvious contradiction to the prescriptions of most of the literature on fiscal federalism. In both countries, the allocation of

the very fast growing revenue from income taxation to lower levels of governments can be explained by the political intention to strengthen the fiscal
position of these levels *vis-à-vis* central government. There are no major
policy discussions of allocative inefficiencies, even of the Swiss system, but
there does exist criticism concerning the stabilization features of the system of
tax allocation in both countries. In my view both the structure and the
dynamics of the fiscal systems of Switzerland and West Germany, two economically very successful countries, may serve as one [more] example of the
primacy of political aspects relative to traditional economic efficiency concepts and the high degree of adaptability of an economy to a politically
determined set of fiscal institutions. (Nowotny, 1983)

This divergence poses a dilemma for anyone attempting to assess the
relationship between economic management and the division of powers.
Typically, economics literature focusses more on institutional redesign
than on ensuring that processes arise so as to render the existing institutional and constitutional arrangements more consistent with the underlying economic principles. One explanation may be that the optimal tax-
assignment literature came to the fore in the context of the formation of the
European Economic Community and the accompanying concern with tax
assignment and tax harmony. Since the EEC represented a new set of
arrangements, it made eminent sense to start from some basic economic
building blocks. But to transfer this analysis to the domain of federalism is
not quite as straightforward as it might seem since, as Claude Lemelin
correctly points out, "association treaties (like the EEC's Treaty of Rome)
are essentially *economic documents* [whereas] federal constitutions are
primarily *political documents*" (Lemelin, 1981). The point of this focus on
the assignment problem in federations and, more generally, on the typical
economic approach to federalism is not to downplay the resulting economic insights. Far from it. Indeed, in Chapter 9, pertaining to the Canadian economic union, the thrust of the analysis will, for example, be to
devise institutions or arrangements to ensure that the existing division of
powers does not lead to the negative sorts of repercussions predicted by
economic theory. Rather, the purpose of this section has been to show that
a single-minded pursuit of economic principles as they relate to the
structure of federalism is apt to be a misleading policy endeavour —
misleading in that economists are unlikely to convince the Swiss that they
ought to turn over the responsibility for direct taxation to their central
government or to convince the Canadian provinces that they should return
the authority to tax corporate income to Ottawa and ensure that all tax
rates are uniform across provinces. What it does suggest is that history,
culture, politics and the Constitution, as well as economics, have com-
mingled to produce the status quo with respect to various policy areas.

However, there is also a danger in simply accepting "what is" and
ignoring "what ought to be." The Royal Commission on the Economic

Union and Development Prospects for Canada has a mandate both to review and rethink our structures and policies across the entire political, economic and constitutional fronts.

My approach with respect to this dilemma will probably not be very consistent. In most cases I shall respect the status quo and direct the analysis toward those issues and/or processes which can render the status quo as consistent as possible with the underlying economic goals. In other words, the emphasis will be on "process" rather than "redesign." In some cases, however, the analysis will rely on economic principles to indicate where changes in constitutional design would be beneficial. Thus, even apart from any inherent bias that I may bring to the analysis, much of the monograph will of necessity be subjective in the further sense that there will also exist the trade-off between structure and process.

Chapter 2

The Centralization/Decentralization Spectrum: *An Overview*

As was pointed out in Chapter 1, there are many alternative ways in which a federal nation can approach centralization or decentralization. Likewise, there are many ways in which a federal nation can approach the design and implementation of economic policy. The purpose of the first part of this monograph (Chapters 2 and 3) is to present a framework which attempts to integrate these two subject areas. In turn, this outline will provide a backdrop for the analysis later in the monograph of specific policy areas; it will also address the question of whether an altered division of powers within these areas might enhance the economic management of the federation.

The present chapter[1] begins by focussing on the "federal continuum" — the notion that there is some degree of decentralization (or centralization) in all political structures and that on this score federal states are really part of a continuum of alternative political structures. The analysis then attempts to "rank" some of the major federations in terms of the degree to which they are decentralized. To emphasize the difficult nature of this task, some attention is directed to a brief historical assessment of the tides of centralization and decentralization in the Canadian federation. The last section of the chapter focusses on the important role that interprovincial transfers can play in determining the de facto division of powers, irrespective of the formal wording of the Constitution. In brief, in considering this centralization/decentralization spectrum we will incorporate the concept into a range of alternative economic strategies.

The Federal Continuum

Figure 2-1 depicts what I refer to as the federal continuum. The far right

FIGURE 2-1 The Federal Continuum

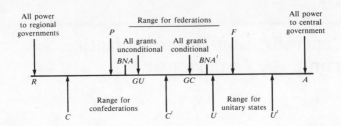

of the spectrum (labelled A) corresponds to a situation where all power rests with the central government — it represents the antithesis of federalism. Perhaps city-states like Monaco fall into this category. At the extreme left of the spectrum (labelled R) all power resides with the regional governments: in effect, there is little or no role for the central government. I find it difficult to conceive of political organizations that would fall into this category, but perhaps the United Nations comes close. In any event, whether or not points R and A are empty sets is not important, since the analysis is concerned with what lies between these extremes and not with the polar cases themselves.

Range UU' is intended to indicate the location of unitary states along this centralization/decentralization spectrum. The existence of local government implies that even unitary states must be to the left of A, and the range itself suggests that there can be considerable variability in the degree of decentralization associated with unitary states.

The range allocated to federations, PF (with P and F denoting more power to the provinces and to the federal government, respectively), occupies the middle ground in the figure. The overlap with both unitary states and confederations is deliberate and is designed to convey the message that the distinction between political systems may on occasion be more a matter of degree than of substance. Finally, the range for confederations, CC', occupies the leftmost portion of the spectrum indicating the likelihood that confederations will be characterized by more decentralized forms of government. In the present world, the confederation category may also be an empty set. Although the CH on Swiss automobiles stands for Confédération Helvétique, Switzerland is appropriately classified as a federation. If the EEC moves toward political union, it would presumably start out as a confederation.

Although no precise meaning can be attached to the horizontal distances in Figure 2-1, the range allocated to federations is deliberately broad. In order to breathe some reality into the federation component of the centralization/decentralization spectrum, the figure incorporates the interval $BNA–BNA'$, intended to suggest the range of the Canadian federation. As even a casual acquaintance with the history of our federation will reveal, the BNA Act (Constitution Act, 1867) is consistent with both considerable decentralization and centralization. While the present study is not intended to provide a detailed historical overview of the shifting fortunes of federal versus provincial supremacy, later in this chapter some attention will be directed toward the broad historical trends relating to centralization and decentralization.

The final piece of information in Figure 2-1 relates to the nature of intergovernmental grants. Range *GU–GC* (to depict unconditional grants and conditional grants, respectively) is intended to suggest that where federal-provincial transfers are unconditional in nature the likelihood is that they will lead to greater provincial autonomy (decentralization), and vice versa. The role of intergovernmental grants will also be dealt with later in the chapter. Prior to utilizing Figure 2-1 as a backdrop to elaborate on certain aspects of the Canadian federation, it seems appropriate to focus initially on some cross-federation comparisons.

Ranking Federations

In principle, we might want to rank federations according to their degree of decentralization. For example, Prime Minister Trudeau in his opening remarks to the televised 1980 First Ministers' Conference on the Constitution noted:

> We . . . know that a much higher proportion of public funds are spent in Canada by the provinces and the municipalities . . . than by the federal government and in this we are far and away the most decentralized . . . of any country in the world. (Trudeau, 1980, p. 94)

"Far and away" may be an exaggeration, but Canada has the most decentralized federalism in terms of state and local expenditures as a percent of total government expenditures. The 1981 data are as follows: Canada, 55.4 percent; Switzerland, 53.2 percent; Germany, 42.9 percent; United States, 41.2 percent; Australia, 40.9 percent; and Austria, 31.8 percent (Bird, 1985, Table 2). The decentralized fiscal position of the Canadian provinces is even more evident if we focus on "own revenues" of provinces or states as a percent of total government revenues: Canada, 39.2 percent; Switzerland, 25.1 percent; Germany, 21.9 percent; United States, 21.1 percent; Australia, 18.6 percent; and Austria, 9.4 percent.

However, these comparisons often hide as much as they reveal. For example, it is important to recognize that overseeing a given percentage of expenditures is not the same as having the freedom to allocate these expenditures in accordance with provincial/state priorities, as the section on conditional versus unconditional grants will make clear.

Moreover, even if it could be demonstrated that the Canadian provinces do have more powers than, say, the U.S. states, it still does not follow that Canada should necessarily be classified as more decentralized. Any classification would also depend on the powers of the federal government. Consider Canada and the United States. Most students of federalism would probably agree that the Canadian provinces have, today, more powers than the U.S. states. But Ottawa can also do some things that Washington can not. The Canadian government has a well-established tradition of providing regional subsidies (e.g., Department of Regional Economic Expansion (DREE) and the regional Unemployment Insurance Commission benefits) and regionally differentiating both the personal and corporate income tax systems. Whether by custom or constitution, the U.S. federal government has never played a meaningful role in the regional development area, although both countries presumably take regional concerns into account in terms of federal expenditures — e.g., military expenditures in the United States and shipbuilding in Canada.

Australia provides an even better example. Section 51(iii) of the Australian constitution states:

> The Parliament shall . . . have power to make laws . . . with respect to taxation; but not as to discriminate between States and parts of States.

And section 99 reads:

> The Commonwealth shall not, by any law or regulation of trade, commerce, or revenue, give preference to one state or any part thereof over another state or any part thereof.

These provisions have prevented the Australian federal government from creating a monopoly for air transportation, from nationalizing banks, and have inhibited the creation of some marketing boards (Chrétien, 1980, p. 14). Hence, even though we would classify Australia as a more centralized federation than Canada, the Australian central government is more constrained in many areas than is the Canadian Parliament.

Nonetheless, in terms of a loose ranking of the industrialized federations, we would probably classify Germany and Austria as the most centralized, primarily because the role of the second tier of government in these two federations is to implement and administer federal laws. Likewise, Canada and Switzerland would qualify as the most decentralized. Sandwiched in between would be Australia and the United States. Thus, in terms of Figure 2-1, the range permitted by the German constitution would lie to the right but still overlap the *BNA–BNA'* range. Basically, however, for purposes of this study, the relevant cross-federal comparisons are those that relate to specific policy areas. At this level the rankings can be quite different from those enumerated above.

All six federations have centralized monetary policy. Indeed, with respect to this head of power there is little difference between federations and unitary states. Some analysts might want to draw a distinction between the British-style parliamentary federations (Canada and Australia) and the other four federations mentioned above, where the central banks have more autonomy than in the parliamentary federations. Were we to broaden the perspective and focus on overall macro policy (including the ability of the central government to control the major taxation levers and to impose wage and price controls), major differences in the federations would begin to emerge (see Chapter 4).

As a second example, we consider the degree to which the second tier of government has the ability to determine its own tax rates and tax bases for direct taxes (personal and corporate income taxes). Germany and Austria would again be the most centralized, since both tax rates and tax bases must, as specified by their constitutions, be uniform across the federation. The Australian states have the right to mount surcharges for personal income taxation, but since none of the states has as yet taken advantage of this privilege, Australia would also qualify as being very centralized on this score. Canada and the United States would occupy the middle ground, with Switzerland and its so-called "tax-jungle" claiming the right to be the most decentralized.

Up until this point, the determination of where federations are located in terms of the centralization/decentralization spectrum has been conducted, implicitly at least, in terms of how a particular power (or the overall range of powers) is allocated between the federal and provincial governments. But this is probably too narrow a conception of the issue. Another dimension that must be taken into consideration are those powers that reside, by virtue of the constitution, not with a particular level of government but with the people. Under this notion of decentralization (power to the "people"), the Swiss with their referendum process would no doubt emerge as the most decentralized and, until recently, Canada would probably qualify as one of the more centralized. With our new Canadian Charter of Rights and Freedoms there are constitutional constraints on the powers of our legislatures at both levels of government. Just how much the Charter will impinge on the economic powers of government is not as yet clear.

Finally, while this framework may be interesting in its own right, it is important to recall that its purpose is to lend insight to the overall goal of the study — to ascertain the impact of greater or lesser decentralization on the economic performance of a federation.

The remainder of this chapter is devoted to two interrelated features of Figure 2-1 that clearly have had, and no doubt will continue to have, an influence on the ability of the Canadian federation to respond to its political and economic environment. The first point emphasizes the flexibility of the BNA Act (henceforth the Constitution Act, 1867), in that it has over the years allowed for periods of both centralization and decentralization. Indeed, any ranking of federations in terms of Figure 2-1 must be time-dependent. Ten years from now different rankings may be appropriate, just as a few decades ago Canada would have been characterized as being more centralized than it is at present. The second area deals with the interrelationship between centralization or decentralization and the system of intergovernmental grants.

The Ebb and Flow of Provincialism

In his book *Federalism and Decentralization: Where Do We Stand?* Richard Bastien traces the swings in power between Ottawa and the provinces (Bastien, 1981). Figure 2-2, adapted from Bastien, presents an historical overview of these shifts. Panel A plots the distribution of own-source revenues over the period 1925–80 for the federal government and the provincial/local governments. Panel B shows the distribution of revenues after intergovernmental transfers.

From Panel A the provincial/local share of total own-source revenues rises from under 55 percent in 1925 to nearly 70 percent at the onset of the Great Depression. To provide some perspective, the provincial/local share of own-source revenues at the time of Confederation was only 27 percent. In a very real sense the early 1930s was the high point of provincial financial autonomy vis-à-vis the federal government. Even today, the provincial/local government sector has nowhere near 70 percent of own-source government revenues.

In terms of total revenues (Panel B) the provincial/local sector peaked at close to 80 percent in the early 1930s. This figure is also above the current level, but not by nearly as much as for own-source revenues — a consequence of the substantial role currently played by federal grants to the provinces. Once again, for perspective, the division of after-transfer revenues at the time of Confederation was 42 percent and 58 percent for the provinces and Ottawa, respectively. Bastien comments on this pre-Depression period of increasing decentralization:

> The reduction in the relative importance of the federal government at this time was facilitated by the fact that the peacetime priorities were in areas such as roads, education and social welfare, all of which came under provincial jurisdiction. Although the operating expenditures of the provincial governments increased moderately, their capital investment expenditures grew rapidly and provincial debts reached unprecedented levels. The rapidly increasing use of electricity and automobiles required huge public investments by the provinces and municipalities. By the end of the 1920s, the total spending by the provinces and their municipalities was approximately 50 percent higher than federal government spending.
>
> The increase in the provinces' financial responsibilities obliged them to find new sources of revenue. Most of them set up government monopolies for the sale of alcoholic beverages and imposed excise taxes that brought in substantial income. Taxes on gasoline, commercial permits and drivers' licences also provided new revenues. (pp. 4–5)

FIGURE 2-2   The Ebb and Flow of Centralization

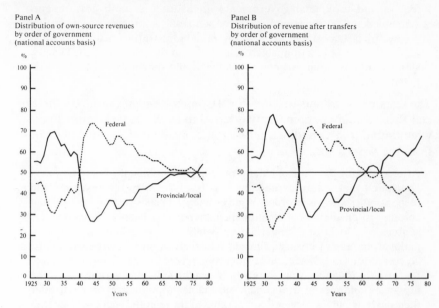

Panel A
Distribution of own-source revenues
by order of government
(national accounts basis)

Panel B
Distribution of revenue after transfers
by order of government
(national accounts basis)

Source: Bastien (1981), Graphs 1 and 2.

As far as the federal government was concerned, despite the fact that it entered the direct taxation field (with a corporate income tax in 1916 and a personal income tax in 1917), indirect taxes remained the principal revenue source. As late as 1921, 90 percent of federal revenue was derived from indirect taxation. Over the decade of the 1920s provincial/local revenues doubled in absolute value whereas federal revenues actually declined.

The dual crises of the Great Depression and the Second World War dramatically reversed this decentralist trend. From Figure 2-2, the federal government's share of both own-source and after-transfer revenues exceeded 70 percent in the early 1940s. In the postwar period the trend is once again toward greater decentralization. While it is not my purpose to undertake a history of this federal-provincial tug-of-war, brief comments on some principal episodes are in order.

Not surprisingly, the Great Depression ushered in an era of fiscal crisis, particularly for the provinces:

> Both the federal and provincial governments attempted to prevent revenues from declining during the Depression by increasing taxes. The federal government increased its sales tax from 1 percent to 8 percent, doubled the personal income tax, and imposed new import duties. The provinces increased the gasoline sales tax by 50 percent and raised succession duties and flat-rate taxes on corporations. By 1940, all provinces were taxing personal and corporate incomes, and Saskatchewan and Quebec had intro-

duced a retail sales tax. There was little or no co-operation between the federal and provincial governments in taxation as both governments scrambled for revenues and produced a chaotic tax jungle of joint occupancy, high tax rates, duplication of administrative machinery, and regressiveness in taxation which contributed to the severity of the Depression by undermining business confidence and incentives. (Strick, 1973, p. 98)

The response to all this was the Royal Commission on Dominion-Provincial Relations, more commonly referred to as the Rowell-Sirois Report, which submitted its findings in 1940. Once again, it is convenient to draw from the work of Bastien:

After analyzing the state of federal-provincial relations, the commissioners concluded that a serious imbalance existed between the revenues and responsibilities of each order of government. They stressed the fact that certain responsibilities of a national character were financed from revenue sources of a local or regional nature, while certain revenue sources of a national character were used almost exclusively by provincial governments. To correct this imbalance, the commission recommended a new division of responsibilities and taxing powers between the federal government and the provinces, and special arrangements to enable the poorest provinces to offer their citizens public services comparable to those in the rich provinces. In particular the commission recommended:
• that the federal government assume the responsibilities associated with unemployment relief and old age pensions, which at that time absorbed a considerable proportion of provincial revenues;
• that the provinces no longer tax incomes of individuals and corporations because these "national" areas of taxation would be more efficiently administered by the federal government;
• that the "chaotic and illogical" statutory grant system be replaced with "national adjustment grants" to be made to the poorest provinces so that they could provide public services of "average" quality without placing an undue tax burden on their citizens. (Bastien, 1981, pp. 10–11)

Several comments are in order. First, one indicator of greater centralization is the transfer of powers from the provinces to the federal government. Following on the recommendations of the Rowell-Sirois Report, the Constitution was amended in 1940 to give the federal government the authority to set up an unemployment insurance scheme and in 1951 to enable Ottawa to establish a nationwide old-age pension plan. Second, at a January 1941 conference to discuss the implementation of the commission's proposals the provinces rejected the transfer of direct taxation to the federal government. Later in the year, however, the financial exigencies relating to the war effort did generate just such a temporary agreement. As R.M. Burns, a prominent analyst of the day, remarked: "Patriotism accomplished what financial reasoning could not" (Strick, 1973, p. 101). Third, in the immediate postwar period the Canadian federal government desired to keep control of direct taxation. In this process it now found a new ally — Keynesian economics. In line with the 1945 federal white paper on employment and income, Ottawa maintained that the different sources of revenue should no longer be considered from a purely constitutional point of view but in terms of their usefulness as macroeconomic management tools (Bastien, 1981, p. 14). What followed was a series of five-year arrangements with respect to intergovernmental finances. Initially known as tax-rental agreements, they are now referred to as the fiscal arrangements acts. The postwar history of these arrangements represents a gradual transfer of direct taxation back to the provinces, as Figure 2-2 reveals.

Most observers would probably view the Rowell-Sirois Report as a very centralist document. Certainly, the thrust of the recommendations outlined in the previous paragraph did lead to a centralization over fiscal resources. However, the report was also a staunch defender of provincial autonomy in those areas that fell under provincial jurisdiction. For example:

> The Commission's plan seeks to ensure to every province a real and not illusory autonomy by guaranteeing to it, free from conditions or control, the revenues necessary to perform those functions which relate to its cultural and social developments. (Canada, 1939, p. 80)

This guarantee was coupled with an even stronger assertion that the proposed National Adjustment Grants (essentially equalization payments) be unconditional, thereby catering to provincial priorities:

> It should be made clear that while the adjustment grant proposed is designed to enable a province to provide adequate services (at the average Canadian standard) without excessive taxation (on the average Canadian basis) the freedom of action of a province is in no way impaired. If a province chooses to provide inferior services and imposes lower taxation it is free to do so, or it may provide better services than the national average if its people are willing to be taxed accordingly, or it may, for example, starve its roads and improve its education, or starve its education and improve its roads. (p. 84)

Even though equalization payments were introduced formally only in 1957, it is likely that their past and present unconditional nature derives in part from the philosophy of the Rowell-Sirois Report.

A further milestone in the evolution of federal-provincial powers occurred in 1954, when Quebec initiated its own separate personal income tax. (For an interpretative view of the role this action has played in federal-provincial fiscal relations see a recent article by Claude Forget, 1984, pp. 187–212.) This initiative helped trigger the movement from the tax-rental arrangements to the tax-sharing arrangements under which the federal government began transferring larger and larger shares of direct taxation back to the provinces. The process of decentralization on the fiscal side was later augmented by the establishment of separate corporation tax systems by Ontario, Quebec, and, more recently, Alberta.

With the dramatic resurgence in the share of funds available to the provincial/local sector, particularly after intergovernmental transfers were taken into account, it was tempting to argue that the federation became correspondingly more decentralized. Indeed, on the basis of these shares, former prime minister Trudeau claimed, as noted above, that Canada was the most decentralized federation in the world. However, as the next section on interprovincial transfers will argue, if these intergovernmental grants are condition-laden, as many of them were until recently and as some still are, then it is not clear that they contribute to the exercise of provincial autonomy. Moreover, in the negotiations leading up to the Constitution Act, 1982, the federal government introduced the notion of securing a domestic economic union in the Constitution. Had Ottawa's initial proposals with respect to this internal economic union found their way into the new Constitution, the net result would have been a substantial erosion of provincial powers in spite of the provinces' large share of overall public expenditures.[2]

Thus, the Canadian Constitution has shown itself to be a remarkably flexible document. It enabled a great degree of centralization in the crisis associated with the Depression and the war. It has permitted a swing back to substantial provincial powers when the regional demands of the country necessitated this shift. Moreover, during this latter process it has also enabled the federal government to initiate and implement something akin to national standards for major social programs such as medicare, hospital insurance, post-secondary education, and welfare. And, except for a few instances, these changes and accommodations were brought about without constitutional amendment.

On the basis of this record, considerable caution should be exercised in any redesigning of Canada's institutional fabric via constitutional amendments in order to meet the economic needs of future decades. If there is a need for either further centralization or decentralization, one way to approach the issue is through constitutional amendment. However, the exhibited flexibility of the Constitution suggests that it is possible, indeed likely, that the needed response can and will arise within the existing framework.

This brief overview has implications for the way in which one interprets Figure 2-1. Specifically, any attempt to locate a particular federation along the centralization/decentralization spectrum has to recognize the time-dependence of such a ranking. For example, in 1945 the Canadian federation would clearly have been located near *BNA'* in Figure 2-1. It is particularly important to keep this time frame in mind in later sections dealing with the allocation of powers for various economic functions. As an indication of what would be involved in a more comprehensive treatment of this area see Appendix Table A-1, which traces some of the principal historical developments in the federal-provincial conflict over the control of the personal income tax.

Interprovincial Transfers and the Division of Powers

As a general rule, the allocation of a given power between Ottawa and the provinces depends on the division of powers as laid down in the Constitution. However, de facto responsibility need not coincide with de jure responsibility. For example, responsibility for monetary policy under the Constitution rests with Ottawa. It is quite possible for Ottawa (or the Bank of Canada) to "regionalize" monetary policy — e.g., the Bank could, if it wished, support the price of bonds of the provincial governments which, in turn, would imply that the provinces could, in effect, conduct open market operations.

There are, however, other ways in which the de facto division of powers can diverge from the de jure distribution. Our interest here centres on the extent to which the magnitude and form of intergovernmental transfers can influence the power spectrum. Because, historically, the federal government collected a proportion of taxes larger than its expenditure proportion, a need arose for some sort of revenue sharing between the federal government and the provinces. These transfers are generally classified into two broad categories — unconditional transfers and conditional transfers. The former increase provincial revenues without any implications as to how the monies should be spent, while the latter impinge on provincial autonomy in one way or another. The most succinct analysis of these two types of transfers still remains that by Jacques Parizeau:

> Unconditional transfers can take all kinds of shapes or forms. They can, for instance, be the result of a change in the shares that each level of government raises in a given tax field, when it has been accepted by both sides that that tax field will be shared and that the total tax burden in that field is set at a certain level. Or, they can result in the complete evacuation by the federal government of a given tax field. Or again, they can be produced by the creation of a new tax field, accepted by both authorities as being allocated permanently to the provinces. Or, they can be straight financial annual transfers from the federal budget to the provincial treasuries. And, of course, there can be a combination of all these formulas.
>
> A conditional transfer implies that the federal authorities agree to pay for all or part of a provincial program, as long as that program, its norms, and possibly its administration, have received federal approval or are subject to federal controls.
>
> Conditional transfers not only maintain federal control but they can also be used to expand it. Insofar as they take the shape of shared-cost programs, in other words, while the federal contribution is only a fraction of the total cost, the provincial contribution constitutes so much that cannot be allocated by provincial authorities to autonomous adventures. If the federal government opens shared-cost programs in existing fields of public expenditures, it can thus "freeze" gradually an increasing share of provincial budgets. *At the limit, provincial authorities become more or less administrative agencies of federally initiated or federally financed programs, irre-*

spective of how the legal documents distribute formal powers between the two levels of government.[3]

In terms of Figure 2-1, it should be obvious that a series of unconditional grants (labelled *GU*) allows for more provincial autonomy. At the other extreme is point *GC*, where the existence of conditional grants enables Ottawa to wield considerable influence in those areas that are constitutionally assigned to the provinces.

In more general terms, Albert Breton and Anthony Scott argue that one key role of intergovernmental grants is to bridge any mismatching between the assignment of taxation powers and the assignment of expenditure responsibilities (Breton and Scott, 1978, chap. 12). Indeed, they point out that the existence of this extra degree of freedom may be used as a means to achieve cost-minimization in the government sector. Suppose, for example, that provinces have the right to mount their own separate personal income tax systems. Because of the administrative, compliance, and co-ordinating costs of such a system, it may be preferable to adopt a system of centralized collection accompanied by a set of federal-provincial grants.

It is also possible to provide a rationale for conditional grants based on the concept of interjurisdictional spillovers. If programs under provincial jurisdiction involve spillovers (benefits which "spill over" to residents of other jurisdictions), it is likely that provinces will underspend on these activities. One solution would be to transfer the spending authority for this expenditure to the national government, which would "internalize" this externality or spillover. Another possibility is to set in place a set of conditional grants to the provinces which would compensate for any spillovers and encourage the optimal degree of spending on the particular category in question.

These efficiency and flexibility arguments aside, it is clear that the nature of intergovernmental grants can and does have an impact on the de facto division of powers between Ottawa and the provinces. Indeed, it is not an overstatement to assert that a major overhaul of intergovernmental grants is tantamount to a change in the Constitution itself.

Equally important, however, is the recognition that these intergovernmental grants need not be viewed as "exogenous" factors in federal-provincial finances. Just as the nature of the financing arrangements can influence the effective power distribution, so too the formal delineation of powers in the Constitution is likely to affect the form of intergovernmental grants. Thus, it is not surprising to find that the transfers from Ottawa to the provinces tend to be of the unconditional variety, whereas similar transfers between, say, Washington and the individual states tend to be conditional. The Canadian provinces have more autonomy than the U.S. states, and this will in all likelihood have an impact on the type of grants that characterize their respective federations.

Summary

The purpose of this study is to assess the degree to which centralization or decentralization will influence the economic performance of the Canadian federation. This chapter attempted to provide a framework for viewing this centralization/decentralization spectrum. By way of summary, the principal arguments are as follows: (a) different federations are located at different places in terms of the federal continuum in Figure 2-1; (b) federations are likely to have occupied different positions on this spectrum at various points in their economic history; and (c) de jure division of powers may differ from the de facto distribution, a consequence in large measure of the form and magnitude of intergovernmental transfers. The analysis also indicates the high degree of accommodation that the Canadian Constitution has provided in terms of adjusting to economic and political necessities. More speculatively, this might point in the direction of the Constitution as an accommodating rather than a determining factor in terms of the reaction to underlying economic and political trends.

However, this framework can only take us so far. It does not have anything to say about whether greater centralization is a good or bad thing from an economic perspective. In Chapter 3 I shall present a framework that will take us some way toward addressing this issue.

Chapter 3

Federalism and
Alternative Economic Strategies

In order to assess the impact on economic management of centralization in the Canadian federation it is necessary to develop some frame of reference for evaluation. Merely to enumerate where Canada or other federations stand with respect to particular policy areas (see Chapter 2) does little to confront the issue in a meaningful way. An enumeration is not the same as an evaluation. Accordingly, in what follows I shall attempt to provide one framework within which such an evaluation might take place. Essentially, the framework embodies a two-tier procedure. The first level addresses the range of alternative goals for the policy issue in question. The second level then draws out the implications of greater or lesser decentralization with respect to each of these goals. In other words, the appropriate division of powers is evaluated with respect to alternative policy goals. For some of the alternative objectives the division of powers will not be very critical. Not so for others. Economic theory also enters the analysis in another way: some of the alternative goals or objectives can be ruled out in terms of basic economic principles. More positively, resort to economic principles provides an avenue for determining what the overall policy goal ought to be.

Although the framework is general, for purposes of exposition the analysis that follows will focus on regional policy. Most of the analysis will be conducted from the vantage point of the federal government — I shall enumerate several federal or national objective functions and then attempt to ascertain what the appropriate role for the provinces might be under each of these objective functions. In this way, we can make some headway in sorting out the interaction between the allocation of powers and the objectives of policy.

This approach is not as "centre-oriented" as it might at first appear, since all Canadians (including the provinces) have a role in shaping the national economic strategies. However, later in the chapter I will also devote some time to the opposite approach — devising objective functions for the provinces and then deriving the appropriate federal strategy. Finally, and often forgotten or neglected, the focus of attention will shift to individual Canadians: What can one say about the division of powers from the vantage point of the economic well-being of individual Canadians? In part, at least, this is the "people prosperity" versus "place prosperity" trade-off that is encountered in most, if not all, federations.

Alternative Federal Objective Functions[1]

As noted above, the framework adopted can be viewed as a two-tier approach: What are the range of alternative goals or objectives that Canadian policy can or might adopt? And how best can any given policy be implemented, where implementation includes the appropriate role for the federal and provincial governments? I shall refer to the former as the "objective functions" of Canadian policy and to the latter as the "implementation strategies."

Table 3-1 presents a menu of alternative federal government objective functions relating to regional policy. The focus is geared toward the interaction between national and regional development goals. In this outline I am employing the words "objective function" in a broad sense. In the terminology of linear programming, the objective function for all seven alternatives in Table 3-1 would be "maximize national income." The seven cases differ from each other because the "constraint set" differs. For convenience, however, I am referring to these seven cases as alternative objective functions.

These alternatives are meant neither to be exhaustive nor necessarily representative of existing policies. Essentially, they are numbered so that, by and large, the level of national income (in per capita terms) will fall as we move down the list — i.e., the constraints are meant to be more and more binding as we move from alternative one to alternative seven. While it should become evident that different objective functions will place different constraints on the sorts of policies that the provinces should be allowed to pursue, the initial task is to elaborate on these various alternatives.

Objective function 1 would require Ottawa to consider only the impact on aggregate Canadian income when designing policy. This focus need not imply that there would be no direct regional aspects to federal policy. However, policies with definite regional effects would have to be justified in terms of their impact on increasing national income. For example, the emerging literature with respect to equalization suggests that in the presence of large provincial resource rents some sort of equalization program may be called for on efficiency grounds (see Boadway and

TABLE 3-1 Alternative Objective Functions for Canada

1. Maximize national income.

2. Maximize national income, subject to the constraints that:

   (a) all Canadians have access to some minimum level of public services;

   (b) there be a minimum level of income for all Canadians.

3. Maximize national income subject to the constraints that:

   (a) all Canadians have access to some minimum level of public services;

   (b) there be a minimum level of income for all Canadians;

   (c) regional income disparities be narrowed.

4. Maximize national income subject to the constraints that:

   (a) all Canadians have access to some minimum level of public services;

   (b) there be a minimum level of income for all Canadians;

   (d) provincial income disparities be narrowed.

5. Maximize national income subject to the constraints that:

   (a) all Canadians have access to some minimum level of public services;

   (b) there be a minimum level of income for all Canadians;

   (e) this income be produced (earned) in each region.

6. Maximize national income subject to the constraints that:

   (a) all Canadians have access to some minimum level of public services;

   (b) there be a minimum level of income for all Canadians;

   (e) this income be produced (earned) in each region;

   (f) that regional production disparities be narrowed.

7. Maximize national income subject to the constraints that:

   (a) all Canadians have access to some minimum level of public services;

   (b) there be a minimum level of income for all Canadians;

   (e) this income be produced (earned) in each province;

   (g) provincial production disparities be narrowed.

Source: Adapted from Courchene, 1973a, Table 1.

Flatters, 1982). More generally, since I have left unspecified whether this is a short-run or long-run maximization problem, federal intervention in providing regional infrastructure could well be consistent with maximizing Canada's income over the long run. If the provinces adopt policies that interfere with objective 1 (e.g., discriminatory purchasing policies, competing industrial location incentives), then the level of income in Canada will obviously be lower than it would be if provincial policies were consistent with overall income maximization. But since the federal government under this objective function would have no policy responsibility for the distribution of regional income (earned or unearned), Ottawa could be indifferent toward the actual economic policies of the provinces. Thus, overall federal policy takes as one of its parameters the existing provincial policies.

It would appear that this objective function is not acceptable to the majority of Canadians. It would certainly be unacceptable to many of the provinces who could probably argue that the costs of such an economic policy would be borne to a large degree by the lagging regions of the country. Indeed, we could see this objective function as being relevant only for two polar cases: a confederation, in which effective power rests with the state or provincial governments and where the role of the national government is primarily one of a co-ordinating agency and a provider of certain national public goods, or a virtual unitary state where the national government assumes most of the powers and is not concerned about the distribution of income, regional or personal, across its citizenry. Both examples would appear to be empty sets.

Objective function 2 incorporates two sorts of distributional constraints. Constraint (a), which appears in all of the remaining objective functions, can be satisfied by some version of an equalization program. Most economists would justify such a constraint in terms of satisfying the dictates of horizontal equity. Moreover, as noted above, an equalization program can be efficiency enhancing, though not all federations have opted for an equalization program (see Chapter 7). However, since Canada has had such a program since 1957 and since the principle of equalization is now enshrined in our Constitution, it is appropriate to incorporate equalization in all viable national objective functions.

Constraint (b), which also appears in the remaining objective functions, could be implemented via some version of the current welfare system or, preferably, via a comprehensive negative income tax. Beyond this concern over the welfare of low-income individuals, federal policy would focus only on overall efficiency. Again, this would require little co-ordination among federal and provincial policies, since there is no "regional" distribution constraint on overall economic policy although some types of provincial policies would clearly lead to higher levels of national income than others. As a final comment on the second objective function, the concern over the eventual size of the overall economic pie would require that any income-support scheme must ensure greater incentives to work than are characteristic of the current income-support network.

The third and fourth objective functions involve the federal government more directly in regional policy. Measures that enhance the equality of opportunity on a regional or provincial basis would contribute toward the achievement of these objectives — e.g., a generous equalization program, an approach to the established programs that embodies equal-per-capita payments to the provinces and perhaps raises the minimum income support level for welfare. Unlike the situation for the first two objective functions, Ottawa would now be concerned about policies initiated by provincial governments that would work against the narrowing of regional or provincial disparities.

Objective functions 5, 6, and 7 are intended to mark a real break in terms of the constraints imposed on the conduct of Canadian economic policy. The previous four objective functions could be accommodated via the tax-transfer system and production could occur where it had a comparative advantage. Not so with the last three objective functions. Here, if the constraints are binding (and surely they would be), the federal government has to step in and interfere with the allocation of resources in the private sector. The means by which this can be accomplished are all too familiar — Department of Regional Economic Expansion (DREE)-type programs and regional differentiation of the federal corporate income tax system for such things as depreciation allowances and research and development.

This interference with resource allocation is carried much further in the sixth objective function where the additional constraint requires a narrowing of regional production disparities. If, to accomplish this objective, the federal government considers it essential to offer subsidies to industry to locate in certain designated areas, then competing subsidies offered at the provincial level for location in non-federally designated areas must be considered, in terms of objective 6, as inappropriate provincial or regional policies.

Objective function 7 introduces a substantial further restriction to the maximizing of national income. It implies that the province rather than the region is the appropriate unit for economic development in Canada. In addition, it increases considerably the possibility of conflicting policies between the two levels of government. The cost, in terms of foregone national output, of measures by Ottawa to negate any "province-building" policies on the part of the richer province might be enormous under objective function 7, since it attempts to ensure that economic development proceeds apace in all the provinces. Even here, however, some caution must be exercised since there is generally more than one way of implementing a given policy — i.e., the choice of policy instruments to implement any given objective may be as important as the selection of the objective function itself.

While not everyone would agree that the alternative objective functions in Table 3-1 are representative of the options available to Canadian policy-makers, there is likely to be more agreement with respect to the underlying issue that Table 3-1 is intended to highlight — that the "appropriate" division of powers is not independent of the overall policy goal. If Canada alters the thrust of regional policy, then it is entirely possible that the existing allocation of powers will frustrate the achievement of the new policy goal. Likewise, a unilateral alteration in the division of powers may result in a situation where the existing policy goals become much more costly to achieve. One implication is, of course, that the policy goals and the division of powers ought to be jointly determined. A second and perhaps more important implication is that the constitutional arrangements ought to be flexible, since it is easier to amend the overall policy goals than the Constitution.

Selecting the Objective Function

Which objective function is the most appropriate for Canada? Fortunately or unfortunately, there is no unique way to answer this question. At one extreme, it is possible to conceive of situations where the exigencies of the global economy literally impose a particular objective function on Canada. At the other, the preferences of Canadians (individually and collectively) may dictate the overall policy goal, quite independently of the underlying economics. Likewise, the constitutional framework may effectively rule out some otherwise viable policy goals. Finally, we can always resort to economic calculus to ensure that, at the margin, the benefits of a particular policy alternative are not outweighed by its costs. It is instructive to focus on some of these alternatives in more detail.

In terms of an externally imposed objective function we might focus on the free-trade issue. Canada is one of the few industrialized countries that does not have access to a "domestic" market of 100 million people. Even though Canadians may not be in favour of, say, greater integration with the United States, the global economic exigencies may be such as to thrust this option upon us. In the regional policy area, continued regional subsidization along the DREE lines may prevent export access to the U.S. market because the Americans would resort to countervail. Canada would then be faced with a difficult trade-off — continue with its regionally interventionist policies and risk being locked out of the U.S. markets or forfeit its regional policies in order to gain access to the U.S. market.

In some cases, the external constraints may mesh very well with what underlying economics would dictate. Consider social policy. The cushion of growth Canada experienced in the 1960s allowed us to mount a generous system of transfers to persons, business, and even provincial governments. The environment in the 1980s is very different. It seems that the rewards will now go to those nations that can allocate or reallocate resources quickly and efficiently to the sunrise industries.

Hence, the role of social programs might now be reversed — to ensure that they facilitate adjustment rather than entrenchment in order to enhance our ability to rekindle economic growth and to penetrate foreign markets.

Not so obvious, perhaps, are the ways in which other factors can constrain or influence the selection of national economic objectives. For example, objective function 7 would not be practicable in federations like Australia or the United States where the constitution severely limits the ability of the federal government to implement pro-regional policies. History and culture can also be potent forces that impinge on the selection of national objectives. Relative to citizens of other federations, Canadians probably have an easy time understanding how cultural and regional factors can influence the selection of national economic priorities; but an example from Switzerland indicates that this element too can be full of subtlety. Most public finance analysts readily point to Switzerland as an example of a "tax jungle," with the various cantons levying a bewildering range of personal income tax rates on varying definitions of what constitutes the tax base. In the popular mind, this is typically associated with the degree of decentralization inherent in the Swiss federation. Yet, as John Hayes points out, although the Swiss constitution gives the federal government the authority to impose uniformity in terms of both tax laws and tax rates, there is insufficient political support across the Swiss citizenry for the federal government to strive for such uniformity (Hayes, 1982, p. 137).

In addition to these various constraints — constitutional, cultural or whatever — on the selection of national economic priorities, there are also economic factors which can impinge on the selection of the appropriate objective function. At one extreme, economic principles can operate in a prescriptive manner with respect to the selection of policy goals. With some degree of misrepresentation, this approach underlay the recommendations of the Rowell-Sirois Commission. The commission's "grand design" included the transfer of responsibility for unemployment relief and old-age pensions to the federal level and the creation of a set of national adjustment grants (essentially equalization payments) to ensure that all provinces would be able to provide their citizens with some average quality of public services. We can view this set of proposals as striving to satisfy both efficiency and equity concerns. The way is clearly open for the Royal Commission on the Economic Union and Development Prospects for Canada, the modern-day equivalent of Rowell-Sirois, to generate a similar policy objective or a series of policy objectives, again based on equity and efficiency concerns.

At the other extreme, economic principles can be used to rule out certain overall objectives. For example, suppose that the federal government opted to peg the rate of interest four percentage points below the prevailing market rate. The result would surely be a monetary explosion, a rapid increase in inflation and a depreciating Canadian dollar. Under such a policy, if the provincial governments ran substantial deficits, the Bank of Canada would be forced to monetize them in order to maintain the artificially low interest rate. This would no doubt exacerbate the consequences of the policy; but it would hardly constitute an argument for, say, curtailing the ability of the provinces to run deficits, since the overall policy was inappropriate in the first instance. Thus, a resort to economic principles can frequently reduce the range of objectives that can be considered to be viable: to argue for increased centralization or decentralization on the basis of facilitating the achievement of an inappropriate set of economic objectives is unacceptable.

The final approach to selecting the appropriate overall policy objective is to evaluate the costs and benefits of the various alternatives where the benefits would include society's preference for both economic and non-economic attributes. Indeed, Table 3-1 was designed with this approach in mind. The underlying assumption is that Canadians have a genuine concern for their fellow citizens. Other things being equal, they would prefer that all provinces enjoy economic development at a roughly equal pace. Thus, setting aside the foregone output costs, the "benefits" associated with each objective function in Table 3-1 would be such that they would rise monotonically from objective function 1 to objective function 7. However, as was emphasized in the previous section on alternative federal objection functions, it is likely that satisfying these successive objective functions will result in progressively greater amounts of foregone output. Ideally, of course, we would want to move through the various objective functions until the marginal benefit of going to the next one falls below the corresponding marginal cost. In principle, it should be possible to make estimates of the costs associated with moving through the various objective functions.[2] It is unlikely, however, that the benefits are amenable to precise measurement in as much as they are largely a function of citizens' perception of what it means to be a Canadian. Consider, again, objective function 7. The economic costs of satisfying this objective function would be extremely high, particularly since the provincial economies have very different economic structures, and if the various provinces were to adopt offsetting policies, the costs of achieving objective function 7 could escalate dramatically.

Yet certain features of the existing policy environment can be seen as consistent with this objective function. For example, the different regional provisions associated with unemployment insurance can be viewed as ensuring that the population base of the various provinces remains essentially intact. To the extent that this reflects a strong preference by Canadians that provinces hold on to their populations or that all provinces share equally in any development, rather than a simple case of policy error, then the nature of the underlying problem is considerably altered. In this case, the fact that economic analysis can show that this objective function embodies substantial efficiency costs may not carry the day. Rather, the notion of the "optimal policy instrument" may come into play — i.e., are there other avenues for satisfying these societal preferences that are less damaging to national efficiency? This is, of course, a general issue because there are many policy areas where the inputs into the objective function embody principles that go beyond economic efficiency. In the particular case of objective function 7, however, it seems that neither the opportunity costs nor the preferences of Canadians could sustain it as a viable policy goal on the regional front. This is a personal reflection.

Recapitulation

This analysis has been somewhat unsatisfactory, but perhaps it could not be otherwise given the inherent intractability of specifying policy objectives and the recognition that more is at stake in doing so than the discipline of economics. Nonetheless, it is important to recognize that the discussion-cum-analysis was designed to be illustrative rather than definitive. In particular, the intent of the exercise was to argue that the assignment of powers is not independent of the overall policy objective, and vice versa; relatedly, that some policy objectives are more constraining in terms of the division of powers than are others; that economic principles can make an important contribution to selecting the appropriate objective function both in a positive (prescriptive) sense and in a negative (constraining) sense; and, finally, if a particular objective function is preordained (for reasons of culture, constitution or whatever), the optimal policy instrument calculus can normally come into play in terms of rendering the objective function more consistent with overall efficiency.

The purpose of the following section is to illustrate some of these principles at a level that is closer to the reality of Canadian regional policy.

Provincial Strategies

In the discussion of Table 3-1, attention was directed to certain types of provincial actions that would inhibit or make more costly the achievement of the overall policy goal. The thrust of the previous section on selecting the objective function was to argue that there can, in turn, be some constraints on the choice of these overall goals. The purpose of this section is to focus on the range of policies of provincial governments and on how they might interact with federal government policies. The analysis is conducted within the context of a more concrete policy environment. Specifically, how might the range of provincial policies affect the ability of the federal government to reduce regional economic disparities? For illustrative purposes I shall assume that this federal objective is appropriate.

The analysis will serve to distinguish two features of provincial policies:

(a) A greater (or lesser) degree of provincial autonomy need not necessarily impinge on the attainment of federal goals. Much will depend on the particular instruments deployed by the various provinces as well as by the federal government. This is, of course, the optimal-policy-instrument calculus.

(b) With respect to the issue at hand — the reduction of regional disparities — it is not only the richer provinces whose policies may prove problematical. Those of the poorer provinces (the provinces toward which the policy is directed) can also generate difficulties for the success of the policy.

While the analysis that follows is specific, the underlying attempt is to highlight general features that can be brought to bear on the policy areas dealt with in the remaining chapters of the book.

The starting point of the analysis is that the federal government's goal is to minimize the variance in unemployment rates across regions. For convenience, Canada is viewed as being composed of two regions — the Maritimes and Ontario. The diagrammatic representation of the analysis is presented in Figure 3-1.[3] The vertical axis represents "numbers of people." Equal distances along this axis, whether above and below the origin (or, for that matter, straddling the origin) represent correspondingly equal numbers of people. The horizontal axis depicts relative wage rates. To the right of the origin wages are higher in the Maritimes than they are in Ontario; i.e., $W_m - W_o$ is positive, where the symbols are self-explanatory. To the left of the origin, the opposite prevails: $W_o - W_m$ is positive, i.e., wage rates are higher in Ontario.

Curve *JJ* represents job creation in the Maritimes. For convenience, it is drawn as a straight line. The positive slope of *JJ* is intuitively plausible — the lower wages are in the Maritimes (relative to Ontario) the greater will be the number of jobs created there. For example, where $W_o - W_m$ equals *OF*, the number of new jobs in the Maritimes will be *OD*. At a relatively lower Maritime wage (*OF*), job creation will rise to level *OB*. Curve *JJ* is drawn so that even when relative wages are equal (at the origin) there is still some positive Maritime job creation.

Curve *OM* is designed to represent the probability of outmigration from the Maritimes. An increase in Ontario wages relative to Maritime wages will lead to a greater outflow of persons to Ontario — for differential *OF*, the outmigration flow is *OC*, and for wage differential *OE*, it is *OA*. The *OM* function is drawn so that even where wage rates are identical there is some outmigration, but this is of no special significance to the analysis.

FIGURE 3-1 A Geometry of Regional Adjustment

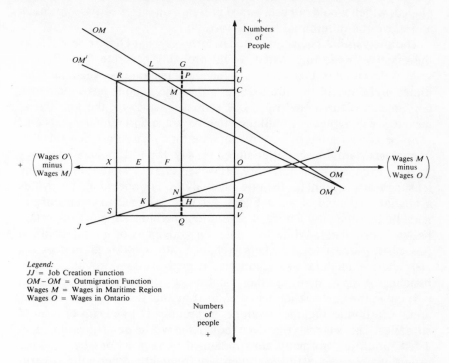

Legend:
JJ = Job Creation Function
OM–OM = Outmigration Function
Wages M = Wages in Maritime Region
Wages O = Wages in Ontario

The starting assumption is that the two economies are currently in equilibrium, and the task at hand is to allocate the new entrants into the Maritime labour force between new jobs and outmigration. Let the number of new entrants in the Maritime job market be equal to the vertical distance *AB* in the diagram. (Note that this is an exogenously determined number of people. While it is represented thus far by the vertical distance *AB*, it can also be represented by any other equivalent vertical distance in the diagram, e.g., *UV*.)

The Optimal Currency Area Solution

If the Maritimes had a separate currency, the system would, in the absence of government intervention, settle down at an effective wage differential equal to *OE* in Figure 3-1.[4] This wage differential is obtained by taking the vertical distance representing the numbers of new entrants into the labour force and sliding it between the curves *OM* and *JJ* until it "fits" exactly, i.e., distance *KL* equals distance *AB*. At this effective wage differential, *OA* new entrants would migrate and *OB* new entrants would find jobs in the Maritimes. Since *OA* plus *OB* equals *AB*, this "looks after" all the new entrants, so to speak. If the actual wage differential were only equal to *OF*, then *OC* persons would migrate, *OD* would get new jobs, and the remainder (*AC* plus *DB*) would be unemployed, which would put downward pressure on the effective wage rates and move the differential back toward *OE*.

The analysis has been conducted in terms of what I have referred to as the effective wage rate. What would probably generate this effective wage differential is a movement in the exchange rate between the Maritimes and Ontario (we are assuming that the regions have their own currencies). If the actual wage differential is, say, *OF*, the Maritimes, currency will depreciate until the effective wage differential equals *OE*.

Since regions and provinces do not have their own currencies, this sort of analysis is obviously better suited to, say, the EEC, where countries do have exchange-rate flexibility. However, there is some value in using it as the starting point for the present analysis. For one thing, it provides a tangible example of what Figure 2-1 was designed to demonstrate, namely, that the very nature of federations precludes the use of certain policy instruments. While the states or provinces of a confederation possess the ability to alter their exchange rate, such freedom does not characterize a federation. Secondly, the analysis does provide a useful benchmark for comparing other solutions to the regional problem. In particular, the next section will demonstrate that the "optimal currency area" solution to Figure 3-1 can be "reproduced" by means of a set of subsidies. This suggests that even though the two levels of government in a federation are normally constrained in certain actions by, say, the provisions of the constitution, there are frequently other policy instruments which can accomplish the same result. For example, provinces are not allowed to mount tariffs against goods from other provinces. However, provincial purchasing preferences have the same impact as a tariff for the goods in question. Indeed, these purchasing preferences can be viewed as altering the province's exchange rate for the protected goods.

The Optimal Subsidy Scheme

Let us bring a bit of reality into Figure 3-1 and assume that the Maritimes does not have its own currency. Moreover, let us further assume that while wage rates are lower in the Maritimes the differential is only *OF*, which is less than *OE*. As noted above, associated with wage differential *OF* is outmigration of *OC* and job creation *OD*, leaving *DB* and *AC* Maritimers unemployed. One obvious solution would be for Maritime wage rates to fall relative to those in Ontario so that wage differential *OE* is reached. But suppose that there are sufficient rigidities in the system (minimum wage laws, nationwide wage bargaining, union strength and the like) such that the wage differential remains at *OF*. Under these circumstances, what is the optimal policy? One answer is that which duplicates the optimal currency area solution.

To see this result, assume that the government has full information with respect to the outmigration and job creation functions and, further, that it can act as a perfect discriminator (i.e., it will pay only what is needed to require the additional migrant to move and to have the additional worker employed). Under these assumptions it will offer subsidies to both outmigration and job creation such that, at the margin, the effective wage differential again becomes *OE*. The cost of having the marginal person migrate (*GL*) is equal to the marginal cost of employing an additional worker (*HK*), where these costs are measured horizontally. The total cost of the subsidy program is the sum of the two triangles *NHK* and *LGM*.

The assumptions underlying this result are very restrictive. If firms and people are able to conceal their preferences, it is possible that all new jobs and all outmigrants will receive a subsidy. In this case the marginal subsidy cost of employing the last person will be *BK*, not *HK*. (This assumes that the job-creation function goes through the origin.) In a C.D. Howe Institute monograph David Springate found, using inter-view techniques, that many recipients of DREE grants would have invested in the Maritimes without the grant (Springate, 1973). Hence, subsidies will often find their way even to those who would not need them to motivate their action. For the present, however, we shall main-tain the assumption that governments have full information with respect to these reaction functions.

Therefore, under the assumption that the federal government is com-mitted to a policy of full employment and that it takes the existing relative regional wage rates as given, an optimal subsidy scheme would involve both outmigration (bringing people to jobs) and job creation (bringing jobs to people) subsidies. What should be clear, however, is that the cost of achieving this goal will be increased substantially if the provinces mount development policies of their own.

Provincial Strategies

Suppose that the Maritime provinces know that the federal government is committed to absorbing any and all new labour force entrants. This sets the stage for the provinces to take advantage of Ottawa's commit-ment. One obvious strategy for these provinces is to attempt to shift the outmigration function downward, e.g., from *OM* to *OM'* in Figure 3-1. One way in which this might be accomplished is to allow the provinces the right to select the training or retraining programs for their citizens. If these programs are designed to train people for within-region skills rather than skills which would equip them better for employment in other regions, the result will be to tilt the outmigration curve downward. Similarly, these provinces can lobby the federal government to incorpo-rate regionally differentiated benefits within employment insurance (as is now the case, since beneficiaries can collect UI for longer periods of time if they reside in high-unemployment regions), which will also move the *OM* curve in the direction of *OM'*.

What happens if the outmigration curve shifts from *OM* to *OM'* in Figure 3-1? The new equilibrium is at *X* — i.e., the effective equilibrium wage differential now becomes *OX*. Outmigration equals *OU* and job creation equals *OV*, where by construction *UV* (i.e., *OU* + *OV*) is equal to *AB* or, what is the same thing, *RS* = *LK*. The marginal cost of employing or moving the last labour force participant is now equal to *QS* (which equals *PR*) compared to the previous marginal cost of *HK*. The net result is that the federal government is enticed to devote more resources to the regional problem and in the process to shift its policy mix in the direction of bringing jobs to the Maritimes rather than sending people to jobs in other regions.

Obviously, the policies of the other provinces can also influence the cost to the federal government of achieving this regional goal. Were the richer provinces to mount barriers to internal migration (via provincial licensing of skill accreditations, for example), this policy would be equivalent to the previous example — i.e., a downward shift in the outmigration function in Figure 3-1. Were the richer provinces to counter the federal initiative by offering competing job-creation subsidies, this policy would shift the job-creation function upward in Figure 3-1. Not only would this result in larger overall costs (as in the previous case), but now more of the adjustment arising from the imposition of an optimal set of subsidies would be thrown on outmigration from the Maritimes and less on job creation in the region.

Free market adherents would probably argue that if the federal government would adopt a non-interventionist stance (and if everyone believed that there would be no intervention), then it is likely that the wage differential would adjust quickly toward *OE*, the equilibrium wage differential. But given the underlying assumption that the federal government commits itself to regional intervention, the analysis demonstrates that the provinces (both "rich" and "poor") can mount policies which have the potential for dramatically escalating the costs of the regional policy and, in the limit, frustrating the initiative altogether. Under these circumstances, one of two things must occur. If the federal government adheres to this policy goal, then the allocation of powers should be altered so as to prevent the provinces from frustrating the policy; but if the provinces maintain their right to legislate in this area, then the federal government should abandon the overall objective.

Prior to taking leave of Figure 3-1, it should be noted that much of what passes as regional policy can be evaluated, at least at a superficial level, in terms of its parameters. Consider the process of deconcentration of governmental activities. Suppose that as a result of moving Veteran's Affairs to P.E.I. the local pay scales increase relative to those of Ontario. This would be shown in Figure 3-1 as a shift of point F toward the origin. In other words, the existing wage differential would be narrowed. As a result, more of the group AB would be unemployed in the absence of any subsidies and, therefore, both the marginal and total costs of "accommodating" these people would increase. And so on.

Regional Policy Goals from a Provincial Perspective

To this point the analysis has accepted explicitly the existence of national goals for overall policy. Within this framework, the focus then turned to the degree to which actions by either level of government (but particularly the provincial level) might interfere with accomplishing these goals. However, it is possible to approach policy from the opposite vantage point. The objective function would then be a composite one — the set of provincial preferences. Assuming, as is likely, that these preferences could not be satisfied simultaneously, the role of the federal government would then be either to render consistent these preferences by such measures as deft implementation of conditional and unconditional grants or to take the lead in constitutional reform so that the existing provincial preferences would become consistent with Canadian unity.

There are some advantages to this alternative way of approaching overall policy formation. First of all, for many policy areas it may be a more realistic representation of the political economy of the federation. Relatedly, it emphasizes two salient features of the country: first, provincial priorities with respect to critical economic variables and economic objectives (e.g., the exchange rate, free trade, the trade-off between employment and inflation) may differ, and, second, even where the preferences are essentially similar, they may not be satisfied to the same degree. It is instructive to elaborate on this second point. Suppose that all provinces desire the same inflation-unemployment trade-off. With inflation running at comparable rates throughout the country but with widely varying rates of unemployment, it is obvious that some provinces would not only find themselves far off their preferred positions but would also be desirous of a different overall policy mix with respect to these two variables.

The Role of the Constitution

With some degree of misrepresentation we can view the alternative approaches of national or provincial dominance in terms of the roles that can be played in the analysis by the Constitution or the division of powers. At one extreme would be what could be referred to as "constitutional determinism." The existing division of powers will determine the range of federal objective functions that are viable, and the system will somehow be made to work in accordance with this existing division of powers. This might be equated to the Table 3-1 approach. At the other extreme, we can entertain the notion of "constitutional endogeneity." This might be associated with the approach discussed in the previous section on provincial goals. The division of powers would be modified to reflect the perceived needs and preferences of the various governments. However, the analogy does not hold in practice because of the role that can be and is played by the set of intergovernmental transfers. As noted in Chapter 2, a change in the nature and form of these transfers is effectively a change in the Constitution itself. Is this constitutional endogeneity or is it working within the existing formal framework? While the answer is not clear, the distinction between constitutional determinism and endogeneity will be broached in Chapter 10, which is devoted to the notion of "balance" in federations.

Summary

Most of the remainder of the monograph will focus on specific policy areas and address the issue of whether a move toward either greater centralization or decentralization of responsibility for the area in question will enhance economic management of the federation. The policy areas selected for detailed study are quite diverse so that no one framework for evaluation is applicable across the board. Nonetheless, the analysis in Chapters 2 and 3 suggests that there are a few general questions and/or issues that are likely to be applicable across a fairly broad spectrum of policy issues. In summary form, these considerations would include the following:

- Since federations differ in their degree of centralization (or decentralization), it is likely that the approach and institutional arrangements associated with a given policy area will also differ.
- Over time, individual federations may well approach a given policy area in different ways.
- De jure allocations of power for given functions may differ from de facto allocations, and one of the principal reasons for this difference relates to the form and magnitude of the system of intergovernmental transfers.
- The set of factors that will determine the objectives of policy may differ across federations and across time. Some federations are more "open" than others. Some are more constrained than others by the judicial interpretation of their constitutions. Some have regional/cultural/linguistic cleavages that impact in various ways on determining policy objectives.
- As a result of these various factors, resort to economic principles in determining policy objectives will likely be more important in some

federations than others. This reservation need not be as constraining as it might at first appear, since there generally exist alternative ways to implement a given policy objective (i.e., the optimum-policy-instrument calculus). Moreover, some of the alternative objectives can normally be ruled out in terms of economic principles.

- What is clear, however, is that the appropriate institutional arrangements (e.g., the allocation of powers) is not independent of the selection of the overall policy objective.
- For other specifications of the policy objective, failure to constrain the allocation of powers may be very costly.
- In the limit, where the policy objective is determined exogenously, viable economic management will probably have to entail some constraint on the allocation of powers (i.e., constitutional endogeneity). At the opposite extreme, where the allocation of powers is immutable, viable economic management suggests that the objective function may have to be constrained (i.e., constitutional determinism).
- Since it is generally much easier to alter policy objectives than to alter constitutions, this suggests that a premium be placed on the ability of a given constitutional framework to accommodate change.

The last few observations would appear to be particularly important for purposes of this study. As a result of the recent reform of the Canadian Constitution, particularly the implications that have already flowed and will surely continue to flow from the enshrining of rights and freedoms in the Constitution, there appears to be an impression across the country that constitutional reform may provide an answer to a much wider set of concerns. In my view, there are potential dangers in harbouring this attitude. It reflects a belief in what I have earlier termed constitutional determinism. It may well be that the Constitution is in need of revamping in certain areas. However, what was clear from Chapter 2 is that the Constitution Act, 1867, has proven to be remarkably flexible in accommodating swings to and from the centre. This suggests either a cautious approach in terms of recommending constitutional change or, if change is required, that it be implemented in a way that does not straitjacket future generations of Canadians and their governments. The analysis that follows will argue that where changes are required they can in general be accomplished within the existing legal/constitutional framework.

While I believe that the backdrop presented in Chapters 2 and 3 does provide some useful guidelines for addressing the centralization/decentralization issue, it does not provide a comprehensive framework. For example, there are decentralized federations that function well as there are centralized federations that perform equally well. Relatedly, what is decided with respect to one policy area cannot be independent of what is appropriate for other areas, but this is just another way of indicating that much of what follows has, of necessity, to be subjective.

Because of this I shall attempt, wherever possible, to present both views of the issue. More particularly, my general approach will be to give considerable weight to the way in which responsibility for particular policy areas has evolved over the years and to recommend dramatic changes only when the consequences of maintaining a version of the status quo are equally dramatic. While this may appear, at first blush, to lead to a reassertion of the merits of the existing situation, this will not always turn out to be the case. What it does mean, however, is that the ardent decentralist and the ardent centralist alike may be disappointed with the ensuing analysis and its implications.

Chapter 4

Monetary Policy

The analysis of particular policy areas begins with a focus on macroeconomic or stabilization policy. Later sections of the monograph will deal with allocation and distribution policies. The selection of policy areas within these three broad categories is admittedly arbitrary. Basically, I have tended to focus on those areas where there has been a debate as to which level of government should be responsible for the policy area in question. In terms of stabilization policy, there are probably four areas that merit analysis — monetary policy, fiscal policy, exchange-rate policy, and regulatory policy. The present chapter focusses on monetary policy and, to a limited degree, on regulatory measures (wage and price controls and exchange-rate controls). Chapter 5 deals with fiscal policy.

The approach to each of the areas will follow a roughly similar pattern. First, an attempt will be made to ascertain the present division of powers with respect to each activity. Second, the analysis will then assess those sets of arguments that appear to be motivating a move toward either greater or lesser centralization. At times both of these trends come into play. For example, in the analysis of monetary policy there has been a long-standing discussion to the effect that monetary policy should be regionalized (decentralized). At the same time there is also concern that monetary policy is not centralized enough because, for example, provincially and even federally chartered trust companies are not required to hold reserves with the Bank of Canada. As part of the assessment of these issues, attention will also be directed to their economic implications. Thus, while it is constitutionally problematical to force trust companies to hold reserves with the Bank of Canada, this obstacle may not be of great importance if such a move is not necessary in order that the Bank have adequate monetary policy control. Phrased differently, the reason why certain areas are not more centralized or decentralized may not relate to the provisions in the Constitution; it may be a function of the underlying economics.

The third aspect of the evaluation will be to recommend changes in the institutional or constitutional environment if this seems appropriate. Often, however, there exist no impediments to greater centralization or decentralization. For example, if Ottawa deemed it desirable to regionalize monetary policy, this could in fact be done without constitutional amendment. In other words, the present centralization of monetary policy rests on economic arguments, not on constitutional ones.

The Legislative Authority for Monetary Policy

The federal government has the constitutional power to conduct monetary policy under the terms of section 91 of the Constitution Act, 1867, which confers on the federal government exclusive jurisdiction over currency and coinage, banking, the incorporation of banks, the issue of paper money, savings banks, interest, and legal tender. The principal vehicle for implementing monetary policy is, of course, the Bank of Canada, which was established by an Act of Parliament in 1934. The main legislative authority under which the Bank of Canada operates is the Bank of Canada Act, the Bank Act, the Quebec Savings Bank Act, and the Currency and Exchange Act. This legislation, particularly the Bank of Canada Act and the Bank Act, is subject in principle to decennial revision, although recent practice suggests that revisions take place every 12 years or so.

The Bank of Canada's mandate, as indicated in the preamble to the Bank Act, is:

> to regulate credit and currency in the best interests of the economic life of the nation, to control and protect the external value of the national monetary unit and to mitigate by its influence fluctuations in the general level of production, trade, prices and employment, so far as may be possible within the scope of monetary action and generally to promote the economic and financial welfare of the Dominion.

The relationship between the governor of the Bank of Canada and the minister of finance will be the subject of a later section. In general terms, the Bank has considerable latitude in its day-to-day conduct of monetary policy.

The instruments that the Bank has at its disposal in conducting monetary policy include setting primary and secondary reserve requirements, conducting open market transactions, operating the discount window (as a lender of last resort), and engaging in moral suasion. Basically, however, the Bank's influence stems from its ability to determine the total quantity of high-powered money in the system, and from the requirements of the Bank Act that the chartered banks must hold a certain portion of this high-powered money in the form of primary reserves. These required reserves are currently 10 percent for sight or demand deposits and 3 percent for notice deposits. Once again, practice has modified principle so that some of the instruments have become more important than others. For example, the primary reserve requirements can no longer be changed by the Bank of Canada: the rates for primary reserve requirements are now incorporated in the Bank Act. On a day-to-day basis the principal way by which the Bank of Canada alters the cash reserves of the banking system is by shifting the federal government's deposits between the chartered banks and the Bank of Canada, so that this instrument might well be added to the above four. Moreover, the weight put on various instruments is a function of the underlying philosophy of monetary policy. Under the pre-1975 approach to policy, which placed considerable emphasis on securing "appropriate credit conditions," the exercise of moral suasion and changing secondary reserve ratios became important policy instruments. In more recent years, with the emphasis on controlling monetary aggregates, these instruments fell into relative disuse. Interesting as these issues may be, neither they, nor an analysis of the particular policy stance that the bank is following, are at the heart of the present analysis. The actual policy stance is conceptually quite separate from the issue of whether monetary policy should be less or more centralized than it currently is. It is the latter issue that is the focus of this monograph.

In our analysis of centralization versus decentralization there are at least three general issues in the monetary policy area that merit consideration. The first has a long policy following and concerns whether or not monetary policy should be regionalized. In other words, is monetary policy too centralized? The second general issue relating to the division of powers goes in the opposite direction. The near-banks, such as trust companies and credit unions, are not required to hold reserves with the Bank of Canada despite the fact that their deposits are close substitutes for chartered bank deposits. Does this exception serve to emasculate the Bank of Canada's control over monetary policy? Phrased differently, does efficient monetary control require that all deposit-taking institutions be subject to Bank of Canada control? The third general concern relating to the positioning of monetary policy vis-à-vis the division of powers is of more recent origin: Should the Bank of Canada be responsible to any government or should it derive its authority directly from the Constitution? I shall refer to this issue as the constitutionalist approach to central banking, even though in the context of this monograph this term can be misleading. Each of these concerns will be dealt with in turn. The final section of this chapter focusses on wage and price controls and, in particular, on the issue of whether the federal government should have the constitutional ability to impose controls. This policy area is not normally associated with the exercise of monetary policy. It is included in this chapter principally because it is frequently viewed as an alternative to monetary restraint in combatting inflation.

The Case for Regional Monetary Policy

Monetary policy, unlike fiscal policy, is essentially centralized in all nation states, federal or otherwise. Nonetheless, within Canada, there have been persistent requests that there be a regional dimension to the design and implementation of monetary policy. In general, these arguments founder on one or another basic economic precept. However, some of them are more sophisticated than others so that it is instructive to focus in detail on the more common variants.

Optimal Currency Areas

The notion of "optimal currency areas" was raised in Chapter 3 in the context of alternative ways to view the regional problem. To focus on it again in this section, albeit in more detail, is admittedly repetitive. However, since modern macro theory views exchange rates as absolute rather than relative prices — as an extension of macro or monetary theory rather than a part of micro theory — a consideration of optimal currency areas is a logical starting point for a discussion of regional monetary policy.

The notion of optimal currency areas, and in particular the argument that the national currency area may not coincide with the optimal currency area, was popularized by Canadian economist Robert A. Mundell (1968, chap. 12). He argued that the case for flexible exchange rates was made stronger if the currency area was the economic region rather than the nation state:

> Suppose that the world consists of two countries, Canada and the United States, each of which has separate currencies. Also assume that the continent is divided into two regions that do not correspond to national boundaries — the East, which produces goods such as cars, and the West, which produces goods such as lumber products. To test the flexible-exchange-rate argument in this example assume that the U.S. dollar fluctuates relative to the Canadian dollar, and that an increase in productivity (say) in the automobile industry causes an excess demand for lumber products and an excess supply of cars.
>
> The immediate impact of the shift in demand is to cause unemployment in the East and inflationary pressure in the West, and a flow of bank reserves from the East to the West because of the former's regional balance-of-payment deficit. To relieve unemployment in the East the central banks in both countries would have to expand the national money supplies or, to

prevent inflation in the West, contract the national money supplies. (Meanwhile the Canada–U.S. exchange rate would move to preserve equilibrium in the national balances.) Thus unemployment can be prevented in both countries, but only at the expense of inflation; or inflation can be restrained in both countries but at the expense of unemployment; or, finally, the burden of adjustment can be shared between East and West with some unemployment in the East and some inflation in the West. But both unemployment and inflation cannot be escaped. The flexible exchange rate system does not serve to correct the balance-of-payments situation between the two regions (which is the essential problem), although it will do so between the two countries; it is therefore not necessarily preferable to a common currency or national currencies connected by fixed exchange rates.

The preceding example does not destroy the argument for flexible exchange rates, but it might severely impair the relevance of the argument if it is applied to national currencies. The logic of the argument can in fact be rescued if national currencies are abandoned in favor of regional currencies.

To see this suppose that the "world" reorganizes currencies so that Eastern and Western dollars replace Canadian and U.S. dollars. If the exchange rate between the East and the West were pegged, a dilemma would arise similar to that discussed in the first section. But if the East-West exchange rate were flexible, then an excess demand for lumber products need cause neither inflation nor unemployment in either region. The Western dollar appreciates relative to the Eastern dollar, thus assuring balance-of-payments equilibrium, while the Eastern and Western central banks adopt monetary policies to ensure constancy of effective demand in terms of the regional currencies, and therefore stable prices and employment.

. . . if the case for flexible exchange rates is a strong one, it is in logic, a case for flexible exchange rates based on *regional* currencies, not on national currencies. The optimum currency area is the region. (pp. 180–81)

This notion of separate exchange rates for the various regional economies was bandied about principally in academic rather than policy circles. In full bloom, the proposal would involve not only regional currencies but, as well, regional central banks. There is a certain consistency to this idea, since a separate currency (a flexible regional exchange rate) is a sine qua non for an independent and activist monetary authority.

From a practical as distinct from a theoretical standpoint, however, this notion has always been a non-starter. The provinces, singly or in regional groupings, obviously do not have a constitutional right to embark on such an initiative. More generally, while there do exist a few nation states (or quasi-nation states) that do not have their own currency, I do not know of an example of a subnational entity having its own currency.[1]

Nonetheless, the notion of separate currency areas is a valuable conceptual, if not practical, construct. The latest flurry of interest in separate regional currencies occurred in the context of the Quebec sovereignty-association debate. One of the more convenient ways of focussing on the impact of Quebec's separation on the various regional groupings in Canada was to work out its implications for the values of currencies. In general, the consensus view was that the currency of a separate Maritime nation would depreciate vis-à-vis Ontario, whose currency would, in turn, depreciate vis-à-vis western currency. What might happen to a Quebec currency was more problematical, although most analyses felt that it would settle between the Ontario and Maritime values. In any event, the point is that by focussing on the exchange-rate implications of separate regional currencies we can often come up with insights that are more difficult to obtain by focussing on other variables.

It is not difficult to see why the exchange-rate issue looms large in a country which has as economically disparate regions as does Canada. In a country of only 25 million people, the exchange rate plays the role of short-term arbiter in an economy that aspires to be both a major natural resource exporter and a major secondary manufacturing centre. Thus, exchange-rate variations in the short term become a substitute for more fundamental adjustments and, as such, tend to get translated into arguments for regional exchange-rate variation.

As a matter of historical interest, it is instructive to recall that it was western Canadian concern over the value of the exchange rate in the early 1930s which led, in part, to the striking of the Royal Commission on Banking and Currency whose recommendations led to the establishment of the Bank of Canada. As a final comment on the notion of optimal currency areas, the fact that separate currency areas are necessary for an activist regional monetary policy will aid in evaluating (more correctly, debunking) the remaining proposals for regionalizing various aspects of monetary policy. The first relates to the proposition that the Bank of Canada act as a buyer of last resort for provincial government bonds.

Bank of Canada Support for Provincial Bonds

The Bank of Canada is the fiscal agent for the federal government. In this capacity its role can vary from providing advice on debt management policies to becoming the lender of last resort for government bonds — i.e., to "printing money." Under a monetary policy stance that incorporates monetary growth targets, the scope for printing money is correspondingly curtailed. Nonetheless, the Bank of Canada does have a special role to play in the financing decisions of the federal government.

Over the years, there have been calls for the Bank to perform a similar service for the provinces. Part of the reason behind these requests is that the interest rates on provincial debt vary considerably across provinces and all of them face higher borrowing rates than does the federal government. Why not have the Bank of Canada also act as fiscal agent for the provinces in the sense of guaranteeing that their borrowing rates stay within some prearranged margins?

The economics of this proposal are clear. If the Bank of Canada agreed to support provincial bonds so as to ensure that their yields bore some constant relationship to federal yields, then there would in effect be 11 central banks in the country. Let us assume that the yield on a particular province's bonds tended to push through the fixed differential. In order to prevent this result the Bank of Canada would have to stand ready to buy all quantities at this fixed yield — it would have to monetize the provincial debt. Thus, each of the provincial governments could, in effect, engage in open market operations. The Bank of Canada would lose control over the supply of money — a totally untenable solution. The rejection of provincial bond support by the Bank of Canada would probably find wide agreement among all economists and not merely those who classified themselves as monetarists.

In any event, the Bank of Canada is, and has been, very careful not to engage in the monetization of any provincial debt. The most interesting instance occurred in the mid-1960s. In return for being exempted from the 1963 U.S. Interest Equalization Charge, Canada was required to ensure that its international (foreign exchange) reserves not exceed US$2.6 billion. In the mid-sixties our foreign exchange reserves were bursting through this ceiling. One obvious alternative was for the federal government to utilize any excess foreign exchange reserves to retire outstanding Canadian debt held by foreigners. The difficulty was that most of the externally held debt was issued by the provinces and their agencies and not by the federal government. Even in this case the Bank refrained from purchasing provincial debt, largely, I suspect, because this would then lead to pressures on the Bank to purchase provincial debt in the domestic context. In the event, the "crisis" was sorted out in 1968 when, through an exchange of letters at the official level, the foreign exchange ceiling was withdrawn.

During this same time frame, roughly the mid-1960s, some provisions were enacted which gave the provinces access to substantial borrowing at rates identical to those on long-term federal bonds. This occurred in connection with the establishment of the Canada Pension Plan/Quebec Pension Plan (CPP/QPP). By design, contributions were to exceed benefits in the early years of the plan, and these funds were to be accessed by the provinces in accordance with their share of overall contributions. Table 4-1 shows the total provincial indebtedness to the CPP, as of 1983. The interest rate on these provincial issues is set equal to the current level on long-term federal bonds. It is not my purpose to evaluate the merits of this policy (i.e., has it encouraged deficit financing on the part of the provinces?); rather, it is to point out that this CPP approach may have been motivated, at least in part, by the concurrent pressures for Bank of Canada support for provincial bonds. Obviously, the CPP scheme is vastly different from a policy where the Bank of Canada acts

TABLE 4-1 CPP Provincial Indebtedness, March 1983

Government	Amount Owed ($ millions)	% of Total	% of Total Provincial Debt Held by CPP
Newfoundland	472.3	2.1	14.8
P.E.I.	98.0	0.4	20.8
Nova Scotia	901.9	3.9	27.9
New Brunswick	680.9	3.0	29.7
Quebec[a]	99.1	0.4	0.5
Ontario	12,299.7	53.7	45.8
Manitoba	1,313.0	5.7	33.2
Saskatchewan	1,026.5	4.5	29.8
Alberta	2,436.2	0.6	38.4
British Columbia	3,436.5	15.0	96.3
Canada	171.4	0.7	—
Total	22,935.5	100.0	—

Source: Health and Welfare Canada. March 1983. *Canada Pension Plan Statistical Bulletin.*
a. The figures relating to the QPP are not shown in this table.

as the fiscal agent for the provinces in a bond-support role. The province of Quebec did not follow this route. Its pension fund can and does buy some of the debt of the province, but it pays market prices for it.

Regional Credit Allocation

A more frequent variant of the call for greater regional monetary policy relates to regional credit allocations. There are many possible approaches, but I shall consider only one — that the lending in a given region bear some proportion to the deposits of that region. There are basically two concerns with such a recommendation. First, if all it is meant to accomplish is that bank loans be "booked" on a regional basis, then it will have little impact, since money and credit are simply too fungible to have their optimal allocation deterred by such a policy. It is a simple matter for companies to set up regional "corporate shells" in order to become eligible for the borrowing allocations. Second, if the intention is to require that any loans be reflected in capital actually being put in place in the regions, then this plan would run squarely against the notion of a common internal capital market. Other provinces and regions would quickly reciprocate in one way or another, and the net result would likely be more akin to an overall "deadweight loss," in the economists' jargon, than a significant alteration in the patterns of economic activity.

Underlying these concepts of sectoral or regional credit allocations must be some notion of regional capital market imperfections. The degree to which these imperfections exist is an on-going topic of policy debate. In this regard it should be noted that the postwar history of the Canadian banking system has generally been in the direction of removing the various impediments to the free flow of capital within the country. For example, this was certainly a theme of the Royal Commission on Banking and Finance (the Porter Commission, which reported in 1964) when it called for the removal of the 6 percent asset ceiling on the lending side of the chartered banks' balance sheets. Indeed, one of the characteristics of the Canadian banking system is the absence of these credit regulations, in stark contrast to the banking systems of countries like France and even the United States.

However, from a constitutional standpoint, it is also clear that the credit allocation route can be followed if Canada is willing to accept the accompanying costs. A similar result can be accomplished in other ways, too. All provinces now have loan agencies of various sorts, and the federal government also operates regional development and lending facilities. In other words, much of this concern now falls under the general rubric of regional development rather than monetary policy. While many analysts look more kindly on these regional development incentives than I do, the majority would probably prefer that the banking system be permitted to operate on a nation-wide basis and that any regional lending preferences be carried out under the auspices of regional rather than monetary policy. Nonetheless, it should be noted that on more than one occasion the Bank of Canada has, via moral suasion, requested the chartered banks to minimize the likelihood that their lending policies would have a deleterious effect on the less-buoyant regions of the country (e.g., in 1973).

While there has been no formal attempt to utilize the monetary system to ration credit along regional lines (and quite appropriately so, in my view), there have been several developments that might be viewed as distant substitutes. Provincially regulated near-banks have grown rapidly, as have credit unions and the caisses populaires. Indeed, some of these financial institutions dominate the deposit scene in certain provinces. For example, in the mid-1970s cheque clearings through credit unions in Saskatchewan were in the order of four times those through the largest chartered bank. Moreover, in the recent Bank Act, provincial governments were allowed to take a major share position in a newly chartered bank. This was in response to the recommendations emanating from the 1973 Western Economics Opportunities Conference where, once again, the expressed concern was the insensitivity of the existing nationally chartered banks to the perceived needs of the western provinces.

Regional Input into Bank of Canada Policy

A separate issue from formal regionalization of the central banking function is the filtering up of regional concerns into the Bank's decision-making process. The directors of the Bank of Canada are chosen to reflect both the geographical and industrial diversity of the country. There is at least one director from every province. Generally, these directors are not experts in monetary matters, but they presumably do reflect their respective provincial and occupational concerns in the Bank's board meetings. This is in marked contrast to the U.S. experience where experts are brought in as consultants to the Federal Reserve. The Bank of Canada does not follow this practice, perhaps because it might run afoul of the parliamentary framework in which the Bank operates. This would presumably also rule out Bank directors appointed by the provinces. However, it is consistent and sensible for the Bank to ensure that some of its directors have more than a passing familiarity with monetary theory and policy. Once again, there exist other avenues for provinces and regions to bring their concerns to the attention of the Bank: the televised First Ministers' Conference on the Economy in February 1982 saw premier after premier level a broadside against the Bank's high interest-rate policies.

My own view on these matters is that while it is appropriate on occasion to take into account regional concerns, control over monetary policy must rest at the centre, as it presently does.

Recapitulation

Other countries have experimented more with regional monetary policy than has Canada. In general, however, there are other avenues for meeting any special financial needs of regions and provinces — avenues that are preferable to wholesale interference with the national banking system.

There is precious little that the provinces can do on their own to alter this system, since monetary policy falls clearly in the federal domain. If, however, the federal government did wish to devolve some powers to the provinces or regions it seems equally clear that it could do so. However, the rationale for a centralized monetary authority is based on sound economic principles, and I would expect this is, and will continue to be, the reason why it is centralized.

This does not mean that the status quo has to be viewed as the optimal policy. For example, there are few theoretical reasons for the current practice of excluding provincial treasury bills as satisfying the chartered banks' secondary reserve requirements. Moreover, Canada could well follow the Swiss practice of allocating a portion of the profit (seignorage) of the central bank to the cantons (provinces). In other words, the institutional environment may take many forms, as it currently does across countries, but the key point is that there be only one monetary authority.

Extending Reserve Requirements to Near-Banks

Given that there is ample economic reason for not regionalizing monetary policy, the obvious next question is whether monetary policy is sufficiently centralized. The context within which this issue has arisen most frequently is whether or not adequate monetary control requires that provincially chartered or at least provincially regulated near-banks be brought under the aegis of the Bank of Canada. The most recent arena in which the matter has come up was in relation to the new Canadian Payments Association: Should all financial institutions accepting deposits transferable by "order" (cheque) be required to join the Canadian Payments Association? I shall deal with each in turn.

Reserve Requirements for Provincially Regulated Intermediaries

Many Canadians do their banking with trust companies and credit unions. For some, the attraction is the greater range of services (such as longer operating hours and higher interest rates on transactions deposits) that these near-banks provide. For others, the attraction may be that they want to belong to a credit union which might cater more to the needs of its members than would a branch of a large national bank. At any rate, the issue at hand becomes the following: With the rapid growth of these near-banks, which are not required to hold cash reserves with the Bank of Canada, is it likely that they will pose a problem for monetary control? Put differently, does effective monetary control require that near-banks be brought under central bank control?

One answer to this question was given by the Economic Council of Canada (1976) in its special report, *Efficiency and Regulation: A Study of Deposit Institutions*. Underlying this valuable report is a "functional" approach to the financial sector:

> [A]ny institution will be able to perform activities open to deposit institutions if it meets the qualifications and abides by the rules governing those activities. In contrast to other approaches towards revising the framework governing deposit institutions, our functional approach permits reform without requiring changes in the division of powers between federal and provincial authorities, provided agreement is reached on the development of regulation relating to each function. (p. 126)

Hence, consistent with this functional approach, the Economic Council of Canada recommended that if reserve requirements are imposed on the chartered banks, similar requirements should be required of any other deposit institutions engaging in similar activities:

> We recommend that cash reserve requirements be applied to all deposit institutions on an equal basis according to the nature of their liabilities.

Reserve requirements should only be levied against demand deposits, notice deposits, and term deposits with an earliest maturity of less than 100 days and should be set at a level of no more than 4 percent of the relevant deposit liabilities. The holding of such reserves should be made a condition for direct access to the clearing system and for coverage under deposit insurance. Depending on the institution, these reserves could be held at either the Bank of Canada or an approved depository. (p. 69)

The implications of this functional approach to financial intermediaries go well beyond the issue at hand, whether near-banks should be required to hold reserve requirements. It also has implications for the manner in which Canada ought to approach the regulation of the "four pillars" of the financial sector (banking, brokerage, insurance and trusts) which will be dealt with in Chapter 8. What the functional approach says is that any one deposit institution can cross over into other areas provided that it fulfils the regulations and requirements of this area. This important question — the regulation of financial and capital markets — will be dealt with in Chapter 8.

Returning to the issue at hand (whether monetary control requires that all financial institutions offering deposits transferable by cheque be required to hold deposits with the Bank of Canada), the accepted answer is that rendered on several occasions by Governor Gerald K. Bouey. From the September, 1974, *Bank of Canada Review*:

To return to the legislative framework for banks and near-banks, an admission that the present arrangements are anomalous in certain respects does not mean that they fail to work reasonably well in practice so far as monetary policy is concerned. The technical powers given to the Bank of Canada have in fact proven broadly adequate for the Bank's purposes. Largely through its control over the supply of cash reserves to the chartered banking system, the Bank of Canada has unquestionably been able to exert sufficient influence over the process of monetary expansion to have a major impact on the degree of ease or tightness of financial markets. So much is evident from the record. It is clear that the effects of Bank of Canada operations on the growth of money and credit and on the level of interest rates have not been confined to chartered banks but have been felt pervasively throughout the financial system . . . the Bank of Canada can, by varying the supply of chartered bank cash reserves, influence the operations not only of the banks but of the near-bank financial institutions as well. . . .

The basic character of these responses is not altered by the fact that the near-banks are not required to maintain a stipulated minimum level of cash reserves nor indeed to hold part of their cash in accounts with the central bank, as chartered banks must do. The function of the banking system's cash reserve requirements is simply to increase the short-run precision and predictability of their response to changes in the supply of central bank money. So long as the banks are required to hold somewhat larger non-earning cash reserves than they would by choice, they will respond rather sensitively to excesses as well as to deficiencies in their cash reserve positions. And so long as the institutions that are subject to these legal requirements bulk large in the financial system — and in particular in the business of issuing chequable deposit liabilities — their response to changes in their reserve positions will have prompt and substantial effects on other financial institutions and markets.

These conditions for a reasonably effective implementation of monetary policy are met in Canada as things stand at present. The chartered banks are dominant enough in the relevant areas of deposit-taking and short-term credit extension to give the Bank of Canada through its management of their cash reserves, an adequate degree of leverage and precision for monetary control purposes.

Up to present, then . . . I cannot blame any shortcomings in monetary policy on the technical arrangements that link the Bank of Canada to the rest of the financial system. The absence of cash reserve requirements applicable to depository institutions other than chartered banks has never, to my knowledge, frustrated the efforts of the Bank of Canada to bring about as sharp of a curtailment of the pace of monetary expansion and as large an associated rise in short-term interest rates as we were prepared to contemplate in the circumstances of the time.

Whether this would continue to be the case in future years if a growing proportion of the country's banking business were taken on by institutions other than the chartered banks is another question. In thinking about the adequacy of our present cash reserve arrangements for purposes of monetary control, one does have to consider the implications of a further possible decline in the chartered bank's share of chequable deposit business. A progressive loosening of the relationship between the amount of cash reserves supplied by the central bank and the probable responses of the institutions which provide the public with most of the money it uses for transactions purposes would undoubtedly make the effects of central bank operations less predictable. (Bouey, 1974, pp. 22–23)

It is possible that the march of events will require second thoughts on this issue. The pressures may not arise so much from the near-banks as such but from the computer and informational revolution and the overall restructuring of the financial system. In Canada, the Toronto Dominion Bank is leading the way in terms of moving in on the brokerage business, while brokerage houses have for some time engaged in banking functions, and Trylon has the potential of becoming an omnibus financial institution. In the United States, the demarcation lines within the financial sector are being eroded far more quickly. Merrill Lynch has effectively become the first nation-wide bank, short-circuiting the 50-year old law that limits multistate banking. Sears-Roebuck with its nation-wide system of outlets will soon be a major "one-step" financial intermediary. It is simply too early to tell what the outcome is likely to be and whether or not in the Canadian context similar pressures will serve to erode monetary control. As a model for financial regulation, the Economic Council of Canada (ECC) proposals with respect to functional regulation make eminent sense. Our approach has tended to resemble functional separation, even to the extent of applying restrictions on cross-ownership for some intermediaries. Along with functional separation has been a separation of regulatory authority. As noted above, securities firms are provincially regulated while banks are federally regulated. Within this context, there is a problem of regulatory overlap. Even if the ECC's notion of functional regulation is recognized as meritorious on economic grounds, it would still run into political or constitutional roadblocks, since it would imply that the federal authorities (via the Bank of Canada) would be regulating, say, securities firms with respect to their deposit-taking activities. In recent years, however, matters have become considerably more complicated. For example, federal deposit insurance now applies to some provincially regulated intermediaries so that the regulatory lines of authority are becoming progressively blurred. Developments such as this on the regulatory front, in addition to the movement toward integration of the financial intermediation function on the part of the intermediaries themselves, have brought matters to a head. Both Ottawa and Ontario are now engaged in framing proposals for regulatory reform. These concerns transcend the narrower issue of whether non-bank deposit-taking institutions ought to hold reserves with the Bank of Canada. However, they are relevant in the sense that, until the larger issues are sorted out, it is likely that practice and not principle will carry the day with respect to reserve requirements: as long as the Bank of Canada feels that the existing framework is workable, there will be little attempt to engage in regulatory warfare in order to ensure that all deposit-taking institutions hold reserves with the Bank. This concern over jurisdiction also played a role in the structure of the Canadian Payments Association.

The Canadian Payments Association

As part of the 1980 Bank Act revision, a new institution, the Canadian Payments Association (CPA), was established to oversee all cheque-clearing and cash-settlement requirements of the financial system. Previously this task had been performed by the Canadian Bankers' Association and only the banks had direct access to the clearing system. Near-banks had to clear through one or another of the chartered banks. Not surprisingly, there was considerable opposition to this approach by the near-banks. Partly as a result, the white paper on banking legislation, tabled in 1976, proposed the CPA. Under this proposal all institutions in Canada accepting deposits by "order" (chartered banks, trust and mortgage loan companies, credit unions and caisses populaires, Quebec savings banks, Alberta Treasury Branches, etc.) would be required to join the CPA and all would be required to maintain minimum cash-reserve deposits with the Bank of Canada.

The near-banks objected to this proposal and the provinces, led by Quebec, argued that this requirement was unconstitutional since the CPA was in effect making provincially regulated institutions subject to federal legislation. As the federal background paper points out, these white paper proposals related to the near-banks in terms of their "payment activities," an area of federal jurisdiction, and not in terms of any regulations relating to the chartering of these institutions (Canada, Department of Finance, 1979). However, because mandatory deposits with the Bank of Canada were not considered essential for purposes of monetary control, the federal government modified its CPA proposals rather than have the matter settled in the courts.

The CPA is now conceptually separate from the Bank of Canada. Deposit-taking institutions have the option of becoming full members and clearing directly through the CPA (in which case they will have to hold clearing balances with the CPA), or they can, as previously, clear indirectly through a member of the CPA. Local credit unions need not be members. Rather, the credit union "centrals" of each province or perhaps an umbrella organization of these centrals can become full members. In terms of the chartered banks, any clearing balances that they hold with the CPA will count toward their primary reserve requirements.

Thus, the CPA represents one more in the long line of "constitutional" compromises. What it does do, however, is narrow the difference between a bank and a non-bank — both can now obtain direct access to the national clearing system. As long as the Bank of Canada continues to conduct policy in terms of its post-1975 philosophy — to rely on variations in interest rates to restrain the demands for money and credit — this narrowing of the difference between banks and non-banks is not likely to erode the ability of the Bank of Canada to implement monetary policy.

However, this may pose a problem if the Bank ever reverts to its pre-1975 philosophy which placed substantial emphasis on controlling the availability of credit. It is instructive to devote a paragraph or two to this issue because it will serve to illustrate one of the key messages in this monograph — that there are undoubtedly many activities in the stabilization area where the Constitution constrains federal action, but as long as these activities do not make economic sense or can be done in preferable ways, then they should not be viewed as a constitutional constraint on the federal government's ability to implement stabilization policy.

Credit Controls

In the 1960s and early 1970s the Bank of Canada tended to conduct monetary policy with an eye to developing "appropriate credit conditions" (Courchene, 1976, Part II). This approach included focussing on both the cost and the availability of credit. On occasion, the Bank recognized that the particular setting for the cost of credit was inconsistent with the market clearing rate of interest, but it hoped to get around any problems by simultaneously influencing the availability of credit. It is in this context that there can be considerable slippage in monetary policy because, if the Bank's credit restrictions apply only to chartered banks, the way is open for the near-banks to thwart the thrust of policy.

Not surprisingly, there was some recognition of this problem by the Bank. Indeed, in January 1970, in a rare extension of its power of moral suasion beyond the chartered banking system, the Bank of Canada "asked a number of other financial institutions not to frustrate the effect of the ceiling on 'swapped' (foreign currency) deposits by arranging similar transactions in other ways" (*Bank of Canada Annual Report, 1969,* p. 18). To the best of my knowledge, this edict was not challenged. However, shortly afterward the then minister of finance, Edgar Benson, proposed that Parliament enact controls over the terms under which credit could be advanced. These controls would have applied to a wide range of institutions. While the measures were dropped once Canada floated its dollar on June 1, 1970, the underlying issue remains unresolved: Has the Parliament of Canada the right to enact a broad set of credit controls? If not, should it have such authority?

Let us focus initially on the second concern. Credit controls would have an impact on private sector demand through their effect on the availability of credit. In the pre-1975 philosophy of the Bank of Canada (i.e., prior to the advent of monetary gradualism) the modus operandi of the Bank was to generate "appropriate" credit conditions. In turn this meant instituting desired changes in both the cost and the availability of credit. In this context the ability to extend controls over the availability of credit beyond the chartered banking system would appear to be of some value in the conduct of monetary policy.

This issue has diminished in significance in the post-1975 era. With the Bank of Canada placing more emphasis on monetary aggregates and in the process allowing interest rates to settle at their market clearing levels, it is no longer as important to worry about the availability of credit, as distinct from the cost of credit. This is so because the Bank is more likely to prefer the less interventionist and more market-oriented alternative of raising interest rates to restrain spending. Thus, the possible constitutional inhibitions in the use of credit controls are not currently viewed as a problem, and the possibility of introducing a constitutional amendment in this regard has effectively disappeared from the policy scene.

In terms of the first question — whether the Parliament of Canada does have the ability to enact a broad set of credit controls — any answer can be speculative at best. It seems likely that such a move would be challenged by the provinces as impinging on their right to regulate the near-banks. And it also seems likely that the courts would respond in much the same way as they did to the Anti-Inflation Act challenge (elaborated later in this chapter), namely, that credit controls can be supported in times of economic emergency but not in the normal course of events. It seems to me that this state of affairs is appropriate, i.e., no additional federal powers are needed here.

Nonetheless, it is instructive to note that there is more scope to apply credit controls in most other federations. As Zysman (1983) has noted recently, the German financial system can be viewed as credit based, as distinct from that of the United States and Canada which is best described as market based. In a credit-based system (which would include the systems of some unitary states like Japan and France) it is typically the case that governments play a major role in the allocation of credit. Thus, my suggestion that the federal government does not need additional powers in this area reflects in part at least a preference for the operations of markets and not a reflection of what is characteristic of other federations.

This analysis ties in closely with some of the issues dealt with in the previous chapters, especially those related to the selection of the overall policy objective for a given policy area. In this particular case the potential constraining influence of the Constitution was minimized because the existing policy goal was altered. Naturally, the concern may arise anew if the thrust of monetary policy once again reverts to focussing on the availability of credit rather than the cost of credit. Indeed, this interaction between the distribution of powers and the selection of policy goals will occupy centre stage in Chapter 8 on capital markets. To anticipate the analysis somewhat, the existing constitutional framework does constrain what can be done. However, in my view, the real issue at stake is to decide what ought to be done — to decide on the appropriate structure and role for the various market intermediaries. Only then, it seems to me, can one come up with an appropriate division of powers.

A Constitutionalist Approach to Monetary Policy

The above analysis focussed on the arguments for centralizing or decentralizing monetary policy. There is, however, a strand of analysis that suggests that monetary policy should be independent of any level of government (Parkin and Bade, 1978). One of the forerunners of this analysis is a series of papers by Canadian economists Keith Acheson and John Chant (1972, 1973a, 1973b) that focusses on central bank behaviour in the context of the theory of bureaucracy. Because the Bank is not independent, but is, rather, a bureau, it is likely to gear its policy actions so that they tend to be consistent and accord with the interests of its parliamentary "master" — the minister of finance. This has been carried further by others who argue that central banks will always tend to conduct policy in ways that will serve their bureaucratic aims, often at the expense of conducting appropriate monetary policy. The "solution" to this problem normally involves a set of constitutional arrangements which gives the central bank an existence independent of the government of the day but at the same time limits its freedom to manoeuvre. I shall refer to this arrangement as the "constitutionalist approach" to central banking. It has its counterpart on the fiscal side in terms of the recent efforts, particularly in the United States, to amend the constitution to require that governments balance their budgets.

As Canadians are aware, this issue came to the fore in the late 1950s and early 1960s when both governor James Coyne and the then finance minister Donald Fleming argued that the final responsibility for monetary policy rested with the other. The upshot of the crises was that a bill calling for the removal of the governor passed the House of Commons, but Coyne resigned prior to its being ratified by the Senate. Immediately upon taking over as the new governor, Louis Rasminsky clarified the relationship between the Bank and the government:

> In order that the relationship between the Bank of Canada and the Government can be clarified in law, an amendment to the statute governing the Bank of Canada is now being considered by our Parliament. The amendment makes it clear that there must be, as there is now, continuous consultation on monetary policy between the Government and the Bank. It provides a formal procedure whereby, in the event of a disagreement between the Government and the Bank which cannot be resolved, the Government may, after further consultation has taken place, issue a directive to the Bank as to the monetary policy it is to follow. Any such directive must be in writing, it must be in specific terms, and it must be applicable for a specified period. It must be made public. The amendment makes it clear that the Government must take ultimate responsibility for monetary policy and it provides a mechanism for that purpose. But the central bank is in no way relieved of its responsibility for monetary policy and its execution. It can be assumed that if the Governor were directed to carry out a monetary policy which, in good conscience, he could not regard as being in the national interest he would, after taking steps to ensure that the issues involved were placed clearly before the public, resign.[2]

Interestingly enough, Rasminsky also indicated that this had always been the Bank's (and indeed former governor Coyne's) understanding of the relationship. More recently, Governor Bouey commented on Rasminsky's clarification, noting that the former governor "stressed the advantages of arrangements which give the central bank a sufficient measure of independence within government to be held responsible for monetary policy, and also make it clear that the elected representatives of the people have ultimate responsibility and have a suitable mechanism through which to exercise that responsibility" (Bouey, 1982, p. 4).

With this as a backdrop, I return to the question at issue: Is there a need to make the Bank more independent of the government of the day? Two considerations influence my answer. First, an independent central bank does not fit well within the context of a parliamentary system. Those central banks that have more independence than has the Bank of Canada tend to be found in non-parliamentary systems. If the Charter of Rights and Freedoms serves to erode Parliament's authority (as surely it will), there may be some future increased independence in other areas as well, but that day has not yet arrived. Second, it is not clear from recent experience that the Bank necessarily knuckles under to government demands. In my own research I have argued that over the 1972–74 period the overall fiscal stance influenced Bank policies. However, in the recent period the Bank of Canada has held firmly to its tough policy stance despite widespread public criticism. Thus, my conclusion at this time is that the existing constitutional arrangements are satisfactory.

Controls

Wage and Price Controls

Wage and price controls can be defined as "detailed sets or regulations regarding allowable increases in wages, prices, profits and other sources of income administered by a government agency with mandatory powers of enforcement (Canada, Department of Finance, 1979, p. 17). Over the last few decades many, perhaps most, of the industrial nations have seen fit to impose wage and price controls as part of their struggle against inflation. Canada's major experiment with mandatory controls occurred over the 1975–78 period, usually referred to as the AIB period, named after the Anti-Inflation Board which was the agency responsible for monitoring the controls.

For purposes of this monograph, the intriguing feature of this controls experiment was that, in response to substantial pressure from the public and in particular from the labour unions, the government of Canada asked the Supreme Court to rule on the constitutionality of the Anti-Inflation Act, the legislative underpinning for the controls. By a seven to two decision the Supreme Court ruled that the Anit-Inflation Act was intra vires. However, the written arguments suggested that there were limits on the federal government's ability to legislate in this area. There was consensus among the Justices that in times of a national emergency the Parliament of Canada had the authority to override the division of powers. The split in the decision revolved around the issue of whether Parliament had to specify, in the act itself, that it was enacting the legislation on an emergency basis. Since Parliament did not so specify, the minority ruled that the legislation was unconstitutional. The majority view was that it was not necessary for Parliament to label legislation as emergency in order that it be constitutional as emergency legislation. But a subgroup of the majority argued that while the Anti-Inflation Act was constitutional on emergency grounds, it was also consistent with the peace, order and good government provision because inflation was a subject matter that transcended local or provincial concerns.

This judgment raises two general issues. First, constitutionally, what can the federal government do in the future in the way of imposing controls? Second, should the Constitution be altered so as to allow Ottawa standby powers to impose wage and price controls? I shall deal with these in turn.

It is obvious that the federal government can enact controls to apply to the federal public sector and to that part of the private sector falling under federal jurisdiction (e.g., banking and transportation). If the provincial governments were to enact parallel legislation and in the process agree that the administration of the controls be conferred on, say, a federally created agency, then the way would be clear to re-create the sort of Anti-Inflation Board system of controls even if there were no economic emergency. The problem is, of course, that it may be difficult to get provincial support and co-operation in a non-emergency environment.

The other alternative is for the federal government to enact wage and price controls on the basis of its emergency powers and to leave itself open to a court challenge as to whether or not the inflation environment warrants designation as an economic emergency.

The 1982 round of wage restraints — generally referred to as the 6 and 5 program — reflects this constitutional dilemma. Ottawa imposed these guidelines on those sectors falling within its constitutional authority, essentially the federal civil service and federally regulated industries. For their part, most of the provinces enacted similar sorts of programs for their own employees, but there was no attempt on their part to apply the controls across all industries.

Interestingly enough, prior to the imposition of 6 and 5 there was a flurry of economic literature relating to tax-based income policies, or TIPS for short. The essence of such schemes is that the income tax system is used to provide incentives to keep wage increases in check. One of the advantages claimed for this type of control scheme was that it provided more flexibility (particularly for exporting industries) than did a universal regime of controls. In my view, however, a major part of the appeal of the TIPS approach to wage restraint was that it did not run up against a constitutional problem — TIPS did not attempt to regulate wages directly but only through the provision of income tax incentives. Hence, it probably could be enacted by the federal Parliament.

However, the issue remains: Should the Constitution be amended to allow the federal government the authority to implement (in non-emergency situations) wage and price controls? After all, this would be giving the Parliament of Canada the power that the U.S. federal government has. On this question there is unlikely to be unanimity because it essentially becomes an issue of whether we believe that wage and price controls are an appropriate and effective anti-inflation policy instrument. We can find economists on both sides of this issue. My own view is that to the extent that controls are needed, they are necessary in the public and not the private sector. The federal government clearly has the constitutional right to impose controls on its own employees, as the 6 and 5 program has demonstrated. Moreover, a set of wage and price controls is likely to be effective only when the economic situation is such that most groups are willing to co-operate with such an initiative. In turn, this is likely to be a period that would qualify as an emergency in the constitutional sense; but Ottawa already has the right to enact controls in such a situation.

In general, then, it is my view that the federal government already has adequate powers in respect of implementing wage and price controls. However, I readily admit that part of this view is based on my belief that the imposition of controls is as likely to do harm as to do good. Accordingly, the system ought to ensure that they can be imposed only in real emergency situations.

Exchange Controls

The existence of high interest rates over the recent period have brought occasional calls for adopting a low interest rate policy for Canada supported on the external front with a regime of exchange controls. As is the case for wage and price controls, the federal government could obviously enact exchange controls under its emergency powers, but Ottawa's powers extend beyond this. It is likely that the combination of the trade and commerce power (section 91.2) and the responsibility for currency and coinage (section 91.14) could support an exchange control regime. Unlike the case for wage controls and credit controls, exchange controls do not regulate intraprovincial transactions and, hence, would not be likely to run afoul of provincial powers such as property and civil rights (section 92.13). Thus, it is likely that:

> [E]xchange controls can be made to apply to provincial governments as long as they are of general application and do not single out provincial actions for special regulation. On the other hand, controls over provincial borrowing and lending abroad in the absence of general exchange controls would appear to be ultra vires. (Canada, Department of Finance, 1979, p. 19)

The question that arises in this context is whether it is desirable to have a constitutional amendment or some enabling legislation which would allow the federal government to regulate foreign borrowing and lending by provincial governments. As was noted earlier in the chapter, it is the provinces and their agencies (such as the hydros), rather than the federal government, that have made extensive use of off-shore funds, and frequently these bond issues have been denominated in foreign pay. In 1976, for example, provincial governments obtained more than $4 billion in foreign markets. There are substantial risks to this borrowing, particularly if the issues are denominated in foreign currency. If the federal government allows the exchange rate to fall by, say, 5 percent, then the Canadian dollar debt-servicing of this foreign debt will also increase by 5 percent and so will the redemption cost if the dollar remains at this lower level. In the early 1970s the federal government went as far as to exhort all potential foreign borrowers to do their utmost to place their issue domestically. But this plea was more an exercise in moral suasion than in regulation.

Other federations approach this issue differently. For example, the Australian Loan Council controls and co-ordinates all borrowing by the Australian states. However, to introduce the concept of a loan council in Canada would represent a dramatic alteration in federal-provincial powers because the implications of restricting provincial borrowing would reverberate on provincial budgets and federal-provincial transfers. At the very least the larger provinces would probably insist on more flexibility in altering their portions of the shared income tax system (see Chapter 5). Thus, while an amendment giving Ottawa the power to oversee and regulate provincial access to foreign markets is probably out of the question (or at least could not be contemplated without major alterations in other aspects of the federal-provincial financial interface), it does appear to be eminently sensible to strive for more federal-provincial co-ordination in this area. Indeed, it is somewhat anomalous that the federal government, with its preferential credit rating, should be tapping domestic savings via Canada Savings Bonds and at the same time driving provinces off-shore for investment funds. It might make for more appropriate federal macroeconomic policy if any exchange-rate changes affected federal debt servicing rather than the present situation where federal actions on the exchange-rate front impact principally on the provinces' debt servicing.

Summary

Chapter 4 completes the brief review of monetary policy issues and the division of powers. I shall turn to an analysis of fiscal policy and the division of powers, following which the general implications arising from both monetary and fiscal policy will be highlighted.

Chapter 5

Fiscal Policy

Chapter 4, in focussing on one of the two "big levers" of stabilization policy, showed that monetary policy was effectively centralized in Canada. The story is somewhat different for the other major macro policy tool — fiscal policy. Not only do the provinces and municipalities share in the overall decisions to spend and to tax, but they also account for a greater share of both revenues and expenditures than does the federal government. This is clear from Table 5-1, which presents an overview of the distribution of own-source revenues in the postwar period. The shrinking proportion of federal taxation is even more apparent in the data which relate to revenues after transfers: for 1982, provincial revenues exceed federal revenues, and the combined provincial-local revenues account for nearly two-thirds of overall revenues.

The picture is somewhat different if the federal presence over time is expressed relative to gross national product, as in Table 5-2. While the federal role in terms of both revenues and expenditures has shrunk vis-à-vis the provincial-local role, it is not the case that the federal presence has diminished with respect to GNP. As the lower panel of Table 5-2 indicates, Ottawa's expenditures as a share of GNP have remained in the 16–17 percent range since 1975. This is slightly below the Organization for Economic Co-operation and Development (OECD) average for the proportion of spending accounted for by central governments.

With this information as a backdrop, I now turn to a discussion of the division of powers and fiscal stabilization. Given that there is almost universal agreement that the federal government must play the major stabilization role, the relevant issue as far as the federal government is concerned is whether Ottawa has sufficient room to perform adequately its fiscal stabilization role.

TABLE 5-1 Distribution of "Own-Source" and "After-Transfers" Revenues, Selected Years 1945–82

	Own-Source Revenues			Revenues after Transfers		
	Federal	Provincial	Local	Federal	Provincial	Local
			(percent)			
1945	71.4	6.1	12.4	69.2	16.7	14.1
1950	64.1	21.9	14.0	59.8	22.8	17.5
1955	63.6	22.0	14.4	61.1	20.3	18.6
1960	58.2	24.5	17.3	51.6	24.3	24.1
1965	54.5	29.7	15.9	45.9	29.3	24.8
1970	50.9	34.6	14.5	39.8	35.4	24.9
1975	51.8	36.3	11.9	39.2	38.0	22.8
1980	46.2	41.5	12.3	34.5	42.6	22.9
1982	46.8	41.0	12.2	35.5	42.0	22.6

Source: Department of Finance, *Economic Review April 15, 1983*, Tables 64 and 66.

TABLE 5-2 Government Expenditure as a Percent of GNP

	1967–74	1975	1976	1977	1978	1979	1980	1981
				(averages)				
Total Government								
Canada	36.1	41.3	40.2	41.3	42.0	40.7	41.7	42.7
OECD	37.3	42.4	42.6	43.3	44.3	44.2	45.2	N/A
Federal Government								
Canada[a]	14.6	16.8	15.8	16.2	16.6	15.7	16.4	17.4
OECD	16.2	18.0	18.1	18.3	18.9	18.9	19.4	N/A

Source: Department of Finance, *Economic Review, April 1983*, Table 47.
a. Excludes CPP/QPP.

There are three aspects to this general question. First, does the federal government have sufficient leverage in the area of government expenditures? Much more complicated is the second aspect: Does Canada's decentralized approach to personal and corporate income taxation limit the ability of the federal government to utilize these key instruments for stabilization purposes? Finally, the exercise of stabilizing fiscal measures frequently requires the running of deficits. Is there a difference in the ability of Ottawa and the provinces to float debt, internal or external? These three areas will be addressed in turn. At the same time we should recognize that although there is general agreement that the federal government ought to have the principal role in fiscal stabilization, the provinces can also contribute to the stabilization effort. Interspersed through the analysis will be an evaluation of the provincial adjunct to the overall stabilization effort.

Expenditure Policy

As Table 5-2 suggests, on a national accounts basis, the provinces and municipalities now account for the bulk of government spending. However, much of this spending is not amenable to the pursuit of active stabilization policy. Expenditures on health and primary education are not good candidates for offsetting cyclical fluctuations. Nonetheless, the provinces and their agencies (e.g., hydros) probably oversee more of those types of capital expenditures that can be accelerated or retarded to offset swings in economic activity than does the federal government. However, the issue at hand is whether or not this implies that Ottawa is left with too little influence.

In my view the federal government still has ample room to manoeuvre. The federal spending power under the Constitution is exceedingly wide. Indeed, it is plenary. Over the past two decades Ottawa has been able to exert its expenditure influence in areas that are not even under its own legislative jurisdiction (e.g., health and education) via the instrumentality of conditional grants. Ottawa's inventory of mega-projects unveiled in connection with the February 1982 First Ministers' Conference, some of which were to be entirely federally funded, others joint ventures with the provinces, but all of which could be initiated as part of a co-ordinated counter-cyclical policy, indicates that the federal role is still or at least can be pre-eminent.

As was the case with monetary policy, it is important not to confuse the current stance of federal fiscal policy with what the stance could be under the existing arrangements. There is at the time of writing a good deal of disagreement among Canadians as to whether the federal deficit is too large or too small (Conklin and Courchene, 1984). However, this dispute is irrelevant to the issue at hand unless it can be shown that the present federal fiscal stance is somehow constrained by the division of tax or expenditure powers.

There are two other areas that merit attention in terms of the interaction between expenditure stabilization and the Constitution — unemployment insurance and welfare.

Unemployment Insurance

Unemployment insurance is the most sensitive of the cyclical expenditure programs. Under the Constitution Act, 1867, responsibility for UI rested with the provinces, but in 1950 this obligation was transferred, via a constitutional amendment, to Ottawa. In the spring of 1984 UI was the largest federal expenditure program, roughly $12 billion. If we assume that the responsibility for achieving high employment rests with the federal government, then UI ought to be a federal responsibility. What is easy to overlook in these days when federal-provincial confrontation tends to occupy centre-stage is that the transfer of UI to the federal level represents a mutually agreed-upon alternative with respect to the division of powers that has in principle worked in the direction of enhancing economic management (stabilization) of the federation.

However, to argue in favour of federal responsibility for UI is not tantamount to approval of the structure of the actual UI program. It is obvious that there are defects in the design of the current UI program. Indeed, we could go as far as to argue that the allocative distortions in UI (such as the lack of experience rating in setting premiums and the existence of regional benefits) would be unlikely to exist if the programs were provincially run. Moreover, the fact that the federal government increased UI premiums dramatically in the midst of the recent recession clearly undermined the program's stabilization potential. Nonetheless, the position I have taken throughout this monograph is that we must distinguish between which level of government ought to be responsible for a given program and the actual characteristics of the program. On this basis UI ought to be a federal responsibility. We might argue for centralization on the basis of allocative and distributive reasons as well, but our present concern is with stabilization. Given that the federal government should accept the major responsibility for ensuring high employment in a growing economy, it follows that the costs of failing to achieve this goal (i.e., unemployment) should also fall primarily to the central government rather than to the provinces.

Welfare

If UI is appropriately centred at the federal level, should welfare be federal also? Under the current arrangements, the Canadian Assistance Plan (which is the overview program for welfare) is a 50 percent shared-cost program with responsibility resting with the provinces. There are really two quite separate components to CAP — the income-support component and the social services component. The latter deals with rehabilitation, counselling, case-work and the like, and is more amenable to decentralization and provincial control. In terms of stabilization policy, the interest centres on the income-support component. While a substantial proportion of welfare recipients are not sensitive to the business cycle (e.g., female-headed families), it is nonetheless true that as the economy goes into recession the numbers on the welfare rolls increase. Compounding this situation is the fact that even though the federal government pays 50 percent of overall costs, the number of persons per capita receiving welfare does vary considerably across provinces. In particular, the "have-not" provinces (in an equalization sense) have a greater percentage of their citizens on welfare than the richer provinces.

Should this asymmetry generate a financial problem for some of the poorer provinces, in spite of the generous nature of the equalization program, there are several avenues of recourse. One would be for Ottawa to "equalize" the Canadian Assistance Plan — to pay a greater percentage of the program costs for those provinces which have a higher proportion of welfare recipients. There are two ways in which this could be done. First, the federal government could vary the shared-cost component (the federal share) of CAP in accordance with, say, the unemployment rate in the province. This variation would introduce an equalization component into CAP in the form of a conditional grant. Second, the federal government could introduce the notion of "fiscal need" into the formal equalization program so as to deliver increased equalization flows to high-unemployment provinces. In this case the additional funds would come in the form of unconditional grants. Since both the Canada Assistance Plan and the equalization program are federal programs, either of these modifications could presumably be implemented under the existing constitutional arrangements.

A second avenue would be to transfer the income-support aspect of CAP to the federal level. The stabilization argument for this approach would be roughly the same as for UI. Since the number of welfare recipients is a function of the phase of the cycle, it makes eminent sense for the federal level to bear the cost of welfare.

There exists, however, a counter-argument. Under present arrangements, welfare is decentralized. Normally, it is administered at the local level, and frequently there are differences in levels of support as between rural and urban areas, and, as well, support levels differ across provinces. Unemployment insurance has this feature inasmuch as benefit levels are related to earnings levels, and the latter are related to regional or local wages. Were welfare administered on a national level, the support level would presumably be uniform. Herein lies a potential problem: if the level of support for families were geared to that necessary for Toronto, for example, it would be far too generous for families in rural Saskatchewan. This imbalance would surely generate incentives for migration that may well be perverse. A compromise would be to have Ottawa responsible for some minimum acceptable level (geared perhaps to rural areas) and allow for provincial top-ups where they are deemed appropriate (Courchene, 1973b). The underlying problem here is that the responsibility for welfare has been a provincial responsibility. As such, it has become intricately bound up with other aspects of each province's socio-economic policy — minimum wages, housing policy, development policy and so on. To argue for transferring welfare to the federal level is to argue for a wholesale alteration in the nature of the socio-economic policy of the several provinces — an alteration which would probably have substantial implications for a wide range of other provincial policies in the socio-economic area. Moreover, unless it were accomplished through the income tax system it would probably require a constitutional amendment.

As a final comment, the interaction among UI, welfare and the personal income tax system ought to be rethought at both levels of government. For one thing, were the federal government to restructure UI and put it more on an "insurance" basis, it is likely that some of the UI beneficiaries would have to fall back on welfare. In this sense the two programs are closely interrelated. Moreover, there is an extensive literature that argues for integrating these programs into a single overarching program along the lines of a negative income tax. Were this to occur, then the case for federal control would seem to be obvious. Nonetheless, this route does pose problems that will be aired in Chapter 6.

The present welfare arrangements represent an intriguing constitutional compromise — a program under provincial jurisdiction administered by the provinces (and often at the local level), subsidized by federal cost-sharing under the aegis of the federal expenditure power, subject to certain federal regulations, such as the disallowance of a period of residency as a condition for eligibility, and a requirement that the provinces put in place adequate appeal procedures.

Recapitulation

In summary, while Canada is probably one of the most decentralized nations in terms of the proportion of goods and services expenditures under the constitutional control of non-federal governments, the federal government nonetheless has wide latitude deriving from its expenditure power. Moreover, because of the system of intergovernmental transfers, the federal government maintains some say as to the manner and conditions under which the provinces can exercise their spending responsibilities. There is, no doubt, room for improvement in the system, but in general, Ottawa retains enough scope and flexibility to pursue adequately its stabilization role on the expenditure side. The one potential area for increased federal control is the income-support component of the present welfare system. Were UI and welfare to be integrated into a single program, the argument for transferring this overview program to the federal level would be persuasive. Indeed, I believe that a majority of the provinces might go along with a constitutional amendment if there were federal-provincial agreement on the format of the new program.

However, the principal stabilization role relates not to expenditures but to taxes and, in particular, to the cyclically variable taxes like personal and corporation income taxes. Prior to focussing on this complex area, it is useful to devote some time to the provinces' role in stabilization policy.

The Provinces' Role in Fiscal Policy

Recently, the Ontario Economic Council (1983b) published a position paper directed to the issue of whether Ontario should initiate its own separate personal income tax. This publication will provide part of the backdrop for the later analysis of income taxation. For present purposes it is also of interest because it directs some attention to the role of the provinces in stabilization policy. University of Toronto economist Thomas A. Wilson, who did the research for this section of the report, begins his overview with the following comments:

> Because the favourable external effects of provincial fiscal policies will be given little weight by provincial governments, provincial fiscal policies will likely either be too weak, or be designed to increase the impact of the policy within the province at the expense of other provinces. Hence primary responsibility for stabilization policy should be assigned to the federal government. However, this does not mean there is no role for the provinces to play. The involvement of the provinces in stabilization policy should lead to improved performance with respect to regional economic objectives. Canada has faced for some time a chronic problem of regional imbalance, coupled with greater cyclical patterns in some regions than in others. In many instances, expansionary fiscal policies could be more effective in countering recession if they were focussed on the more depressed regions. In other situations, restrictive fiscal policies would be more effective in reducing inflation (at lower cost in terms of employment and growth) if these policies would be focussed on the expanding regions. However, political tolerance of federal moves to accommodate regional disparities via a regionally discriminatory federal stabilization policy appears extremely limited, particularly in the case of restrictive fiscal policies. It follows that the use of provincial fiscal policies as an adjunct to federal policy — supporting federal policy in those provinces where the cyclical problem is more

acute, and offsetting fiscal policies where the cyclical problem is less acute (or indeed opposite to that of the nation as a whole) — could improve the overall average performance of stabilization policy. (Wilson, 1984, p. 141)

This assessment does not differ much from that by the University of Manitoba's Clarence Barber nearly two decades ago:

It has been a conclusion of this analysis that provincial governments in Canada should develop an active fiscal policy directed toward the objectives of low levels of unemployment, reasonable stability of prices, and an adequate rate of economic growth. The traditional view, that fiscal policy is appropriate only at the central government level, cannot be supported. Most of the differences between the position of the central government and that of a province are differences of degree rather than kind and should not prevent an active fiscal policy on the part of provincial governments. This is particularly true of the larger provinces such as Ontario, Quebec, and British Columbia, but even the smaller provinces could take a much more active interest in these questions than they have in the past. Moreover, the differential impact of cyclical fluctuations on the various provinces and the inability of federal fiscal policy to adequately take account of those differences makes possible a valuable and useful role for provincial fiscal policy.

To be fully effective, provincial fiscal policy should be carried out in coordination with federal fiscal policy and there should be some arrangement made to help ensure that the policies of the various provincial governments are complementary. There is a need, too, for policies designed to secure effective co-operation at the municipal level, particularly in respect to municipal capital expenditures. In some measure the policy recommended here may involve the provinces in pursuing a fiscal policy that runs counter to that of the federal government. If the difference is due to a belief by the provinces that federal policy is inadequate, such policy measures might well be supplemented by direct pressure on Ottawa to change its policy. Such pressure would be more likely to occur if the provinces were actively interested in the fiscal policy area and were equipped with an economic staff capable of making informed judgments on policy questions. But at times, individual provinces might find it necessary to take policy steps to supplement or offset federal measures.[1]

We have to be careful in interpreting these passages. Neither author is necessarily arguing for more decentralization of the stabilization role. Both recognize the necessity for the federal level to take on the primary responsibility for fiscal stabilization. What they are saying is that the existing decentralization of fiscal policy need not be a cause for too much concern and indeed can be beneficial. Because of the wide regional economic variations, there is a role for provincial stabilization efforts since a single unified federal stabilization thrust may not be appropriate for all regions. Moreover, this provincial role need not always be in the direction of enhancing the federal thrust because on occasion federal stabilization policy may be inappropriate for a given region or province.

Nonetheless, some federal-provincial forum should exist where overall fiscal decisions can be formulated and even harmonized. The reverse side of the last point is that provincial stabilization policies should not be designed so as to increase the impact of the policy within the province at the expense of other provinces, to use Wilson's phraseology. This is consistent with the Report of the Royal Commission on Banking and Finance in 1964 which noted that provincial and local governments must increasingly concern themselves with the effects of their activities in the extraprovincial sphere.

Wilson estimated the income multipliers of Ontario tax and expenditure policies and compared them to their national counterparts. While the numerical estimates are not reported here,[2] he concludes:

> While the (Ontario) income multipliers for fiscal action are typically somewhat smaller than their national counterparts, the multipliers are not so low as to render provincial fiscal policy ineffective, at least under a floating exchange rate system. The simulations (for Ontario) also indicate that the multiplier effects of government capital expenditure changes are considerably larger than the corresponding effects of equivalent general income tax changes. Of course, these broad aggregates tell us little about possible supply-side effects of policies. But if one's principal concern is impact on real aggregate demand, expenditure changes appear to have the edge over income tax changes. (Wilson, 1984, p. 149)

Wilson's simulations were carried out for the province of Ontario. It is likely that the stabilizing fiscal actions by some of the smaller provinces would generate lower, perhaps considerably lower, multipliers because their economies are at the same time smaller and more open.

These results and the analysis of the previous section suggest that the federal government still retains adequate room to manoeuvre on the stabilization front with respect to government expenditures, and that the provincial/local sector can, via expenditures, provide a valuable supplementary stabilization thrust. There is, however, one crucial difference between the two levels of government. Because of its greater access to tax revenues as well as ultimate recourse to the printing press, the federal government is able to finance larger deficits (in proportional terms) than are the provinces. During 1983 two of the provinces (Quebec and British Columbia) had their credit ratings downgraded, and, to some degree at least, the concern over their ability to float debt led to the turmoil associated with their respective policies toward public-sector wages. This is part of the reason why, in general, principal responsibility for stabilization policy ought to be entrusted to the federal government.

Having dealt briefly with the expenditure aspect of stabilization, our attention is now directed to tax policy, in particular to personal and corporate income taxation.

Tax Policy

Canada's Personal Income Tax System

Personal income taxation is a pervasive policy instrument. Its structure has important ramifications for all three functions — stabilization, allocation and distribution — as well as for the operations of an internal common market. While the focus in the present section is only on the stabilization role, it is useful to devote some time to outlining the structure of Canada's personal income tax (PIT) system. This outline will be more detailed than would be necessary for purposes of investigating the stabilization issue, but it will facilitate the later analyses involving the relationship between the income tax system and the pursuit of the allocation and distribution objectives.

Under the provisions of the 1962 Tax Collection Agreements the PIT in Canada is shared between the federal government and the nine provinces that are signatories to the agreements. (The Province of Quebec has its own separate personal income tax system, some details of which will be presented later.) Under these agreements, the federal government collects the taxes for both levels of government. Because the tax filing process flows through the federal government, employers need make only one deduction for employees from source income, and taxpayers need file only one return despite the fact that roughly one-third of their total PIT bill eventually ends up in provincial coffers. The entire administrative cost of both the collection and audit processes is borne by the federal government. In this sense the provinces "piggyback" on the federal tax system.

However, there is a cost to the provinces. The nine participating provinces must accept the federal structure for income taxation. In particular, the federal government defines virtually all aspects of the tax structure such as the types of income subject to tax, the allowable exemptions and deductions, and the underlying marginal tax rates including bracket width and the indexation factor. For their part the provinces can set their own tax rate, to be expressed as a percent of "basic federal tax."

Table 5-3 outlines in more detail the structure of the shared income tax system. The table is designed to follow the steps that a taxpayer would go through in filling out his/her tax form; the rightmost column of the table lists the level of government that has jurisdiction over the particular stage.

Table 5-4 contains the provincial tax rates corresponding to item 7 of Table 5-3, as of 1982. There have been some recent alterations in these rates. For example, Alberta has raised its tax rate and Ontario has a temporary 5 percent surcharge on Ontario tax payable. On average, the provincial rates are roughly 50 percent of federal taxes. As a result,

TABLE 5-3 A Schematic Approach to the Operation of the Personal Income Tax

Conceptual Step	Elaboration	Jurisdiction
1. Definition of income	e.g., Employment income, business income, capital gains, investment income	Federal
subtract		
2. Allowable deductions	e.g., RRSPs, pension contributions, UI contributions, union dues	Federal
subtract		
3. Personal exemptions	e.g., Spouse exemptions, child allowance, charitable deductions	Federal
equals		
4. Taxable income		Federal
multiplied by		
5. Federal marginal rate schedule	Tax brackets indexed each year	Federal
equals		
6. Basic federal tax		Federal
multiplied by		
7. Provincial rate of tax on basic federal tax	Must be a single percentage (e.g., 48 for Ontario); applied to "basic federal tax"	Provincial
equals		
8. Provincial tax payable before credits		A product of 6 (federal) and 7 (provincial), so controlled by both levels
less		
9. Provincial tax credits	e.g., Property tax credits, political contribution credits, tax surcharges or reductions	Provincial
equals		
10. Provincial taxes payable		Obviously, jointly determined

Source: Ontario Economic Council, 1983b, Table 4.
Note: Federal tax credits which appear *after* the calculation of basic federal tax (item 6 in the table) do not affect provincial revenues. These can range from general tax credits to specific (e.g., political contribution) tax credits.

TABLE 5-4 Provincial Income Tax Rates, 1982

	Tax Rate as a % of Federal Tax	Combined Federal-Provincial Marginal Tax Rates[d]		
		$10,000 Taxable Income[a]	$35,000 Taxable Income[b]	Maximum Tax Rate[c]
Newfoundland	59.0	30.2	47.7	54.06
P.E.I.	52.5	29.0	45.7	51.85
Nova Scotia	56.5	29.7	46.9	53.21
New Brunswick	55.5	29.5	46.6	52.87
Ontario	48.0	28.1	44.4	50.32
Manitoba	54.0	29.3	46.2	52.36
Saskatchewan	51.0	28.7	45.4	51.34
Alberta	38.5	26.3	41.5	47.09
British Columbia	44.0	27.4	43.2	48.96

Source: Ontario Economic Council, 1983b, Table 3.

Note: These marginal rates do not take the various provincial surcharges into account. With surcharges, the maximum rates would obtain as follows: Manitoba, 56.03 percent; Saskatchewan, 53.42 percent; B.C., 50.46 percent. Corresponding percentages for the three provinces for the $35,000 column would be 49.4, 46.4, and 43.5, respectively.

a. Federal marginal rate equals 19 percent.
b. Federal marginal rate is 30 percent.
c. Maximum federal rate for 1982 is 34 percent for taxable income in excess of roughly $61,000.
d. Combined marginal rates equal the federal rate plus the product of the two rates.

about one-third of the overall personal tax take goes to the provinces and two-thirds to the federal government.

There is a further degree of freedom that the provinces have with respect to the shared PIT. They can institute various tax credits which the federal government will, for a fee, administer and collect for them. These tax credits must receive federal approval, which means that they must satisfy the three criteria laid down in the tax collection agreements: the tax credits must be administratively feasible; they must not alter the essential harmony of the overall tax system; and they must not jeopardize the efficient functioning of the Canadian economic union. In Chapter 9, dealing with the internal common market, some attention will be directed to the manner in which provincial initiatives with respect to these tax credits may erect barriers to the free flow of goods, labour and capital across provincial boundaries. For present purposes, it is sufficient to note that these tax credits, which began in 1972, have given the provinces considerable flexibility in terms of gearing the overall PIT to their perceived needs. Table 5-5 presents the range of tax credits and surcharges in the various provincial tax systems as of 1981.

Appendix Table A-1 presents a brief history of the PIT and thereby demonstrates the flexibility of the Constitution Act, 1867, in accommodating the wide range of practices over the years in terms of taxing

TABLE 5-5 Special Features of Provincial Personal Income Tax Systems, 1981

Province	Tax Credits	Tax Rebates	Tax Deductions	Surcharges
Newfoundland	—	—	—	—
P.E.I.	—	—	—	—
Nova Scotia	—	—	—	—
New Brunswick	Political contributions	—	—	Negative surtax of 5.5% of provincial tax otherwise payable
Ontario	Property tax, sales tax, political contributions	—	Selective	—
Manitoba	Property tax, cost of living, political contributions	Royalties	Selective	—
Saskatchewan	Mortgage interest	Royalties	Selective	Surcharge, of 11% on provincial tax in excess of $4,000
Alberta	Royalties, renters, political contributions	Royalties	Selective	—
British Columbia	Renters, political contributions, cost of living	Royalties	Selective	Surcharge of 10% on provincial tax in excess of $3,500

Source: MacEachen, 1981, Table IV-1.

personal incomes. While the federal government is unrestricted under the Constitution in terms of its taxing authority, section 92 does give the provinces the right to engage in direct taxation. As Table A-1 indicates, the federal government was the last to enter the personal taxation field: the municipalities and some provinces were already taxing personal incomes when Ottawa levied its first PIT in 1917. Indeed, a Quebec cabinet minister took the federal government to court over its entry into the personal tax field. In 1927 the Privy Council ruled that the Constitution Act, 1867, envisaged a joint federal-provincial occupancy of the direct tax field. Quebec has exercised this constitutional prerogative and has set up its own PIT system. It is instructive to focus briefly on some characteristics of the Quebec system.

The Quebec Personal Income Tax

In 1954 the province of Quebec instituted its own separate PIT, which it retains to this day. The details relating to the Quebec system — some of the reasons why it was established, its impact on the evolution of federal-provincial financial relations, and the estimates of the administrative and compliance cost of running the system — are available elsewhere (Ontario Economic Council, 1983b, chap. 3; Forget, 1984, pp. 187–212). Unlike the other provinces, Quebec does have the ability to alter the structure (to define income, establish deductions and control progressivity) of its own PIT. For example, Quebec did not follow the federal government's lead in 1973 in indexing the tax system for inflation. The nine other provinces were required to incorporate indexation since, as noted above, the federal government defines the overall structure of the shared PIT.

As might be expected, over time several important differences have arisen between the two tax systems. Table 5-6 presents the major variations in the systems. Of particular importance is the Quebec Stock Savings Plan under which Quebecers can deduct, for Quebec tax purposes, up to $15,000 for purchases of new shares issued by Quebec-based companies. Other provinces attempted to mount similar programs via the tax credit route, but the federal government refused to collect them on grounds that they represented barriers to the free flow of capital. This on-going controversy will be highlighted in Chapter 9 relating to the Canadian economic union.

Corporate Income Taxation

The tax collection agreements also cover the corporation income tax, although three provinces with 75 percent of corporate taxable income earned in Canada (Quebec, Ontario and Alberta) have opted out of the arrangements and now run their own separate corporate tax systems.

TABLE 5-6 Ways in which Quebec Personal Income Tax has Departed from Federal Personal Income Tax

Revenue
Non-indexing of tax rate table.

Equity or Redistribution
Higher basic exemptions.
Higher top rate.
Different relief for children.
Real Estate tax refunds.
Different rate progression.
Higher benefit for company cars.[a]
Lower deductions for personal cars used to earn income[a]
No eduction deduction.
No housing loan exemption.[a]
Benefit from employee loan not computed on same basis.

Saving and Investments
Current service contribution to RPP $5,500 rather that $3,500.
Deduction up to $15,000 in stock savings plan.
Investment credit of 25 percent on SODEQ shares.
Capital gains not eligible for $1,000 deduction.
All interest expense deductible re $1,000 deduction.
Capital loss deduction of $1,000 not $2,000.

Special Incentives
$3 for $1 RHOSP contribution for 1982 only.
Quebec does not exempt employees' stock option benefits from tax as the federal measures do for private Canadian-controlled corporations.
Contribution to RRSP limited to $3,500 if employee member of DPSP (federal now has the same limit when contributions to DPSP made in the year).
RHOSP cannot be used to buy a house from the spouse in Quebec.
For 1983 and following years contribution may be made to RHOSP but no deduction.

Miscellaneous
Unpaid balance is always subject to interest charge; interest on refund starts only 60 days after filing or April 30, whichever is later.
Child care expense limits $2,000/child and $6,000/family instead of $1,000 and $4,000, federally.
Limitation in deduction of legal fees to obtain maintenance payments (Que. 133.3); may be allowed by federal authorities (IT-99r).
Differences in interpretation of the same legistation.

Source: Ontario Economic Council, 1983b, Table 7.
a. Before budget of November 12, 1981.
SODEQ: Quebec Business Development Corporations
RHOSP: Registered Home Ownership Savings Plan
RRSP: Registered Retirement Savings Plan
DPSP: Deferred Profit Sharing Plan (IT-99R) — Interpretation Bulletin 99 Revised.

For the seven provinces that remain in the tax agreements for corporate taxation, the provisions are roughly comparable to those in place for the PIT — Ottawa defines the structure, and the provinces have flexibility to mount their own tax credits (administered by Ottawa) and to set their own corporate tax rates. Unlike the PIT, where the provincial tax is a given percentage of the federal tax, the provisions relating to the corporate income tax (CIT) allow the provinces to levy their tax rates against

TABLE 5-7 Special Features of Provincial Corporate Income Tax (CIT) Systems, 1981

Province	Tax Credits	Tax Rebates	Small Business Rate Reduction	Tax Rates[a] (%)
Newfoundland	—	—	3 points	15 (12)
P.E.I.	—	—	—	10
Nova Scotia	—	—	3 points	13 (10)
New Brunswick	—	—	5 points	14 (9)
Manitoba	Political contributions	—	4 points	15 (11)
Saskatchewan	—	Royalties	4 points	14 (10)
Alberta	Royalties, political contributions	Royalties	6 points	11 (6)
British Columbia	Logging tax, political contributions	Royalties	8 points	16 (8)

Source: MacEachen, 1981, Tables IV-2 and IV-3.
Note: Special features in effect as of November 23, 1981.
a. The first figure relates to the general corporate tax rate and the second refers to the small business tax rate.

federal corporate taxable income. Put somewhat differently, they can levy a "tax on base." Most provinces impose a preferential (lower) rate on small corporations.

Table 5-7 presents data on both the provincially mounted tax credits under the shared CIT as well as the provincial tax rates. Since these data refer to 1981, Alberta is included in the table although it now has its own corporate tax system.

The provinces with their own corporate tax systems are free to define both their tax structure and tax rates as they see fit. Table 5-8 presents a summary of the major differences between the Ontario and federal corporate tax systems. In its 1982 budget, Ontario declared a two-year tax holiday for small corporations, i.e., the small business tax rate for Ontario is zero. Since the provinces who are signatories to the collection agreements can set their own tax rates, there would appear to be nothing preventing these seven provinces from following Ontario's lead in this area should they so desire, even though they do not have their own separate corporate tax regimes.

There is one further feature of Canada's overall corporate tax system that merits attention. Despite the fact that three provinces now have their own systems, there is a uniform procedure for allocating the profits of multijurisdiction corporations across the provinces. The allocation formula is as follows:

TABLE 5-8 Summary of Differences between Ontario and Federal Corporate Tax Systems

Liability for Income Tax:
  Residency status
  Non-resident entertainment corporations

Calculation of Net Income:
  Capital property
  115 percent depreciable cost incentive
  Beef cattle stabilization program
  Interest on loans to non-resident persons
  Treatment of management fees, rents, royalties, etc.
  Capital cost allowances
  Reserves — capital gains
  Income revenues
  Foreign taxes
  Taxable Crown corporations
  Deductible corporate taxes
  Payments received under the Employment Support Act
  Foreign tax carry-over on amalgamations
  Partnerships and their members

Computation of Taxable Income:
  Political contributions

Calculations of Taxable Income Payable:
  Small business deduction
  Foreign tax credit
  Incentive tax credit for investment
  Manufacturing and processing profits credit
  Political donations credit
  Employment tax credit

Resource Corporations:
  Resource allowance
  Depletion allowance
  Foreign resource property
  Development expenses

Source: Ontario Economic Council, 1983b, Table 8.

$$\text{Share of profits allocated to province } i = \frac{1}{2} \left[\text{Province } i\text{'s share of Canadian payroll} + \text{Province } i\text{'s share of Canadian sales} \right]$$

In the United States there is no uniform allocation formula adhered to by all the states. The recent U.S. Supreme Court ruling to the effect that California's "unitary tax" system (which allows California to tax a given share of the worldwide profits of corporations doing business in the state) is constitutional is currently wreaking havoc with the U.S. corporate tax system, particularly since there are close to a dozen states which are attempting to follow California's lead. Canada's allocation formula is more in the nature of a gentleman's agreement between Ottawa and the provinces than a binding arrangement. Nonetheless, while it lasts it does contribute substantially to the overall harmony of the corporate tax system.

With this institutional material as a backdrop we are now ready to address the interaction between income taxation and stabilization.

Stabilization Policy and Income Taxation: The Federal Perspective

Shortly after Canada entered the Second World War, the provinces agreed, as part of the overall wartime economic policy, to surrender the direct taxation field (corporate and personal) to the federal government. After the war, Ottawa desired to maintain control over direct taxation, buttressing its position by resorting to the spreading Keynesian view that control over direct taxation was essential in order to stabilize the economy at high rates of employment. Nonetheless, the postwar history of direct income taxation is essentially one of a transfer of an increasing share of the PIT back to the provinces. The latest transfer occurred in 1977 when the federal government turned over roughly 9 personal income tax points (9 percent of the then-existing federal PIT revenues) to the provinces.

What proportion of the overall PIT should be under federal control in order to guarantee that Ottawa has sufficient leverage for stabilization purposes? There are two sorts of "answers" to this question. The first approach would be to attempt to establish the minimum portion that the federal government would need for stabilization purposes. This issue arose in the context of policy discussions in the early 1970s; there was no firm answer then, and there is not likely to be one now. In the intervening period, however, the federal government has transferred additional PIT revenue to the provinces. Presumably the federal authorities felt that the remaining portion would still leave them sufficient scope on the stabilization front.

There is another approach to this question. Even though the provinces now receive about one-third of the PIT revenues, except for Quebec, the federal government can generally have its way with respect to the stabilization properties of the entire PIT. Suppose that as part of a stabilization policy thrust geared to increasing investment Ottawa decides to exempt capital gains from taxation. Since this is a change in the definition of income for tax purposes, the nine provinces must incorporate this change in their own PITs. Potentially more troublesome would be a federal tax cut designed to spur economic activity. The provinces, singly or as a group, have the option of increasing their own tax rates to take up the vacated federal tax room and leaving the taxpayers, on average, unaffected. It was partly to ensure that this would not happen that the federal government, in the context of tax reform in the early 1970s, offered the provinces a "revenue guarantee" if they would initiate parallel reform measures. Thus, even though the federal government collects only two-thirds of all personal income tax revenues, it has generally been able to determine the structure (and, hence, the stabilization features) of the entire PIT.

When it comes to corporate income taxation, Ottawa has much less leverage on the system because Quebec, Ontario and Alberta operate their own independent systems. For example, Ontario did not parallel those features of Finance Minister MacEachen's 1981 budget that it felt were detrimental to the provinces — e.g., the federal initiative to limit the first-year capital cost allowance deductions.

We can still argue that the federal government needs a larger share of these direct taxes in order that it fulfil adequately its stabilization role. However, I think it would be difficult to document this need.[3] More importantly, it is not the critical issue of the moment in the relationship between stabilization policy and direct taxation. What is far more problematical, from Ottawa's standpoint, is the possibility that several more provinces will go their own way on direct taxation. The federal government does not have the authority to restrict the provinces' powers in the area of direct taxation nor is there anything in the Constitution that requires the harmonization of provincial taxation. This issue will be dealt with in the context in which it arose most recently — the provincial (particularly Ontario's) concern relating to the 1981 federal budget.

Stabilization Policy and Income Taxation: A Provincial (Ontario) Perspective

The Ontario Ministry of Treasury and Economics reacted strongly to the 1981 federal budget (Ontario, 1982, p. 25). It was concerned about several aspects of the personal income tax proposals contained in the budget: the restricted deductability of interest expenses related to various types of investment would discourage individuals from risk-taking; the new income-averaging proposals would impact seriously on taxpayers with irregular or cyclical income receipts such as farmers and small businessmen; the proposals relating to investment income accrued in annuities would require taxpayers to pay tax on income that would not be received for a couple of years. Ontario was also concerned with a number of provisions in the federal budget that pertained to corporate taxation. However, the province realized that there was a significance in the manner in which it could react to these corporate tax proposals:

In the area of corporate income taxation, Ontario has at least one course open if its views are not heeded in Ottawa. Since the Province administers its own corporate income tax, it need not parallel federal policies and thus does not have to burden corporations with inappropriate taxation policies. However, current arrangements with respect to the personal income tax compel Ontario to parallel federal measures even though they may not be in the best interest of the people of Ontario. Not only may Ontario be an unwilling partner in policies it feels are misguided, but it actually magnifies their impacts simply by virtue of sharing the common tax base. (p. 25)

Two comments are appropriate here. First, as noted above, Ontario did not parallel the recent federal initiatives affecting the corporate income tax. Second, the last sentence of the quote refers to the circumstance that although the federal government receives only two-thirds of total personal income tax revenues, the fact that Ontario must accede to any changes means that Ottawa's tax changes automatically affect Ontario's share of PIT revenues as well.

Largely as a result of these concerns the Ontario treasurer asked the Ontario Economic Council to examine the economic implications that would attend a decision by the province to withdraw from the tax collection agreements and institute its own collection system for the personal income tax. The council's overall assessment of this issue was that while a separate PIT for Ontario was a viable alternative, there were several more desirable avenues to pursue within the existing system prior to opting for a separate PIT. What is of interest here is that part of the council's analysis pertaining to stabilization policy and the PIT.

In focussing on the manner in which a separate PIT might enhance a province's flexibility with respect to stabilization policy, the council noted that under the existing legislative framework, it is difficult if not impossible to treat corporate and unincorporated enterprises equally. For example, the province of Ontario refused in its corporate income tax provisions to follow the federal government's lead in limiting first-year capital allowance deductions. In the absence of its own personal income tax, this provision could not apply to the unincorporated business sector. Likewise, the two-year tax holiday for small business in Ontario applied only to incorporated enterprises. With either a separate PIT or a more flexible joint system, this type of non-neutral treatment of incorporated and unincorporated business enterprises could be avoided.

More generally, a separate PIT might provide valuable stabilization flexibility in the case where Canada's regions are experiencing different economic fortunes. In the council's words:

[I]t is clear that increased flexibility in policy design would permit some improvement in the effectiveness of provincial fiscal policies in dealing with multiple objectives of stabilization policy. How important this improvement is cannot be readily determined, because it depends on the state of the national and provincial economies, and upon the impact of federal actions on the Ontario economy. For example, if there were little problem of conflict between the objectives, and if the performance of the Ontario economy closely parallelled that of the rest of the country, there would be little advantage to increased flexibility of policies at the provincial level, provided that federal policies were appropriate. In this situation, the piggy-backing of Ontario tax changes on federal tax changes could well be sufficient for stabilization purposes. An opposite example would be a situation in which Ontario's growth prospects were much weaker than the rest of Canada's, with investment strong in the West and/or East and weak in Ontario. Under these circumstances, a regionally neutral fiscal policy initiated at the federal level might not be optimal. If political concerns or constitutional constraints limited the adoption of regionally discriminatory federal policies, a flexible Ontario fiscal policy would permit the province to provide appropriate stimulus to capital investment, should it so desire.

(Ontario Economic Council, 1983b, pp. 82–83)

Impact on Federal Stabilization Policy

The council also recognized that an independent Ontario PIT or a series of separate provincial PITs could have a significant impact on the federal government's ability to pursue stabilization policy:

Specifically, a separate provincial PIT would reduce the *leverage* of any federal tax change that affected "basic federal tax" (e.g., changes in deductions, income definitions, indexing, dividend integration). This is so because changes initiated at the federal level would no longer be automatically carried over into the provincial PIT structures.

In the extreme, one could argue that the existing shared PIT system biases the federal government's choice towards stabilization measures that apply leverage at the provincial level (i.e., that force the provinces to follow suit). For example, in a recession a tax cut that decreases basic federal tax may be preferred to a cut in other federal taxes, since the federal government can achieve the same aggregate demand impact with an income tax cut but with the important difference that an income tax change has only two-thirds of the impact on the federal deficit — the other third of the deficit occurs at the provincial level. This circumstance may bias expansionary federal fiscal policy to take the form of reducing federal basic tax and bias restrictive federal policy to take the form of increasing taxes that fall solely under federal jurisdiction. The other side of this coin is, of course, that if the provinces are in favour of such a tax cut, they can reap the benefits and still blame Ottawa when it comes to explaining the resulting provincial deficit to their voting citizens.

It might be argued that it would be far better to remove this controversial leverage completely. This could be accomplished in two ways. One obvious way would be for Ontario to opt for its own PIT. Then leverage would exist only if Ontario decided to go along with the federal tax changes. An intermediate step would be an understanding between the federal government and the provinces that the former would not introduce structural changes that affected "basic federal tax" without full consultation with the provinces. An agreement of this nature would preclude the federal government from tinkering with such features of the tax system as indexing, the capital cost allowance, and income averaging without provincial consultation. Yet it would not seriously hamper the federal government, which could use federal income tax credits and surtaxes to implement its stabilization policies without having to alter basic federal tax. Obviously, if the provinces welcomed the changes, they could then be introduced into the basic structure of the tax system. (Ontario Economic Council, 1983b, p. 83)

The council went on to recommend that Ontario not opt for its own separate PIT. Even if Ontario or some other provinces felt that the status quo was unacceptable, the council pointed out that there existed several alternatives to both the status quo and a separate PIT. Table 5-9 summarizes these alternatives.

Recapitulation

The reader may well question the substantial emphasis on the Ontario perspective in the above analysis. After all, other provinces may view the issue from an entirely different perspective. However, in the wake of the passage of the Canada Health Act, the province of Alberta signalled its intention to explore the possibility of adopting its own PIT. Presumably, some of the pros and cons for Ontario of a separate PIT would carry over to Alberta as well.

The provinces, then, do have a constitutional right to engage in direct taxation. Within this context, the tax collection agreements represent an ingenious compromise that has permitted the development of a decentralized yet very harmonized approach to direct taxation. Indeed, Canada's approach to direct taxation is often held up as a model for federal nations (Thirsk, 1980).

One way of investigating the interaction between economic stabilization and the division of powers is to focus on the economic principles relating to the assignment of tax powers. This approach would probably lead us to argue for greater centralization of the CIT system and perhaps even the PIT system.

I have not followed this route in the above analysis. It seems to me that the immediate practical problem relating to the system of direct taxation in the Canadian federation is to ensure that the existing system does not unravel. The apparent belief by the federal government that it can unilaterally and arbitrarily alter the basic structure of the shared income tax systems has generated substantial concern in provinces as to whether they should remain as signatories to the tax collection agreements. It may well be that adequate exercise of the stabilization function requires more federal control over the structures of direct taxation in Canada (although I personally doubt this need). But the first step in this direction must be to ensure that the existing arrangements do not degen-

TABLE 5-9 Alternatives to a Separate PIT

Alternatives	Characteristics	Elaboration
1. The status quo	Centralized federal collection. Minimizes administrative and compliance costs. Provincial flexibility limited to applying single tax rate to basic federal tax and to implementing a restricted set of non-discriminatory tax credits. Provinces required to accept all federal changes in underlying tax structure. Consultation on such changes limited or non-existent. Limited and temporary revenue guarantee.	Provinces are expressing increased concern over lack of consultation with respect to major and sudden federal changes. Provinces also appear to be constrained in implementing development tax credits. New B.C. tax credits may provide a precedent.
2. A federal-provincial committee on the structure of the shared tax base	No changes in the current Tax Collection Agreements. Provinces would have equal status on the committee, reflecting the joint occupancy of the tax field and the constitutional rights of both parties to engage in direct taxation.	Could run into problems relating to federal budget secrecy in spite of recent initiatives to open up the process. Would not prevent federal action, since there would be plenty of scope for Ottawa to enact changes after the calculation of basic federal tax (e.g., federal tax credits). After some period of notice (say three years) these federal changes would become part of the shared tax structure, even if there were no agreement on the part of the provinces. A stronger version of this option would require joint federal-provincial agreement prior to all changes in the shared structure. Hence all controversial federal changes would have to be implemented "below the line" as it were.

TABLE 5-9 (cont'd)

Alternatives	Characteristics	Elaboration
3. Tax on base	Provinces would tax the federal base instead of piggy-backing on the federal tax. Provinces would have control over their own rate and bracket structures. Federal changes in tax rates would no longer affect provincial revenues. Common structure for the base would still obtain. A slight increase in compliance and administrative costs. Would appear to fit easily within the Tax Collection Agreements.	Federal government would still have the power to alter the base and thereby bind the provinces, since base changes would affect their revenues. Federal government would lose some control over vertical equity in the tax system; but if the provinces utilized the currently allowable tax decreases and surcharges they could come close to duplicating a tax on base.
4. An extension of the tax credit	All regionally or provincially non-discriminatory tax credits would be allowed. For example, savings and investment credits that did not discriminate against assets in other provinces would be allowed. Compliance and administrative costs would rise somewhat. Provinces could offset some federal changes so that lack of consultation is less of a problem. Current federal collection fee for provincial tax credits would continue to apply.	Could be combined with a joint consultative process and/or a tax on base. Would change the current structure more in terms of degree than of substance.
5. An extension of the tax credit system: II	Items under 4 would continue to apply. Provinces could opt for tax on base (i.e., their own rate and bracket structure).	Would require less federal-provincial co-ordination, since the provinces could in effect chart their course. Indeed, extending the tax credit

TABLE 5-9 (cont'd)

Alternative	Characteristics	Elaboration
	Tax credits or surcharges applicable by type of income (e.g., business income, property income, employment income) would be allowed.	system to this degree would give the provinces most of the flexibility they would gain from having their own PITs. Apart from their
	Compliance and administrative costs might rise substantially, but still much less than under a separate PIT.	inability to impose regionally discriminatory tax credits, the provinces would also be unable to tax sources of income not included in
	No tax credits or surcharges that discriminate against other provinces would be allowed.	the federal income tax base.
6. Separate provincial PITs	No restrictions on provincial PIT flexibility.	Would require substantial horizontal (interprovincial) harmonization in order to minimize efficiency losses.
	Maximize compliance and administrative costs.	
	Minimize necessity for federal-provincial consultation on tax matters.	

Source: Ontario Economic Council, 1983b, Table 14.

erate into eleven separate corporate and personal income tax systems. Moreover, it is probably important for all Canadians to recognize that the virtues of the present system should not be underestimated. In the view of one of Canada's foremost public finance analysts, the lesson we can take from the Swiss and American experiences with direct taxation is that a federal system of government can tolerate much more diversity and decentralization in direct taxation than that which characterizes our federation (Bird, 1985). Therefore, if the status quo with respect to direct taxation is altered at some point in the future, there is nothing to indicate that any changes will be in the direction of more federal control over direct taxation. It would be wise on Ottawa's part to ensure that the status quo is secure before pressing for more centralization.

Fiscal Balance

I want to conclude this overview of fiscal stabilization by focussing on "fiscal balance," an issue that loomed large in the 1982 renegotiations of the fiscal arrangements. In the context of the present chapter, fiscal balance refers to "vertical" fiscal balance — the allocation of revenues relative to expenditure responsibilities between the two levels of government.[4] In the federal overview document relating to the 1982 negotiations Finance Minister MacEachen argued that the "fundamental issue" had become fiscal balance (MacEachen, 1981). His argument was simple — with the federal budget in deficit by some $24 billion and the provincial governments roughly balanced, the time had come for the provinces to shoulder a larger revenue-raising role in the federation. It was partly on the basis of this argument that Ottawa pared some $6 billion from the Established Programs Financing (EPF) transfers over the 1982–87 period. (This move will be discussed in more detail in Chapter 6 on social policy.)

The Economic Council of Canada (ECC) addressed this issue in its report *Financing Confederation: Today and Tomorrow* (1982, pp. 6–9). The council noted that during the 1960s and 1970s the most rapid growth in government expenditures occurred in areas of provincial jurisdiction (health, education, etc.) while provincial revenue sources were less responsive to economic growth than those of the federal government. As a result, Ottawa tended to run surpluses and the provinces to run deficits in terms of "own-source" revenues, and there were large increases in intergovernmental transfers from Ottawa to the provinces.

The issue addressed by the ECC was whether or not there was evidence of a "structural" problem:

> In order to say that there is a "structural" economic problem relating to fiscal imbalance, it must be argued that one of the levels of government does not have access to the revenues required to fulfill its obligations to the citizens of the nation under the Constitution. There is no question, however, that both levels of government in Canada today have access to all major revenue sources. Thus the correction of a fiscal imbalance at one level of government is primarily a matter of raising taxes, restraining expenditures, or both. In Canada, then, the issue of a fiscal imbalance can hardly be called a long-term "structural" economic problem. (p. 7)

The council concluded that, in terms of fiscal balance, there was "no compelling argument in support of the federal government's proposed reduction in net transfers to the provinces" (p. 9). Nevertheless, as noted above, Ottawa did pare the system of transfers from what a continuation of the then-existing arrangements would have generated.

However, it is not obvious that the provinces do have access to the full range of revenues. Ottawa's taxing powers are plenary. The provinces are allowed to engage in direct taxation and, through court interpretation, the retail sales tax has been viewed (inappropriately, from an economic standpoint) as a direct tax. With the Constitution Act, 1982, the provinces now have some ability to engage in indirect taxation with respect to resources, but there are many taxes or revenue sources that they cannot access (e.g., tariffs). Hence, we could make an argument that it is possible for the provinces to suffer from a long-term fiscal balance problem. Moreover, if they were put under a long-term fiscal squeeze some of the provinces might respond by opting for their own separate personal income tax systems (à la Québec) in order to increase the flexibility in those areas of taxation which, constitutionally, they can access.

In any event, with the deficit levels much higher today than they were in 1982 (indeed, the provinces as a whole are now also running substantial deficits), the fiscal balance issue can be rephrased in terms of who should run the deficit: Should Ottawa shift some of the deficit to the provinces? On allocative grounds the answer might be yes, if the process is staged with adequate lead time. It may well be appropriate over time for the provinces to raise a greater share of overall revenue than they currently do. One of the public finance maxims is that the level of government responsible for the spending decision ought also to be responsible for the revenue-raising decision. Thus, I could see the provinces becoming responsible for raising an increasing proportion of their overall expenditure needs.

However, Ottawa has the greater ability to run deficits. The provinces are under the watchful eye of credit-rating agencies and it could be argued that the dramatic measures enacted by both British Columbia and Quebec had more to do with the dictates of Dunn and Bradstreet than with ideology. Moreover, the federal government, unlike the provinces, also has recourse to the printing press. Since a substantial part of the recent deficit run-up can be attributed to both inflation and recession (macroeconomic factors), it seems appropriate on stabilization grounds that Ottawa ought to bear the bulk of any fiscal deficit.

Conclusion

This part of the monograph has focussed on macro or stabilization policy and the division of powers. The issue addressed was whether or not an alternative division of responsibilities or authority would provide a better basis for the effective delivery of the stabilization function in the federation. By way of summary, the analysis leads to the following observations:

• Monetary policy is centralized in virtually all countries, federal and unitary states alike. Canada is no exception. The frequent pleas for a regional component to monetary policy in Canada do not make economic sense. To the extent that special help must be given to regions, this is best handled by separate programs and not via a decentralization of the monetary policy function.

• Monetary control will probably be centralized even further. Not all deposit-taking institutions are subject to the monitoring provisions of the Bank of Canada. Governor Bouey has stated that the present provisions are adequate as far as monetary control is concerned. However, as Chapter 8 on financial markets will reveal, there is in process a rapid integration of the financial system mirroring the integration taking place south of the border. If this erosion of the traditional "four pillars" (banking, underwriting, insurance and trusts) continues, as technology appears to dictate, then the time may come when Canada will move toward a functional approach to the financial system. Under such an approach, all financial institutions accepting deposits transferable by cheque would be subject to Bank of Canada primary reserve requirements.

- The present division of powers is such that the federal government may not be able to implement comprehensive wage and price controls, except in the context of an emergency. Since some other federations are not so constrained, there would be a case for increasing federal powers in this regard. However, under the present arrangements, the federal government can impose controls on the civil service and those sectors that fall under its jurisdiction; in tandem with the provinces it can impose comprehensive controls; and in an emergency or economic crisis it has the power to implement controls. In my view, the federal government's powers are adequate in this regard.

- Ottawa has a free hand in terms of implementing exchange controls, although the economic implications of doing so would suggest that this power is unlikely to be invoked except perhaps in wartime. What is of more interest is the extent to which the provinces access foreign sources of funds. The Australian Loan Council approach to regulating the external borrowing of the Australian states does not seem appropriate to Canada, in large measure because it would represent a drastic curtailment of provincial flexibility on the financial front and would lead to significant moves by the provinces to increase their fiscal flexibility. Nonetheless, there is probably a need for greater co-ordination in this area. Moreover, the anomalous situation wherein the provinces and their agencies typically borrow in foreign pay while Ottawa oversees the value of the dollar, often places the provinces at the mercy of Ottawa. There may be a case for having the federal government tilt its borrowing more toward foreign sources and to vacate some domestic room to the provinces.

- The fiscal side of the stabilization area is very different from the monetary side in the sense that a good deal of decentralization already exists. Indeed, Canada may well qualify as the most decentralized of federations in terms of subnational-level government spending and revenue raising.

- Nonetheless, the federal government's expenditure powers are plenary, so much so that it is hard to argue that it needs more authority in order to carry out expenditure stabilization.

- Many analysts would argue that decentralization has already proceeded too far in terms of the responsibility for direct taxation. But this is not the experience of the fiscal systems in other federations, such as Switzerland or the United States. Moreover, the reality of the situation suggests that the principal concern in this area ought not to be a move toward re-centralization but rather a commitment to ensure that the present system of direct taxation does not fragment into eleven separate personal and corporate income tax systems. While our system of direct taxation is very decentralized, it is also very harmonized.
- The decentralization of taxation probably does complicate the exercise of stabilization policy on the tax front. In turn, there is a premium on consultation and co-operation with the provinces in the formation of tax policy. This is hardly a constraint, since it is desirable in its own right.
- The decentralized taxing and expenditure authority also implies that the provinces can and do have an important role to play in stabilization policy. In order that this role be exercised effectively, co-operation and co-ordination are also essential.
- Over time the situation has developed in Canada where own-source revenues at the federal level have tended to exceed expenditure responsibilities, with the opposite tendency characterizing provincial budgets. As a result there has been a marked escalation in the role of intergovernmental transfers, allowing the federal government to maintain greater control over the system of taxation than if the provinces were responsible for raising revenues in line with their expenditure requirements.
- It is difficult to argue that the federal government suffers from a structural fiscal imbalance — that it suffers from a structural revenue shortfall. Moreover, stabilization considerations suggest that the federal level ought to bear the brunt of any short-term deficits occasioned by either recession or inflation.

In general, then, the analysis suggests that the responsibility for monetary policy is appropriately located at the centre; to the extent that changes are required they tend to point in the direction of even greater centralization. The responsibility for fiscal policy is quite decentralized in the federation. The principal concern in this area is that the present degree of decentralization not degenerate into a veritable tax jungle. There are two important caveats that must be highlighted in this context. First, a later chapter will argue that there needs to be stronger guarantees to secure the internal common market. Such guarantees would enhance the effectiveness of overall fiscal policy. Second, the tabular history of the personal income tax (Appendix Table A-1) reveals that over the years there have been swings to and from a centralized approach to direct taxation. Hence, it is possible to argue that if the need arises for a more centralized system of direct taxation the existing constitutional framework can readily accommodate this centralization.

Finally, economist Richard Musgrave's six precepts relating to the assignment of taxing authority highlighted in Chapter 1 have not played a role in this analysis. This neglect is not because they are deemed to be irrelevant but because the principal challenge on the taxation front is to ensure that the current system does not fragment further. Once this goal is achieved, it then may make sense to work toward an overall approach that has "optimal tax assignment" as the ultimate objective.

Chapter 6

The Social Programs and the Division of Powers

The focus of the third part of this monograph is on selected aspects of the interaction between income distribution and the division of powers. In principle the two chapters in this part — the present chapter on the social programs and Chapter 7 on equalization payments — are designed to focus, respectively, on interpersonal and interprovincial aspects of income distribution. In practice this distinction is not able to be sustained, since the ability of, say, Quebec to provide adequate welfare programs for its citizens is dependent on the level of intergovernmental transfers. Moreover, the chapter on equalization will, of necessity, have much to say about interprovincial allocative efficiency as well as the distribution of funds across provinces. Nonetheless, if we had to categorize these two policy areas somewhere in the triumverate of stabilization, distribution and allocation, the distribution classification is the most obvious.

For purposes of this chapter the "social programs" will include the health-care system, post-secondary education and the income-support system, where the latter encompasses unemployment insurance, the Canada Assistance Plan (CAP; welfare) and the public pension system. I shall focus on each of these areas in turn, addressing the issue of whether some altered division of powers would be desirable in its own right or, more generally, would enhance the economic management of the federation. Prior to turning attention to these issues, it is useful to take a broader view of these programs, particularly since their interaction with the federal-provincial power struggle has been quite similar. This overview will be followed by some general prciples that provide a useful backdrop against which to evaluate any long-term alterations in the division of powers. The final section of the chapter focusses on the issue of "fiscal balance," the distribution of powers relative to the distribution of revenue access.

The Postwar Interaction of the Social Programs and Federal-Provincial Responsibilities

Rowell-Sirois Report

The Rowell-Sirois Report is often viewed as a very centralist document, and to a substantial degree it was, recommending the transfer of all direct taxation to the federal level. However, for those programs that the Rowell-Sirois Commission deemed to be the responsibility of the provinces the report constituted a staunch defence of provincial rights. To ensure that the provinces had access to sufficient funds in order to fulfil their constitutional responsibilities, the commission recommended a system of national adjustment grants (essentially equalization payments). The following excerpts from the Rowell-Sirois Report reflect its thinking:

> In considering the relative fiscal needs of provincial governments, we are mainly concerned with a few divisions of expenditures: on education, on social services, on development. It is of national interest that no provincial government should be unduly cramped in any of these respects. Education is basic to the quality of Canadian citizens of the future and it is highly undesirable that marked disparities in the financial resources available for education should exist as between Canadian provinces. Social services, like education, cannot be subjected to marked disparities without serious reactions on the general welfare and on national unity. An appropriate developmental policy is required in each province, and the only standard which can fairly be applied is the policy of the province itself. (Canada, 1939, p. 83)

In terms of the provincial autonomy in this sphere the commission noted:

> It should be made clear that while the adjustment grant proposed is designed to enable a province to provide adequate services (at the average Canadian standard) without excessive taxation (on the average Canadian basis) the freedom of action of a province is in no way impaired. If a province chooses to provide inferior services and impose lower taxation it is free to do so, or it may provide better services than the average if its people are willing to be taxed accordingly, or it may, for example, starve its roads and improve its education, or starve its education and improve its roads — exactly as it may do today. But no provincial government will be free from the pressure of the opinion of its own people. (p. 84)

The careful reader will note that there is no specific reference in the above quotations to health care, although one might reasonably assume that it falls under "social services." Likewise the commission, in referring to education, is not explicit as to whether university graduate programs, for example, ought to fall under provincial jurisdiction. And in terms of the income support function, elsewhere in the report there is a recommendation that unemployment insurance be transferred from the provincial to the federal domain (as it was). Despite these important caveats, the report mounted a strong defence for provincial autonomy in the social policy area and it recommended a system of equalization-like grants in order that this autonomy be "real and not illusory" (p. 80).

The Rise of National Programs

In the 1950s and 1960s the federal government initiated a series of conditional-grant programs that in effect turned several provincial social programs in the direction of "national" programs. In some cases the conversion was entirely harmonious: the Canada Assistance Plan of 1966 has been described as "probably the most harmonious product of federal-provincial relations of the decade."[1] The introduction of medicare was more tension-ridden: Ottawa made an offer that the provincial governments simply could not afford to refuse.

The nature of the cost-sharing arrangements differs sufficiently from program to program to make it useful to document each separately.

Hospital Insurance

In June 1958 the federal government embarked on a conditional-grant scheme relating to hospital insurance. Overall, Ottawa contributed 50 percent to the financing of the provincial programs. Each province received 25 percent of the national average per capita cost plus 25 percent of its own per capita cost. Hence, the per capita amounts received by the various provinces differed. Those provinces spending less than the per capita national average on hospital insurance would receive more than 50 percent of their total per capita costs, and vice versa. As Moore, Perry and Beach (1966, p. 33) note, the arrangements for hospital grants represents the "first important departure from the federal stand that the question of fiscal need should be taken care of in the unconditional grants only."

Medicare

The conditional grant scheme for medicare emerged roughly a decade later. Again the overall federal share was 50 percent. However, the manner in which Ottawa distributed this 50 percent differed from the hospital insurance format. Specifically, all provinces were to submit their medicare expenses to the federal government. Overall, the federal share would equal the provincial total (this is the 50 percent sharing). The federal government would then pay out its share on an equal per capita basis to the provinces without regard to the actual per capita expenditures in the various provinces.

In return for these monies, the provinces agreed to adhere to five underlying principles with respect to health care: comprehensiveness of coverage; universality of coverage; accessibility to service uninhibited by excessive user charges; portability of benefits across Canada; and non-profit administration by a public agency.

Post-Secondary Education

The financing arrangements for post-secondary education followed the more traditional shared-cost format: Ottawa paid 50 percent of the provinces' operating costs. However, there was an alternative option available to the provinces: they could choose $15 per capita in the initial year, with this per capita transfer escalated over time in tandem with the average growth of post-secondary expenditures. Three provinces chose this option — Newfoundland, New Brunswick and P.E.I.

Unlike the health grants, part of the federal funding for post-secondary education came in the form of a transfer of four equalized personal income tax points and one equalized corporate income tax point. Except for an initial period, this funding had little impact on the overall flows under the program, since the 50 percent federal sharing exceeded the value of the tax-point transfer so that the shortfall came in the form of cash transfers.

Canada Assistance Plan

The shared-cost program for welfare essentially followed the pattern for post-secondary education — 50 percent of provincial costs for eligible expenses. One important aspect of the conditionality of these grants was that the provinces could not impose lengthy waiting periods for eligibility.

Quebec

Prior to focussing on the impact of these programs, it is important to note that Quebec insisted on and received additional income tax points in lieu of cash grants. The federal government offered this "opting out" provision to the remaining provinces but none chose the option.

Implications for the Division of Powers

What was the overall impact of these arrangements in terms of the division of powers? First of all, the provinces still administered the programs. Moreover, they maintained considerable flexibility in many aspects of program design. Welfare levels across provinces (and within provinces between rural and urban centres) need not be, and were not, the same. University programs differed across the provinces — e.g., Saskatchewan had 12 years of public schooling and a three-year general Bachelor of Arts degree while Ontario had 13 years and also a three-year general BA. Physician pay scales varied both within and between provinces, and so on.

However, the conditions did have an impact. In the health-care area, only certain types of institutions and practitioners qualified for federal funding. For example, convalescent homes instead of hospitals did not qualify. Nor did services by paramedics. As a result, the conditional-funding format generated a particular type of health-care system across the country. In the area of post-secondary education the argument is frequently heard that since the provinces were spending 50 cent dollars this lead to an overexpansion of the system.

In general, however, it is fair to say that the use of federal conditional grants, supported constitutionally by the federal spending power, did indeed shift the division of powers in this area toward the federal government. In some cases, however, the provinces were more than anxious that Ottawa play this role (e.g., CAP). In others, such as medicare, a few provinces were "dragged" into the program. In spite of these differences, it is worth recalling a portion of Jacques Parizeau's comments, cited in full in Chapter 2:

> If the federal government opens shared-cost programs in existing fields of public expenditures, it can thus "freeze" gradually an increasing share of provincial budgets. At the limit, provincial authorities become more or less administrative agencies of federally initiated or federally financed programs, irrespective of how the legal documents distribute formal powers between the two levels of government. (Parizeau, 1970, p. 83)

In spite of this loss of provincial sovereignty (which was of more concern for some programs than for others and even then applied only to selected provinces), many Canadians then and now supported the infusion of federal money and the resulting rapid development of the social programs, including those conditions that allowed these programs to take on aspects of national programs. It is worth emphasizing once again that the authority that enabled Ottawa to take the initiative with respect to these social programs, even to the point of harmonizing the programs across provinces in some cases, derived from the federal spending power (Forget, 1985).

1977: Block Funding and Unconditionality

The fiscal arrangements of 1977 represent the next watershed in the evolution of the social programs — the open-ended, cost-sharing format for the established programs (health care and post-secondary education) was replaced by block funding and unconditional transfers. Both Ottawa and the provinces appeared to be in favour of the move. In addition to some of the inefficiencies alluded to earlier, which probably had more to do with the inflexibility in the program design than the fact that they were centrally monitored, the provinces were concerned that their spending priorities were being distorted by the existence of federal subsidies for some areas of expenditures. For its part, Ottawa was concerned about the budgetary implications of the old format: in effect, federal spending on the established programs was being determined by the decisions taken in the ten provincial capitals.

The particular funding compromise initiated in 1977 was very complicated. Essentially, the initial federal payment was set at roughly 50 percent of the per capita expenditures on these programs in the two top provinces. Half of this federal portion consisted of a transfer of equalized income tax points (which required some additional transfer of tax points) and the other half was in the form of cash transfers. Moreover, no province would receive, in total, an amount less than double the cash transfer. Because the federal cash transfer tended (for almost all provinces) to exceed the tax transfer, this meant, in effect, that the overall transfer to the provinces was identical in per capita terms. An equivalent of an additional two income tax points (one in an equalized tax-point transfer and one in cash) was added on to the 1977 funding in order to compensate the provinces for the termination of the revenue guarantee. This total package was to be escalated annually by the three-year average rate of GNP growth. Finally, the payments were unconditional — they could be spent as the provinces wished. However, the five previously enunciated principles associated with the health-care area still remained in force. While these arrangements did not apply to the Canada Assistance Plan, there was an expectation that CAP would also be block-funded within a couple of years.

These developments represented a remarkable turn of events. In effect, the provinces were now given full responsibility for these programs which, after all, came under the provinces' constitutional responsibility. In theory, the provinces gained greater autonomy. In practice, however, some provinces took a different position. In their view, what happened was that the federal government enticed the provinces in the late 1950s and 1960s to embark on federally designed programs (in the health area) and encouraged spending on post-secondary education via conditional grants and then, a decade or so later, Ottawa converted the conditional to unconditional grants. The "autonomy" implied by an unconditional grant was in part illusory in the sense that Ottawa threw to the provinces the full responsibility for controlling what were three of the most rapidly increasing areas of expenditures in the entire public sector. This autonomy was eroded even further for some of the provinces since they found themselves with less, not more, funds in 1977–78 than in the previous fiscal year (if the dollar loss associated with the termination of the revenue guarantee is considered).

Reconditionalizing the Transfers

Almost immediately the federal government appeared to have second thoughts with respect to the 1977 arrangements. In the summer of 1978

Ottawa attempted to renegotiate the financial package. In particular, the minister of finance served notice to the provinces that he wished to have the total payments escalate at a slower rate. The provinces refused to do so (and had the right to refuse since the arrangements were binding for at least five years). In turn, the federal government removed the proposed Social Services Financing Act from the legislation table. (This act was designed to block fund the social services component of the Canada Assistance Plan — to convert it to equal per capita payments following the format of the 1977 Established Programs Financing (EPF) arrangements.)

More significantly, the federal government never respected the spirit of unconditionality. It continued to provide separate cheques to the provinces for health and post-secondary education, and it monitored provincial spending in these areas.

Under the combined banners of visibility, accountability and restraint, the federal government moved dramatically to alter the letter and the spirit of the 1977 arrangements. In the 1982 fiscal arrangements, Ottawa removed the equivalent of the two income tax points that were added to the 1977 arrangements as a compromise for the termination of the revenue guarantee. The provinces argued that these two tax points were part of the "permanent" funding agreed to in 1977, which was also my interpretation at the time. However, the federal government saw it differently, and since the fiscal arrangements are an act of the federal Parliament, Ottawa can always get its way.

The provinces were also surprised to hear that the federal government felt they were not spending their unconditional grants in an appropriate manner. Ontario came under special scrutiny for diverting some post-secondary monies to other budget items. This general issue came to the fore in 1984. The post-secondary education transfers have been made subject to the overall 6 and 5 program and the federal government is undertaking a review of the entire university education field with an eye toward further federal initiatives or conditions that might be introduced.

Ottawa has taken some daring initiatives in the health area. Under the guise of "saving medicare," the 1984 Canada Health Act contains the following provisions:

- it effectively eliminates extra billing (opting out) as a source of funding;
- it rules out the use of deterrent (user) fees;
- it calls into question some previously accepted means of funding, such as medicare premiums;
- it defines in part what ought to be covered under the provincial programs (and in some areas this coverage is broader than what the provinces presently offer);
- it makes it more difficult for those provinces allowing opting out to set the fee schedules for their doctors;

- it is open-ended and unilateral in the sense that its provisions can be altered by the Parliament of Canada if and when it wishes.

I shall comment later on the implications of the Canada Health Act. In general terms, the 1984 act represents a complete about-turn from the 1977 arrangements: not only have new conditions been attached to the cash transfers under the health programs, but also the legislation goes a long way in the direction of telling the provinces what ought to be covered under the universal programs and how these programs ought to be funded.

This "centralizing" process has not been restricted to the health area. The National Energy Program of 1980, the Constitution Act, 1982, the 1982 fiscal arrangements, among others, can also be viewed as reflecting the federal government's desire to locate more power at the centre.

Recapitulation

The purpose of this chapter is to evaluate the implications of altering the division of powers with respect to social programs. While there has been no formal change in the Constitution regarding these programs, the federal government has utilized its spending power over the years to alter the de facto allocation of authority and indeed the nature of the programs. In this important sense the division of powers in this area has been changed on several occasions. We might well ask whether there is a case to be made for either greater centralization or greater decentralization of the social programs. The remainder of the chapter is devoted to this question. The next section on social policy in the 1990s attempts to provide a framework for addressing this issue. The following section then focusses in detail on the federal-provincial overlap in the income security area, an area where we find a variety of jurisdictional arrangements. Finally, the chapter concludes with a discussion of "fiscal balance," which is probably at the heart of the issue.

Social Policy in the 1990s: A Personal Perspective[2]

Canadians tend to cast a longing eye back toward the 1960s. Sustained and stable growth, low inflation and unemployment, and rapidly rising productivity characterized the decade. Moreover, the world economy was relatively stable and expanding. It is not surprising that this buoyant overall environment was conducive to the development of the socio-economic programs. As noted above, this was the era that saw rapid expansion in the established programs. It was also the period of the comprehensive equalization program and other developments on the regional front such as the Department of Regional Economic Expansion (DREE) and the regional aspects of the Unemployment Insurance Commission (UIC) (actually in 1971). In effect, Canada utilized the stable cushion of economic growth to put in place a growing network of transfers to persons, businesses and governments.

The mid-1980s, and the 1990s as well, are likely to be very different. Productivity has been flat for the better part of a decade. Unemployment appears to be stabilizing at double-digit levels. Deficits are staggering at both levels of government. In addition, the world economy is anything but tranquil. Economies everywhere are restructuring and the world trading environment is becoming more, not less, competitive. We no longer have the luxury of designing our social policies independently of the overall needs of the economy. Indeed, the challenge would appear to be precisely the opposite of that of the sixties: How do we now rationalize our system of transfers and social policies in order to help rekindle the failing engines of economic growth? Whereas the bywords of the sixties may have been "equity" and "steady at the helm," those of the eighties and nineties will probably have to be "flexibility" and "adjustment." Indeed, *Challenges and Choices* makes the same point: "How can we better manage and adjust to change? If there is a single major concern among Canadians, it relates to that issue" (Royal Commission on the Economic Union and Development Prospects for Canada, 1984, p. 7).

One way of relating this underlying economic climate to the role of social policy is to focus on three general trade-offs that (while not exhaustive) are implicit in all policy decisions and, hence, those in the social policy area as well. The trade-offs are equity versus efficiency, centralization versus decentralization, and private sector versus public sector.

Equity versus Efficiency

The economic rewards over the next decade will go to those nations that are able to allocate or reallocate resources to the sunrise industries. The role for socio-economic support systems in this context appears rather obvious: they should serve the larger role of enhancing adjustment. They should not become vehicles for rigidifying the existing economic structure.

Frequently this aspect of the overall efficiency/equity trade-off is phrased in terms of security versus adjustment or entitlements versus adjustment. The conflict here is obvious, since an entitlement is, in effect, a property right to the status quo whereas adjustment implies the abandonment of the status quo. However, it is important to put a time perspective on this process. Over the longer term, security and adjustment are likely to be complementary, not competing, in the sense that if the economy fails to adjust, there is no real economic security. The challenge, therefore, arises over the shorter term: is there an acceptable way to modify entitlements in order to facilitate the needed adjustment?

One area where this dilemma has come to the surface is health care.

The thrust of the 1984 Canada Health Act is in part that Ottawa has imposed its own view of equity on the system. This is a questionable policy, if, as a result, it stymies the provinces' ability to seek out more efficient ways to deliver health care. Neither efficiency nor equity is served if the system becomes so overly rigid and expensive over the long term that we are forced to go the British route and, for example, ration access on the basis of age.

The trade-off between equity and efficiency is more severe in some areas than in others. It is inconceivable to me that both equity and efficiency cannot be enhanced by redesigning the income support programs — the CAP-family allowance, UIC, guaranteed income supplement (GIS), old-age security (OAS), Canada Pension Plan/Quebec Pension Plan (CPP/QPP) interaction. Likewise, it would appear that both efficiency and equity would be served if pensions became more portable across industries and across provinces.

More generally, the present status of the economy requires that concerns about adjustment and efficiency rise to the fore across the entire spectrum of government policy. There is no long-term prospect for adequate social programs in the context of a faltering economy. Appropriate policy does not require that social safety nets become sieves. It does not imply rolling back the postwar advances on the social policy front. Indeed, in my view the opposite is true — only by enhancing both the efficiency of the economy and of the social programs themselves are we likely to maintain our hard-won gains in terms of socio-economic policy. What is required, however, is that social policy be reoriented wherever possible to embody features that cater to the incentive to work and to individual incentive; encourage adjustment and flexibility rather than entrenchment; and become more selective (i.e., targeted). Radical surgery is not an answer that Canadians will accept, nor is it necessary. Rather, these goals argue for a series of "successive approximations" (to fall back on Bank of Canada legalese) that will, over the medium term, effectively alter the incentives in these programs. Fortunately, much if not most of this restructuring can be accomplished without violating the generally accepted norms of equity.

To this point, there has been no mention of whether this flexibility is likely to be enhanced more by centralized or decentralized delivery of the social programs. This is the purpose of the next section.

Centralization versus Decentralization

The discussion of centralization versus decentralization is always delicate. Any emphasis on efficiency usually leads in the direction of some decentralization. However, let me begin the analysis of this issue by stating what I do not mean by decentralization in the context of the social programs. Over the years, Canadians have accomplished an impressive commonality of interest in the way their social programs have developed, much of it due to the role played by the federal government. Completely turning over the social programs to the provinces may well destroy this commonality of interest and replace it by ten competing and perhaps inward-looking approaches. This is not what is meant by decentralization. In this context it is instructive to draw from a recent paper by John Graham in which he notes:

> If we look at the issue of decentralization and centralization as one of balance — of never neglecting regional interests when considering general country-wide interests and never neglecting unifying country-wide interests when considering regional (provincial) interests — it is evident that there must be some safeguards to ensure that the interests of the smaller, less politically powerful provinces are not swamped by the promotion of the interests of the large provinces. (Graham, 1980–81, p. 9)

The role of the equal-per-capita funding plus the system of equalization payments can, of course, be viewed as ensuring that the "interests" of the smaller provinces are not trampled upon.

As a result of the recent and still ongoing debate with respect to the Canadian economic union (see Chapter 9), Canadians are likely to be more insistent that policies take on national overtones. While it is important to recognize that for policies to be "national" they need not be "central," it is also the case that this new thrust probably puts the onus on the provinces to show Canadians that they can ensure such things as portability of, and universal access to, the social programs.

Within this general framework of ensuring certain national aspects of the social programs, we can address the issue of whether efficiency and flexibility will be better served by more decentralization or more centralization. For some policy areas covered earlier (e.g., monetary policy) centralization is appropriate; but for other areas of social policy, decentralization is preferable. There are two general arguments for decentralization, both of which apply to many parts of the social policy area. First, decentralization allows regional or provincial preferences to dominate in terms of the characteristics of the programs. Second, decentralization allows the individual provinces the freedom to innovate and experiment in order that more efficient means of delivery services can be found. (This should not be interpreted to imply that there can be no innovation or experimentation at the federal level. After all, we can and probably should view the changing structure of the established programs in this light.) But additional innovation is particularly important for areas like health care where, for example, expenditures on health now account for over 30 cents of every dollar of Ontario's government expenditures and where health-care costs in this province grew by 50 percent over the past three years. Presumably other provinces are under similar sorts of financial pressures in this area. When combined with the fact that the population is aging and the new diagnostic and treatment devices tend to be expensive, this clearly puts an enormous premium on finding ways to increase efficiency while at the same time ensuring the existing level of services. Much in the way of innovative experimentation is clearly ongoing in the provinces. Yet this is probably only the tip of the iceberg as the provinces come to realize that federal monies for health care will probably not be as readily available as they have been in the past.

Ontario's experiment with private-sector management of a few hospitals and Alberta's intentions of following suit represent the sorts of initiatives that we would expect. However, these are likely to be minor innovations compared to what the future will hold. Experimentation with alternative methods of paying physicians and institutions, and with the overall structure and management of the system are not far off.[3] The physicians themselves will probably be moved to action since the alternative to co-operating in enhancing efficiency of the health-care area may be to find themselves as full-fledged civil servants.[4] All of this experimentation is likely to occur within the framework of a public health system. In this context it is useful to recall that the present organization of the health-care system owes much to the experimentation and innovativeness of the province of Saskatchewan; but that was 20 years ago and pressures are again mounting for a rethinking of the manner in which health care is best delivered.

It is probably much easier to argue for a federal presence in post-secondary education, particularly as it relates to graduate programs and research. What is not so clear is whether any federal role should go beyond the provision of funding for these activities. There is considerable concern from various quarters that Canada's system of higher education be world-class, however this status might be defined. In graduate economics, it seems to me that four or so departments have international reputations and are competing in an international (or at least North American) context. While it may be possible to have relatively high standards across the board for undergraduate education (and surely most of the Canadian universities would rank high in any North American comparison), this is probably not feasible at the graduate level.

In this context, would greater federal control enhance graduate programs and research generally? It would probably mean somewhat greater equality across regions (not across each province) in terms of providing opportunities to achieve excellence, but it is not clear that equality of result (as distinct from equality of opportunity to achieve excellence) would ensue. This is particularly the case if students continued to have access to their choice of graduate school. No doubt, there do exist some problems with university education in Canada. However, there is no presumption that greater centralization of the system would solve more problems than it creates. The current diversity between provinces and within provinces does allow for tremendous innovation and specialization. Were the system to move in a more central direction it would be essential that this degree of diversity be maintained.

In the income-support area the situation is more complicated because the jurisdictional overlap is likewise more complex. There has been a long tradition on the part of provinces to tailor welfare levels to perceived differential needs in various parts of the individual provinces, and these payment levels vary across provinces. Since federal control over this area would seem to imply uniform payment levels (unless Ottawa were to provide only the minimum level, with provincial top-ups allowed), the overall result might well be perverse in the sense that net migration would be encouraged into poorer areas. In the one income-support program that is under total federal control (unemployment insurance) the support levels run counter to efficiency: the regionally extended benefits of UI are such that benefit entitlements are much longer in duration in the poorer (and generally lower-income and lower-employment-opportunity) areas. If this pattern were established in any general centralization of the income-support function, most Canadians would probably not opt for greater centralization, on grounds both of equity and efficiency.

In summary, for reasons of regional preference and efficiency-cum-flexibility, there is no call for greater centralization of the social programs. This generalization is subject to two caveats. First, throughout the analysis it is assumed that there is full portability of benefits across provinces. The one key area where this flexibility has not been secured is in the pension area. The problem here relates to occupational as well as geographical mobility. The federal government has played an important role in focussing the attention of Canadians on the issue, principally via the recent parliamentary committee on pension reform. In June 1984 the provincial treasurers, under the chairmanship of then Ontario treasurer Larry Grossman, met with the purpose of improving private-sector pensions, including pension portability. If the provinces prove themselves incapable of ensuring a substantial enhancement in portability, then Ottawa has to step in. The second caveat is related. Much of the progress in ensuring interprovincial access to programs in the social policy area has been secured via the federal spending power — one of the conditions under which federal monies will be transferred relates to reasonable (and sometimes immediate) access to services afforded to interprovincial migrants. While the provinces acting on their own might be able to guarantee such access, it is important for the federal government to continue to conditionalize its transfers in this manner in order to ensure portability and access, unless the provinces agree to guarantee this principle in some ironclad way.

However, beyond these aspects, the twin concerns of efficiency/

flexibility and regional preference would appear to allow for some freedom for provincial experimentation and innovation, particularly for those programs where costs are rapidly escalating.

Private Sector versus Public Sector

By the very nature of our culture and history, Canadians have a greater tendency to look benignly toward government and government intervention than do our neighbours to the south. This has some advantages and some costs. For example, in spite of the concerns I voiced over the direction of the health-care system, it is a far better system than that in place in the United States. At the same time, in a world which increasingly places a premium on initiative and adjustment, Canada and Canadians may too readily seek recourse to government whenever adversity strikes.

The underlying issue here, namely, the appropriate role and magnitude of the public sector, is one which has implications that extend well beyond the social policy area. Nonetheless, even within this area it has important ramifications. With respect to post-secondary education, several provinces may move in the direction of requiring that a greater share of funding comes from tuition fees, particularly for some professional programs. This system may be accompanied by an expanded system of loans (perhaps on a contingent-repayment basis) in order that income level not be an important determinant of access. Ottawa may react negatively to such developments, but in terms of equity and efficiency, let alone the distribution of powers, it is hard to make a case that would justify any federal intervention.

Another aspect of this public/private trade-off centres on the notion of "paternalism." This issue was prominent in the recent pension debate. Recommendations from many quarters to the effect that all pension-related contributions be fully locked in or that governments should assume the principal role for income replacement (as distinct from income support) for the elderly suggest implicitly, if not explicitly, that the typical Canadian is not to be trusted to look after his/her own interests, either because citizens will squander their savings in frivolous pursuits or they will not avail themselves of the opportunities to provide for their retirement. Not only do I find this notion to be far off the mark, but also it is hard to reconcile with the flexibility and initiative that are required by the underlying economic realities.

In summary, therefore, the emphasis on adjustment and flexibility, dictated by the economic exigencies of the 1980s, tends to tip the scales in terms of social programs toward efficiency, decentralization (or at least not more centralization), and private-sector participation. This does not mean that there are not important national objectives that have to be secured in these social programs, but we must recognize that the ensuring of these national aspects does not necessarily require central control.

Admittedly, this analysis is based on my personal biases and on my reading of likely trends in national and international economies. However, what is important for the thrust of the monograph is not whether the reader agrees or disagrees with the analysis, but the notion that the design of social programs may have to be related to the overall needs of the economy. Thus, there is probably an "economic determinism" at work here that will be of more importance to the future of social programs than the recent tendency for these programs to become more centralized. In turn, this suggests that exhibited postwar flexibility in respect of the structure of social programs should be maintained into the future rather than any decision being made on an "appropriate" division of powers.

I now turn to an analysis of the existing division of powers in one area of social policy — the income security area. The purpose of this investigation is to highlight the fact that the allocation of jurisdictional authority not only varies across individual programs but, more importantly, encompasses three different ways in which powers are allocated in federal nations.

The Division of Powers and the Social Programs:
The Income Security Area

The division of powers in the income-support area provides considerable insight into the range of ways in which power can be divided in a federation. As Keith Banting has noted in a recent paper, three distinct types of relationships in the social security area can be distinguished:

(i) unilateralism, which characterizes the major national programs and social assistance;
(ii) bureaucratic symbiosis, which characterizes the CAP;
(iii) a system of multiple vetoes, which governs the CPP.
The fascinating point about this list is that it captures the essence of three different conceptions of the ideal federal state. Unilateralism reflects the concept of classical federalism, in which each level of government acts independently within its own jurisdiction, and few formal mechanisms integrate the policies of the two in a comprehensive way. The bureaucratic symbiosis of the CAP, on the other hand, reflects another conception, often called co-operative federalism, in which the central government influences the policies of provincial or state governments through fiscal mechanisms, and operations involve substantial bureaucratic consultation, coordination and tension. Finally, the multiple vetoes of the CPP approximate, in principle at least, one major variant of intrastate federalism, a conception which envisages provincial governments having a formal place in the legislative process of the central government, with the right to shape or block national legislation in areas of relevance to them. (Banting, 1985, p. 266–267)

Unilateralism

The notion of each level of government acting independently within its own jurisdiction was the dominant theme of Quebec's Tremblay Report.[5] As Bastien noted, this report proposed the "separation and exclusive assignment of functions between the two orders of government" (Bastien, 1981, p. 22). Bastien argues that this concept of autonomy in the spheres of operation of the two levels of government may have been appropriate to the situation in 1867, but with the growth of the mixed economy it is essential and natural that this independence give way to "interdependence" (p. 46). These ideas will be developed in more detail in the context of the overall assessment of the division of powers in Chapter 10.

For present purposes, I am assuming that unilateralism is similar to this notion of autonomy of jurisdiction or independence. This interpretation does some violence to the concept, since what the Tremblay Report had in mind was independence or autonomy with respect to the broad areas of jurisdiction and not independence of action for both levels within a given area, in this case income support. Nonetheless, as Bastien points out, the idea of watertight allocations of jurisdictions runs into trouble, since in the modern integrated economy policy action in one area spills over into most other areas. This spillover is all the more enhanced when there is independence of action within a given jurisdiction as there is in the income-support area.

The federal government has exclusive jurisdiction over unemployment insurance, old-age security (OAS), and the guaranteed income supplement (GIS). The provinces have exclusive jurisdiction over workmen's compensation, the Quebec Pension Plan (QPP), and programs like the guaranteed annual income system (GAINS) in Ontario and similar programs in several other provinces. Programs under joint jurisdiction include the Canada Pension Plan (CPP), the regulation of the private pension system, the Canada Assistance Plan (CAP), and the family allowances (since the provinces now can play a role in allocating these monies within certain limits, although only Quebec and Alberta have thus far taken advantage of this option).

There are of course some advantages of unilateralism. For example, the particular program in question can be tailored according to the desires of the government responsible; but there are also costs. If Ottawa alters the provision of UI, this will reverberate on the provinces; a dramatic reduction in the duration of benefits would likely throw UI exhaustees on welfare, half the cost of which is borne by the provinces. Relatedly, several provinces are unhappy with the notion that under unemployment insurance some $12 billion a year is currently paid out for people not to work. In turn this puts pressures on provincial governments to launch job-creation measures in their own budgets which, to the extent that they succeed, will benefit Ottawa financially as people are drawn off UI into the work force, and so on.

Bureaucratic Symbiosis

As noted earlier in the brief review of postwar developments in the social policy area, the Canada Assistance Plan (CAP) remains the only major shared-cost program. Banting notes that it is a "survivor from the age of cooperative federalism" (Banting, 1985). In terms of the characteristics of CAP as it relates to the division of powers, it seems appropriate to quote at length from Banting's excellent overview paper:

> CAP demonstrates all of the traditional strengths and weaknesses of the conditional grant mechanism. Federal cost-sharing has encouraged an expansion and consolidation of provincial social assistance programs. Although critics lament the lack of national standards in benefit levels, interprovincial variation is probably less marked today than in earlier eras; in 1942, for example, average benefits under provincial mothers' allowance programs varied by a ratio of three to one and the program did not exist in two provinces. And certainly the corrosive effects of residency requirements, so evident in the 1930s, have been neutralized for social assistance, if not for social services. . . . yet the CAP also manifests all of the traditional frustrations of conditional grants. For provinces, it produces regular battles over shareability, and they continually bump against the legislation's outer limits in attempting to supplement the incomes of the working poor and to expand social services. For the federal government, CAP continues to be an element of its budget that is uncontrollable and provides remarkably little political visibility, a commodity highly prized in Ottawa of late. For legislatures and citizens, the shared responsibility inherent in the CAP complicates the process of holding government accountable for welfare policy. (p. 270)

Multiple Vetoes: The Pension Plan

The third approach to sharing powers is exemplified by the CPP and QPP. The rules governing amendments in these programs — described in the last section of Chapter 8 — are such that they have created a system of "multiple veto points," to use Banting's phraseology. Banting (1985) points out that the procedures for amending the CPP are even more demanding than the amending formula adopted for the Constitution and, hence, lend an inordinate degree of inflexibility to the CPP and QPP.

In terms of the recent pension debate, it is clear that if the CPP fell under federal jurisdiction, this level of government would have been sorely tempted to double the size of the program. Fortunately or unfortunately, the set of checks and balances in the system were such that Ottawa could not move unilaterally in this direction. One result is that the GIS has become a much more important program than it was originally designed to be. Introduced in the mid-1960s, GIS "was seen as a transitional mechanism to help elderly people who had little else but the OAS payment to live on and who could not benefit from [the introduction of] the CPP" (Banting, 1984, p. 197). However, because the federal government found it difficult to increase the CPP, it turned instead to the GIS, which was a program under its own control.

While we could view this refocussing as a kind of institutional or jurisdictional determinism, it is also possible to argue that there was an economic determinism at work as well. Given the underlying needs of the economy in the rest of this decade and probably by the 1990s as well, GIS is the appropriate way to go. After all, Ottawa could have increased the OAS component in 1984 (instead of the GIS component), but the general recognition of the need to target income support to those most in need dictated GIS over OAS. Moreover, in the recent parliamentary hearings of the Pension Reform Committee, it is probably correct to say that there was not a groundswell of support for enriching the CPP (although labour and some women's groups did argue in this direction) and the committee itself did not recommend a significant CPP expansion (House of Commons, 1983). Thus, while there may be considerable inflexibility associated with altering the CPP, it is not clear that this has served the nation badly.

System Rationalization: A Guaranteed Annual Income

What lessons can or should be drawn from these alternative jurisdictional relationships in the income support area? Would a different division of powers enhance economic performance? Once again, the answer is far from clear.

At one extreme, responsibility for all these programs could be transferred to one or the other level of government. This transfer would remove some of the intergovernmental spillovers that presently exist in the system. For example, if income support were federal, it would no longer be possible for Ottawa to benefit by a reduction in UI payments thereby forcing more Canadians to fall back on welfare (one-half of which is provincially funded). However, the programs in this area are so broad and diverse that some are more suited to provincial control and some to federal control. As emphasized in Chapter 4 on macroeconomic policy, there is a federal role required in UI (and particularly in the funding of UI) as long as the federal government is held responsible for maintaining high employment in the economy. Likewise, it is inappropriate to have welfare levels identical everywhere in the country, as would likely be politically necessary if CAP were turned over to Ottawa.

Despite these observations in support of the status quo, the majority of Canadians seem convinced that rationalization in the design of support policies would be fruitful:

- The inflexibility of most welfare programs is such that families on welfare are frequently as well off as the "working poor."
- Current UI provisions do not encourage persons to re-enter the work force.
- Regional UI benefits tend to encourage people to remain in low-employment areas.
- The relationship between support levels as a family head moves from 64 to 65 often represents a quantum leap in support.
- The intergovernmental interface is such that one level of government can transfer substantial costs to the other level.

This last point merits elaboration, even though it has been stressed elsewhere in this study. Up until recently, the province of Quebec had the highest minimum wage on the continent, let alone in Canada. As a result, the level of unemployment in Quebec was higher than it otherwise would have been. However, Quebec was able to pass off much of the costs of this high minimum wage to the rest of Canadians since Ottawa came to the province's rescue with increased UI payments, increased equalization payments, and 50 percent of any welfare costs. Moreover, because of Quebec's high unemployment rate it was able to lobby successfully for additional tariffs and quotas for its labour-intensive industries. This ability of one level of government to pass off the costs of its economic decisions to the rest of the country (via Ottawa) is surely not consistent with the emphasis on flexibility and adjustment highlighted earlier in the chapter. (As an aside, it is interesting to note that the Quebec example includes three programs — tariffs, equalization and minimum wages — that have hitherto received no mention in this chapter but, nonetheless, impact on policies in the socio-economic area. This provides further evidence of the extent to which policy areas are now interrelated or integrated, to use Bastien's term.)

One reaction of Canadians to this interrelationship has been to argue for a guaranteed annual income (GAI) program which would rationalize the entire social security system by bringing the full range of programs under a single comprehensive program. At the conceptual level, this is an appealing and useful tactic since it leads one to focus on those aspects of the present system that run counter to the notions of equity and efficiency — such as the substantial portion of UI benefits that accrue to family units with already high incomes. At the practical level, however, we run into several problems, many of which were highlighted in a paper by Michael Mendelson (1985). He focussed on the various delivery mechanisms for a GAI, such as a system of cash payments, a negative income tax (NIT), and a credit income tax (CIT). His analysis and conclusions are represented in the following passages:

> Why is there little hope of implementing of GAI, given that it promises simplification of a system continually criticized for its complexity and that it

is a populist idea, with broad support cutting across normal political group-ings? The short answer to this puzzle is that GAI schemes cannot really do what they seem to do. Their hidden promise is to resolve painlessly the problem of poverty by streamlining the existing flow of income-security payments and reducing the bureaucracy. However, when we look at the nitty-gritty of actual implementation and review the income security system at a level of detail slightly greater than that of a single sweeping generaliza-tion, we find that both the benefits of and the need for simplification may be greatly exaggerated. At the same time the complexity of the supposed solution may be greatly understated. . . . (pp. 230–31)

To get on with the job of improving our income security system, we must recognize finally that it is not a homogeneous, simple system that, but for the timidity of our decision-makers, could be collapsed into one, nice, neat, aesthetically appealing program. Rather, it is a heterogeneous, multi-pur-pose system that must serve a variety of clientele and plays a complex, many-faceted role within our public sector and within the economy as a whole. (p. 250)

However, Mendelson did, in fact, go on to argue for a GAI, not as a single scheme to replace all other income support programs but as a substitute for the existing Canada Assistance Plan. Ottawa would provide some minimum income level, and the provinces would then be left to top it up as and where they perceive the need to do so. This is a variant of a scheme I proposed over a decade ago and have alluded to earlier in this monograph (Courchene, 1973b). Presumably this level of uniform federal support would be at a level appropriate for some of the poorer provinces, with the monies for any provincial top-ups coming from the provinces' own coffers. This scheme would have the added advantage that provin-ces would then think twice about having minimum wages out of line with those in other provinces or out of line with their own economic condi-tions, since they would bear the full financial responsibility for any welfare top-ups.

More generally, Mendelson felt that it was appropriate to consider rationalization and simplification of income security. He concluded that what was needed or, rather, what was possible, was "program rationaliza-tion" and not "system rationalization," even though such an approach was likely to be viewed as "pragmatic and pedestrian" (p. 230).

It is important to recall that over the period 1973–77 Canada did attempt a massive review and revision of the entire social security system. In particular, the original thrust was to attempt to integrate the many social security components into one umbrella program. The trials and tribulations associated with this process as well as its eventual failure were documented by Claude Forget (1984). Some of the diffi-culties encountered parallel the concerns raised by Mendelson; some go further. For example, to rely on the income tax system as the principal mechanism for delivering income support means, in effect, that there will be less flexibility for both Ottawa and the provinces to utilize income tax changes for policies such as stimulating growth. Moreover, since income support is a joint federal-provincial responsibility, there would have to be a degree of co-ordination in the preparation of budgets that has hitherto not existed and indeed may have been problematical within the parliamentary framework.

Even though this attempt at system rationalization did not succeed there is considerable merit to focussing on the "system" implications of the various components of social security. At the very least it provides some guidelines as to how some of the component programs can be revised and restructured.

Recapitulation

In terms of the various jurisdictional arrangements found in the income security area, Banting (1985) draws the following conclusions:

> Classical federalism, cooperative federalism, and interstate federalism all co-exist uneasily in the complex analysis of our modern welfare system. However, the three kinds of relationships in income security highlight an enduring dilemma within federal systems, the apparent incompatibility between flexibility, responsiveness, and accountability on one hand, and coordination and comprehensive planning on the other. The more freedom each level of government preserves to further its own political orientation, to respond to its own electorate, and to adapt to a changing world, the weaker are the integrative capacities of the policy process of the federation as a whole. But the stronger the integrative mechanisms, the less flexible and responsive is the process to the turbulence inherent in economic and political change. Canadians, it seems, cannot have it both ways. (pp. 273–74)

While this general conclusion would appear to hold across a wide range of policy areas, it is not clear what it has to say about the appropriate division of powers. As Bastien notes:

> A government's presence is by no means limited to a few well-defined areas: it intervenes in nearly every field of human activity. In the modern industrial world government is involved in all areas. All its components are interdependent. A government's activities in the education field affect its activities in the area of unemployment, its activities in employment affect its social welfare programs, which in turn affect housing policy, and so on. (Bastien, 1981, p. 47)

Within this context, meaningful decentralization may not imply a separation of powers (as in unilateralism) or an effective series of checks and balances (as in the multiple veto arrangements) but rather co-operation in decision-making. This means that both levels of government must co-operate if coherent action is to be taken. In turn, this implies that federalism must not merely be "a structure of government but also a process" (p. 48). Thus:

> Federalism should not only be seen as a static pattern or design, charac-
> terized by a particular and precisely fixed division of powers between
> government levels. Federalism is also and perhaps primarily the pro-
> cess . . . of adopting joint policies and making joint decisions on joint
> problems. (Friedrich, 1968, p. 7)

Cast in terms of the social programs this definition seems to imply that the issue of the moment ought not to be who has the right to alter this or that aspect of social programs, but rather how and in which direction they ought to be altered or redesigned. Whatever the existing division of powers, the federal government can make life unpleasant for the provinces by wielding its spending power influence. Even if the courts were to outlaw the use of the federal expenditure power as a means of imposing conditions on programs under provincial responsibility, the federal government would still have the authority to pare back the level of intergovernmental transfers. (This issue of vertical fiscal balance will be dealt with in more detail in the next section.) Likewise, the provinces have some weapons in their own arsenal. For example, any province can withdraw from the CPP and set up its own program, following Quebec's lead.

This manipulation potential places a premium on co-operation and co-ordination. Yet over the recent past co-operation has not characterized federal-provincial relations. Among other things, Ottawa's concern over visibility and accountability led in the direction of imposing "conditions" on provincial programs, especially where the federal fiscal position no longer allowed "money" bribes. Moreover, Ottawa no doubt believes that the unconditional aspect of the 1977 arrangements was a mistake. These considerations aside, one of the underlying arguments of this chapter is that the economic requirements for the needs of the 1980s and 1990s are such that both levels of government will come to realize that: the social programs must be geared toward enhancing the overall efficiency and flexibility of the economy; the system should encourage innovation and experimentation in those areas where cost-efficiency is becoming increasingly critical; and they should encourage greater private-sector participation where this is consistent with society's general notions of equity.

In some cases the issue is one of reviewing and updating the various programs — programs which were designed in a period when resources were more plentiful and Canada's position in the international pecking order of nations was both secure and rising. In these cases, governments no doubt realize what has to be done. However, the implementation process is difficult and delicate, since it may imply the rolling back of "entitlements" to regions, individuals or special interests. Governments do many things well, but their Achilles' heel is that they find it enormously difficult to draw back from earlier commitments whether they be regional UI payments, subsidies to Canadair or whatever. In such situations a co-ordinated federal-provincial strategy and decision-making process may make it easier for both levels of government to undertake the necessary changes in their respective programs.

In other cases the process will be more difficult, since one level of government may perceive that it is ceding some authority to the other; yet there are concessions to be made on both sides. The provinces need more freedom to meet the oncoming challenge on the health-care side. The federal government should have the right to insist on adequate portability mechanisms for social programs across provinces. In the wake of the Canadian Charter of Rights and Freedoms, Canadians will insist that their pensions be portable and the access to social programs be virtually immediate no matter where they decide to reside. Federal initiatives to ensure this flexibility are consistent with both efficiency and equity. At the same time, the necessity that social programs be integrated into the needs of an ailing economy and be amenable to innovation and restructuring to ensure that delivery systems are improved will also contribute to efficiency. Moreover, these initiatives are likely to be entirely consistent with long-term equity considerations. It is far preferable for Ottawa and the provinces to fall back on co-operative federalism and develop a coherent, co-ordinated policy to meet these challenges while time is still on their side than to be dragged into a series of stop-gap policies in times of fiscal or social policy crisis.

In summary, therefore, the income support area is particularly instructive for students of federalism because of the variety of jurisdictional overlaps across the various programs. We can attribute some degree of constitutional or jurisdictional determinism to the manner in which various aspects of the social programs have developed over time. However, the major innovations in social programs over the postwar period reflected more basic underlying trends than the specific division of powers in this area. It is possible that a revised division of powers is the answer, but I for one would be hard pressed to outline what this redesigned power structure would look like. What does appear clear is that both Ottawa and the provinces have an important role to play in this area. Even more clear is the fact that in the context of the mid-1980s, economic considerations will dominate in terms of social programs, in spite of what the precise division of powers may be.

Fiscal Balance[6]

Former finance minister Allan MacEachen's 1981 overview document relating to the 1982 revisions of the fiscal arrangements argued that the "fundamental issue" had become fiscal balance or, rather, fiscal imbalance (MacEachen, 1981, p. 19). With the level of the federal deficit moving to the mid-$20 billion range and with overall provincial budgets basically in balance at the time, Ottawa's argument was that the provinces had to shoulder a larger revenue-raising role in the federation. This provided one rationale for paring the level of EPF transfers in the 1982 arrangements. (Note that overall transfers to the provinces represented roughly half the federal deficit.) Since these federal-provincial transfers relate basically to EPF, CAP and equalization, it is appropriate to discuss fiscal balance in the context of the social programs (see also Chapter 5).

In terms of fiscal efficiency or fiscal discipline, we can make a case for greater provincial revenue collection. Other things being equal, the level of government responsible for the spending should also be responsible for collecting the revenues. In large measure, this is also what the federal concern over visibility and accountability is all about — the large federal-provincial transfers allow the provinces to reap the credit for the spending programs while Ottawa bears the costs of being the tax collector. However, the notion that over the long term the federal level can suffer from a fiscal-balance problem is stretching things a bit: Ottawa's taxation powers are plenary; it has greater access than do the provinces to borrowed funds; and, in the limit, it has the option of money creation. Since the provinces are more constrained in these areas than is the federal government, it may make some sense, in theory, to refer to a potential provincial vertical imbalance.

None of these arguments are meant to suggest that it was inappropriate for Ottawa to cut back on EPF funding in 1982. Indeed, there is, in my view, an advantage to the current funding squeeze in that the provinces are forced to take a long hard look at the role and structure of the EPF programs.

If the provinces find themselves in a fiscal bind, they have three general options:
1. to transfer some of the expenditure functions to the federal government;
2. to cut back on expenditure levels; and
3. to increase revenues.
In part, the role of the Royal Commission on the Economic Union and Development Prospects for Canada is to try to isolate areas where powers can be swapped or transferred unilaterally from one level to the other. Some provinces have even welcomed such an investigation. In its submission to the commission the Ontario government argued that "The Commission should address the underlying issue of fiscal balance between the two orders of government, including an examination of possible realignment of program responsibilities" (Ontario, 1983, p. 14).

While there is scope for some reassignment of powers in the income-support area (e.g., the earlier proposal that the CAP be replaced by a uniform minimum federal payment with provincial top-ups), I want to set this avenue aside and focus on the implications of a financial squeeze at the provincial level in terms of the other two options — expenditure cuts and tax increases. In particular, I want to address these options in the context of the provisions of the Canada Health Act. As noted earlier in the chapter, the Canada Health Act can be viewed as defining what ought to be covered under provincial health programs and limiting the flexibility of the provinces in terms of how they can fund these programs. These provisions, combined with the recognition that the act can be altered at will by the federal government, would seem to put the provinces in an incredible straitjacket: they may not be allowed to pare back services, and they are certainly constrained in terms of how they can raise revenues, even to the point where the use of medicare premiums is called into question.

Clearly, something will have to give. The overall intergovernmental financial interface is an extremely complex and interrelated system. Putting the squeeze on the health-care area may generate pressures for the provinces to act, or react, elsewhere in this complex system. For example, some of the provinces may be taking another look at following Quebec's lead and initiating their own, separate, personal income tax systems.

Several years ago the Ontario Economic Council (1976) proposed to utilize the income tax system to help finance health-care services. The council's argument was that such a scheme would be progressive and it would also encourage citizen awareness of use and costs of health services. Briefly:

> In Ontario, it would be quite feasible, with some adjustments to our current administrative and information systems, to establish a given family's use of the health care system, as well as a dollar measure of the benefits received. These benefits, subject to possible exemptions and catastrophic limits, would be subjected to a form of income taxation. This whole process could be integrated with the income tax returns process in a manner such that the following conditions held: (a) taxation and hence financing of health care would be related to use and benefits received; (b) the poor would avoid paying because taxation can be geared to income, exemptions and other ability to pay criteria; (c) ceilings would exist on the amount of taxation, thus building a "catastrophic" insurance feature into the system; (d) averaging provisions would exist to permit a smoothing out of tax payments, and so on. Of course, whether such a system is desirable must be judged in terms of a number of factors including ease and cost of administration and how well it permits the achievement of the social and economic objectives of Ontario's health policies. (p. 15)

Such a scheme would no doubt be easier to mount if Ontario already had its own separate personal income tax system. This rationale of and by itself is probably not enough to argue for a separate tax system for Ontario, but continued federal intrusions along the lines of the Canada Health Act would represent ample cause for provincial governments to search for increased financial and program flexibility.

More generally, Ottawa's insistence on pressing its particular definition of "equity" on the health-care delivery system may run counter to long-term efficiency and equity if, as a result, the provinces are locked into an inefficient delivery system for health.

Therefore, while concerns over fiscal balance (or the allocation of the overall deficit between the two levels of government) in the short term are obviously an important matter for governments, unilateral federal action designed to redress the issue is likely to be met with unilateral provincial reaction. Each level of government has sufficient clout to retaliate somewhere in this complex system. This was in large measure the message of the earlier section — that virtually any division of powers can be problematical in a modern economy where activities are interrelated and integrated. The conclusion is also the same — for a coherent and co-ordinated design of social programs, there is no substitute to developing a co-operative process for redesigning the social policy area.

Conclusion

In lieu of a formal conclusion, the following points are intended to summarize the implications of the foregoing analysis of the interaction of social programs and the division of powers.

- Basically, the de jure division of powers in the area of social programs has altered little in the postwar period (apart from the odd amendment to the Constitution transferring old-age pensions and unemployment insurance to the federal level and the mid-1960s agreement relating to jurisdiction over the public pension programs, CPP and QPP).
- However, there have been marked swings in the relative roles of the two levels of government in both the design and funding of the social programs. The centralizing features of the mid-1960s eventually gave way to the substantial provincial autonomy associated with the 1977 arrangements.
- Recently, there has been a concerted federal effort to exert more control over the social policy area and in particular over those programs falling under the EPF arrangements. This regulation may be related to a general attempt on the part of the federal government to centralize power in the wake of the 1980 Quebec Referendum. The National Economic Program (NEP), the patriation of the Constitution with its Canadian Charter of Rights and Freedoms, and the reorganization of the Department of Regional Economic Expansion (DREE) into the Department of Regional Industrial Expansion (DRIE) are all moves in a centralizing direction that may have set the context for recent moves on the social policy front — the 1982 fiscal arrangements, the 1984 Canada Health Act, and the intended review (by the previous Liberal government) of post-secondary education.

- The substantial expansion of social programs in the 1960s is easier to understand against the background of buoyant and stable real growth of the 1960s.
- The economy is now in a much different and more difficult position. The requirements over the next decade will be for an economy that is flexible and capable of adjusting to the changing patterns of world demands.
- To the extent possible, social policy should be designed or redesigned so as to ensure that the various programs accommodate rather than inhibit the needed adjustment.
- In my view this calls for a greater emphasis on efficiency, decentralization and private-sector input into the design and financing of the social programs.
- Flexibility and innovation are particularly necessary in those areas of social policy that are experiencing rapid expenditure growth.
- Even though this general thrust argues against further centralization, there are important national objectives associated with the social programs that are conducive to both equity and efficiency (e.g., portability of pensions, access to social programs without substantial residency requirements, access to universities of one's own choosing). If the provinces cannot deliver on these national goals, then Ottawa should step in and ensure them.
- In this sense, economic considerations will probably play an important role in determining the characteristics of the evolution of the social programs. Provided there is a general realization of these needs, almost any division of powers will provide the framework for undertaking the needed redesign.
- However, some divisions of powers are more conducive to cooperative decision-making than are others. A review of the jurisdictional overlap in the income security area reveals that three distinct types of divisions of powers exist in this sphere — separation of powers (unilateralism), co-operative federalism, and a series of checks and balances (multiple vetoes). Each has advantages and disadvantages. Nonetheless, the overriding characteristic of the area is the high degree of interdependence or integration between decisions taken at each level of government.
- This degree of integration tends to downplay the particular structure of powers and correspondingly puts greater emphasis on the policy-making process, although process will be dependent somewhat upon structure.
- There is a need for substantial restructuring of the range of programs in the social policy area. In my opinion this restructuring requires the inclusion of features that cater to the incentives to work and to individual initiative; encourage adjustment and flexibility rather than

entrenchment, and allow the programs to become more selective (targeted).

- Grandiose schemes like submerging the entire income support area under the rubric of a single GAI approach may be analytically appealing. However, the pedestrian route of restructuring the system on a program-by-program basis may the more successful and appropriate approach to take.
- Concern over fiscal balance is bound to emerge as an issue in this area, given the size of federal-provincial transfers and the federal deficit.
- Paring federal-provincial transfers, provided the provinces have sufficient lead time to adjust, is probably fair ball in the federal-provincial arena. It has the advantage of impressing on the provinces the enormity of the job they must do in striving for efficiency in areas such as health-care delivery.
- What is not fair ball is cutting back on transfers and at the same time attempting to lay down conditions on both program design and funding, which is my interpretation of what the Canada Health Act does. This stipulation will surely lead to retaliation elsewhere in the federal-provincial system — retaliation that is just as likely to be counter to long-term equity and efficiency as is the Canada Health Act.
- What is needed in the social program area is an emphasis on process that facilitates the adopting of joint policies and the making of joint decisions on joint problems.
- While there is much scope for reallocating powers in this area, it is more important that both levels of government come to appreciate the nature of the problem at hand and tackle it on a co-operative basis. If this approach is taken, one structure of powers is probably as good as another.

Chapter 7

Equalization Payments and the Division of Powers

Chapter 2 emphasized that modifications in the nature and magnitude of federal-provincial transfers were essentially equivalent to modifications in the division of powers. In particular, the existence of unconditional transfers contributes to the exercise of provincial autonomy. Since equalization payments are, in the Canadian context, the quintessential unconditional transfers, it is obvious that equalization is related intimately to the division of powers in the federation. Indeed, part of the analysis that follows will argue that enhanced provincial autonomy is not only the result of equalization but perhaps also the intent of equalization.

The purpose of this chapter is not to focus in any detail on the precise nature of Canada's equalization program or on the manner in which the Canadian system of equalization has evolved since its inception in 1957. Rather, the purpose is to explore the variety of rationales for equalization and how they relate to the degree of decentralization we find in the Canadian federation, both in absolute terms and in terms of what we find in other federations. Toward this end, the first substantive section of the chapter focusses on the relationship between horizontal and vertical balance in federations. The essential point here is that the manner in which a federation handles any vertical imbalance between the federal and provincial (or state) governments will likely have an impact on the magnitude of, and need for redressing, any horizontal (interprovincial) imbalance. The next section then focusses on two "political" rationales for equalization — what I have termed the federalist/constitutional rationale and the nationhood rationale. The economic underpinnings of equalization are the subject of the following section, which addresses questions such as the manner in which equalization might enhance economic efficiency. The next section deals with the relationship between decentralization and equalization and argues that the nature of Canada's equalization program has allowed the federation to decentralize in terms of expenditure responsibility and taxation. The following section presents some numerical evidence of the degree to which the equalization program appears to be achieving its stated goals. The remaining sections of the chapter focus on the role of equalization in other federations including, for example, the U.S. federation which does not have an equalization program. The conclusion consists of a series of summary points relating to the manner in which equalization interacts with economic management and the division of powers.

Although the emphasis in this chapter is not on the features and history of our equalization problem, I have appended to this chapter a chronology of the evolution of equalization payments (see Table 7-A1). This table will provide some backdrop for the analysis that follows. More conveniently still, the last entry of the table provides the appropriate starting point for a discussion of equalization. With the Constitution Act, 1982, the principle of equalization is now enshrined in the Constitution:

> Parliament and the Government of Canada are committed to the principle of making equalization payments to ensure that provincial governments have sufficient revenues to provide reasonably comparable levels of public services at reasonably comparable levels of taxation.

Table 7-1, which appears later in the chapter, will present data designed to assess whether or not the current levels of equalization can be viewed as achieving these stated goals.

The fact that the formal equalization program was initiated in 1957 and that the principle of equalization was enshrined in the Constitution only after 25 years is also of interest to the thrust of the monograph. It demonstrates that the practice of federalism is not constrained by the form and structure of the Constitution. Rather, when the need arises the system can generate new processes (e.g., equalization) or new institutional machinery (e.g., the first ministers' conferences). In my view this supports the proposition, put forth earlier, that over time the Constitution is as much shaped by the needs of the federation as the other way around.

I turn now to an analysis of the role of equalization in federations, beginning with a more detailed discussion of the concept of fiscal balance than that which appeared in Chapter 6.

Horizontal and Vertical Balance[1]

Every federation has to grapple with the two perennial problems of intergovernmental finance — vertical and horizontal fiscal balance. Vertical fiscal balance relates to the allocation of revenues, relative to the allocation of expenditure responsibilities, between the provinces or states and the federal government. Horizontal balance relates to the relative fiscal capacities of the second tier of governments (i.e., provinces in Canada, states in the United States, cantons in Switzerland, laender in West Germany). In terms of vertical balance, the Canadian experience is probably typical of most federations. At the time of Confederation the importance of the expenditure responsibilities allocated to the provinces was minimal relative to those assigned to the federal government. Partly as a result, Ottawa was given the power to levy all manner of taxes and in particular was given exclusive jurisdiction over indirect taxes (including customs), the major source of revenues at the time. The march of economic and social events altered this balance. The expenditure functions allocated to the provinces under the Constitution — such as education, hospitals, welfare, highways — have become progressively more important over the years, a result of the transfer of responsibility to the state for functions previously undertaken by the family or church (welfare and to some extent education) and the advance of technology (e.g., the spread of the automobile and the corresponding need for highways). In any event, as noted in Chapter 5, the provinces and their municipalities currently account for considerably more than 50 percent of total government spending. Accompanying this trend has been an ongoing problem relating to the vertical distribution of revenues in the federation: Ottawa's share of revenues has over much of the postwar period tended to exceed its share of expenditure responsibilities. Apart from requiring the provinces to stay within their own budget constraints (e.g., by borrowing, by increasing provincial taxes, or by paring expenditures), there are three ways to handle this problem of vertical balance:

1. to transfer some expenditure functions to the federal government;
2. to transfer funds or tax room to the provinces with conditions relating to the manner in which these funds can be spent; and
3. to transfer funds or tax room to the provinces in a no-strings-attached (unconditional) manner.

All three avenues have been utilized in the Canadian federation.

Since unconditional transfers can be spent when and where the provinces please, they are more consistent with a decentralized federation than either conditional grants or the transfer upward of expenditure functions. As a theoretical matter, we might want to argue that a transfer of an expenditure function from the provincial to the federal arena is much more of a "centralist" solution than is the adoption of a conditional grant. But, as a practical matter, there may be little difference between the two since condition-laden intergovernmental transfers can effectively emasculate provincial autonomy with respect to the expenditure category in question. However, this is not the place to elaborate on the interaction between centralization or decentralization and the design of intergovernmental transfers. Suffice it to say that in the Canadian federation, where judicial interpretation of the Constitution has assigned greater power to the lower levels of government than has been the case in the United States, inter-governmental grants have tended to be of the unconditional variety relative to those in the United States, thereby enhancing the more decentralist character of our federation. This relationship can go both ways. On the one hand, unconditional grants enhance provincial autonomy while, on the other, the greater autonomy of the provinces relative to the U.S. states may be the reason why intergovernmental transfers in our federation have tended to be unconditional.

Why is there this concern over vertical balance in a federalism when equalization payments are designed to correct horizontal imbalance? The reason is that the distinction between horizontal and vertical bal-ance is not as clear-cut as we might expect. In correcting for vertical imbalance by means of intergovernmental grants, the federal govern-ment can follow two quite different routes. Anthony Scott refers to these two differing approaches as the "principle of derivation" and the "prin-ciple of equalization" (Scott, 1964, pp. 252–53). Under the former, inter-governmental grants are paid to the provinces in relation to the amounts of federal revenues generated in these provinces. Thus, if Ottawa trans-fers additional income tax points to the provinces according to the principle of derivation, the revenues received by the provinces are determined by the yield of the tax points within their respective jurisdic-tions. Almost invariably, this approach to rectifying a vertical imbalance in a federation will generate a substantial horizontal imbalance since, as Scott notes, the principle of derivation is "in essence . . . a negation of geographical redistribution" (p. 252).

This negation does not apply if the "principle of equalization" under-lies the solution to vertical balance. Scott defines the principle of equal-ization (not to be confused with Canada's formal equalization program) to mean that the vertical intergovernmental transfers are related not to the amounts of money derived from these provinces but are distributed to the provinces in a more equal fashion. One obvious example would be to transfer funds on an equal-per-capita basis (which, in essence, is what now occurs under the established programs). With the principle of equalization underlying vertical intergovernmental grants, it is less likely that a resulting horizontal imbalance will be generated.

Intergovernmental grants are, of course, not the only potential source of horizontal imbalance. More important in the Canadian federation are the provinces' own sources of revenues, particularly resource-related revenues. In some federations there exist formal programs, generally referred to as equalization programs, which are designed specifically to offset this horizontal imbalance in revenue across provinces or states. I shall now turn to the various rationales for an equalization program.

Political Rationales for Equalization

The Federalist/Constitutional Rationale

Since the first "official" proposal for an equalization program can be traced to the Rowell-Sirois recommendation for a set of "national adjustment grants," it is not surprising that this report is the source for some of the arguments for equalization.[2] My interpretation of the Rowell-Sirois Report with respect to these grants is that they are argued for on two related grounds: one of these I refer to as the "nationhood rationale," and it will be dealt with below; the other I have called the "federalist or constitutional rationale." Essentially the argument here is that the Constitution has assigned certain powers to the provinces, and it is only by means of a set of national adjustment grants (equalization payments) that these powers can be meaningfully secured. From the Rowell-Sirois Report:

> They [the national adjustment grants] illustrate the Commission's conviction that the provincial autonomy in these fields must be respected and strengthened, and that the only true independence is financial security. . . . They are designed to make it possible for every province to provide for its people services of average Canadian standards. . . . They are the concrete expression of the Commission's conception of a federal system which will preserve both a healthy local autonomy and build a stronger and more unified nation. (Canada, 1939, p. 125)

The report goes on to say that the issue of horizontal fiscal imbalance was not a major concern in 1867, particularly in the light of the specific subsidies that were incorporated in the Constitution Act, 1867. However, over time, conditions altered markedly and the initial conception of subsidies had to be replaced by a more comprehensive and logical approach (i.e., the national adjustments grants):

> The implications for public finance of the economic and social changes which have occurred in Canada are of far-reaching importance. As a result of the transcontinental economy which was deliberately built up, with its notable concentration of surplus income, and later as a result of the disintegration of this economy [because of the depression and the ensuing tax jungle] no logical relationship exists between the local income of any province and the constitutional powers and responsibilities of the government of that province. (p. 78)

One obvious solution would have been to recommend a transfer of these powers and responsibilities from the provinces to the federal government. The report does not opt for this alternative (except for unemployment insurance and old-age pensions). Indeed, it mounts a staunch argument for continued provincial control of the major expenditure functions. Moreover, it argues that in order to guarantee provincial autonomy, the proposed national adjustment grants be unconditional in nature:

> It should be made clear that while the adjustment grant proposed is designed to enable a province to provide adequate services (at the average Canadian standard) without excessive taxation (on the average Canadian basis) the freedom of action of a province is in no way impaired. If a province chooses to provide inferior services and impose lower taxation it is free to do so, or it may provide better service than the average if its people are willing to be taxed accordingly, or it may, for example, starve its roads and improve its education, or starve its education and improve its roads — exactly as it may do today. But no provincial government will be free from the pressure of the opinion of its own people . . . (p. 84)

As a final comment on the commission's emphasis on the role of equalization payments in providing the financial independence needed to ensure a province's ability to fulfil its constitutional responsibilities as well as the necessity for these payments to be unconditional in form, the following is particularly apt:

> The Commission's Plan [for national adjustment grants] seeks to ensure every province a real and not illusory autonomy by guaranteeing to it, free from conditions or control, the revenues necessary to perform those functions which relate closely to its social and cultural development. (p. 80)

The Nationhood Rationale

Existing side by side with the federal or constitutional rationale for equalization payments is a national unity or nationhood rationale. Canadians, wherever they live, ought to have access to certain basic economic and social rights — rights which, as it were, ought to attend Canadian citizenship. The fact that some of these basic economic and social rights are assigned, constitutionally, to the provinces should not mean that individual Canadians should thereby be deprived of these services:

> The constitutional division of taxing powers, applied to the existing regional distribution of taxable income, has produced surpluses in some provincial budgets, and in others deficits which have inevitably been reflected in reductions of those community services which Canadians have come to look on as the minimum which their governments should supply. As a result, Canadian citizens in some provinces are receiving educational, health and other social services much inferior to those in other provinces and (quite apart from any question of governmental extravagance or the provision of unusually costly services). Canadian citizens in some provinces are required to contribute a much larger portion of their income to the government of the province than those in other provinces. (p. 79)

Even more revealing is the following excerpt:

> In considering the relative fiscal needs of provincial governments, we are mainly concerned with a few divisions of their expenditures: on education, on social services, on development. It is of national interest that no provincial government should be unduly cramped in any of these respects. Education is basic to the quality of Canadian citizens of the future and it is highly undesirable that marked disparities in the financial resource available for education should exist as between Canadian provinces. Social services, like education, cannot be subjected to marked disparities without serious reactions on the general welfare and on national unity. An appropriate developmental policy is required in each province, and the only standard which can fairly be applied is the policy of the province itself. . . (p. 80)

A final quote from the report puts more emphasis still on the national unity issue:

> It is important to note that some of the provinces are quite unable to meet their obligations and at the same time provide the social and educational services which Canadians have come to look upon as essential. Such a situation cannot leave other provinces unconcerned. The investors in other provinces will suffer in the case of private or public insolvency among their neighbours. The producers in other provinces might suffer if markets are destroyed. Migrants must be admitted from depressed provinces, and it is not merely a nuisance and an expense but a positive danger to the more prosperous provinces if the migrants are illiterate or diseased or undernourished. Nor is the danger of competition from substandard labour in a distressed province a peril which can be disregarded. More important than all these considerations taken together is the danger to national unity if the citizens of distressed provinces come to feel that their interests are completely disregarded by their more prosperous neighbours, and that those who have been full partners in better times now tell them they must get along as best they can and accept inferior educational and social services. (p. 79)

It is appropriate to note that while these two approaches are quite closely related, the implications for equalization are somewhat different. In particular, the nationhood rationale might be satisfied with conditional transfers related to the achievement of certain levels of basic services whereas the federalist or constitutional rationale would imply unconditional transfers. The transfers associated with the established programs would appear to satisfy the "nationhood" rationale. Although not formally viewed as an equalization program, the equal-per-capita transfer embodied in the Established Programs Financing (EPF) program does embody an equalization feature. Cast in terms of the previous section, the EPF transfers represent an approach to the vertical balance problem that is associated more with the principle of equalization than with the principle of derivation.

Economic Rationale for Equalization

Fiscal Equity

Economists have rationalized equalization on grounds of both equity and efficiency. The starting point for both these arguments is the recognition that the market income of Canadians living in different provinces does not reflect the additional benefits (or costs) that result from the operations of the provincial public sectors. This leads to both equity and efficiency concerns. I shall deal with the former first.

The Economic Council of Canada (1982) summarizes the equity case for equalization as follows:

> [Consider the case where] the net fiscal benefits of most persons within a given province are not zero and there are interprovincial differences in net fiscal benefits between persons in similar financial circumstances. In this case, the requirements of equity would not be met by a federal tax and transfer system based solely on personal market incomes. Horizontal equity would not be achieved because persons with identical real incomes (including net fiscal benefits from provincial budgets) would be treated differently under such a tax and transfer system. Nor would such a tax and transfer system produce vertical equity in the country as a whole. Provincial net fiscal benefits affect the real incomes or living standards of provincial residents (positively or negatively), but that impact is not taken into account by the federal income tax system (or the system of personal transfers). Hence, even if the federal tax system embodied in principle the desired amount of vertical equity, such equity would not be achieved because one important source of personal income is not taken into account by the federal tax system.
>
> What is required to solve these problems is some form of transfer policy that takes account of these differences between provinces. The two main types of instruments that might be considered to achieve this goal are the personal transfer and income tax system and the intergovernmental transfer system.
>
> The personal transfer and income tax system could be adjusted in several ways to achieve the desired goal. For example, each federal taxpayer could be required to adjust his taxable market income by adding or subtracting his amount of provincial net fiscal benefits. Alternatively, the federal tax rate could be adjusted for each province to take account of the effect of net fiscal benefits.
>
> An alternative approach could involve the establishment of a system of intergovernmental grants that would provide transfers to provincial governments, the net value of which would be positive in provinces whose residents have relatively low per capita net fiscal benefits and negative in provinces with high net fiscal benefits. The latter approach, of course, is that embodied in the existing Equalization Program. (p. 27)

As the council points out, to correct the problem with the personal tax-transfer system might undermine the federal system. Hence, the appropriate route to follow is the intergovernmental transfer route, i.e, equal-ization.

Most economists would view the earlier nationhood rationale, and perhaps the constitutional rationale as well, as falling under the rubric of fiscal equity. In my opinion, however, they are conceptually distinct. Indeed, elsewhere I have challenged the notion that an equalization program follows directly from an argument based on horizontal equity — a system of mobility subsidies would appear to be equally consistent as a solution to equity concerns (Courchene, 1984c, chap. 3).

Efficiency

Because equalization payments reduce the tax-price of public goods and services in the recipient provinces they will also serve to inhibit out-migration from these provinces. Of this, there is little doubt, analytical or empirical. However, what is in some considerable doubt are the resulting implications for economic efficiency. One long-standing approach to this issue argues that equalization runs counter to efficiency because it inhibits the natural adjustment forces: labour is less inclined to seek higher rewards elsewhere because of the subsidy for public-sector output provided by equalization.

The more recent argument is that equalization does serve to enhance efficiency (Boadway and Flatters, 1982). Because of differential provin-cial fiscal capacities and, particularly, differential resource rents, net fiscal benefits (NFBs) vary considerably across provinces. As a result, prospective migrants will take account of both market income and NFBs in their calculus. Hence, it is possible that an individual or family would move to a province and accept a lower level of market income if this was more than offset by larger NFBs. This phenomenon has come to be referred to as "fiscal-induced" or "rent-seeking" migration. While this migration may be optimal behaviour for the individual or family, it runs counter to national efficiency. An equalization program which serves to "equalize" these NFBs across provinces would ensure that migration becomes dictated more by market than by fiscal considerations.

There is an important element of truth in both approaches. Were P.E.I.'s equalization payment reduced from its present near $1,000 per capita level to zero it seems clear that the exodus of people would include some who, on productivity (efficiency) grounds, ought to remain in P.E.I. Similarly, the fact that P.E.I. and Newfoundland do receive $1,000 per capita in equalization surely inhibits the migration of persons who, on efficiency grounds, ought to be located elsewhere.

What is clear, however, is that the recent Canadian equalization pro-grams cannot be defended on grounds of efficiency. Consider the repre-sentative national-average standard (RNAS) approach to equalization that prevailed over the 1977–82 period. The existence of massive resource rents in the western provinces led to the situation where Ontario qualified as a have-not province under the RNAS formula (even with only 50 percent of resource rents entering the equalization formula). The fact that Ontario was denied equalization implies, in terms of the notion of fiscal-induced migration, that too many Ontarians migrated to Alberta. Based on similar reasoning, too few Atlantic residents would have migrated to Ontario. Hence, it is difficult to make the case that the manner in which Canada has implemented equalization is motivated principally by efficiency concerns.

In this context, it is interesting to note that the United States does not have a formal equalization program. As Wallace Oates has remarked, there are no doubt differential net fiscal benefits across the U.S. states but just as likely these differential benefits will be capitalized so that there is no need for an equalization program on efficiency grounds. He concludes that equalization systems are basically a matter not of efficiency but of "taste" (Oates, 1983, pp. 94–97). It is true that to the extent that differential NFBs across provinces become reflected in differential land prices or rents, then the case for eliminating these NFBs on efficiency grounds (to prevent fiscal-induced migration) is correspondingly weakened.

Equalization and the Distribution-Allocation Trade-Off

There is one further efficiency aspect of equalization that merits discussion — the manner in which equalization relates to overall regional policy. As matters now stand, equalization is far from the only program designed to alter regional or provincial fortunes. The personal income tax system is frequently utilized to provide differential provincial incentives. For example, the incentives for research and development expenditures are more generous in the poorer provinces. There are regional benefits associated with the unemployment insurance program. The Department of Regional Economic Expansion (DREE) programs provide incentives for industry to locate in certain designated regions. There is pressure for Ottawa to provide an equalization feature to the Canada Assistance Plan since the incidence of welfare (on a per capita basis) varies across the provinces. And so on.

The issue that arises is whether the equalization program should be the principal policy avenue for regional or provincial distribution or whether there should be an equalization component in a wide variety of policy areas, including some that clearly alter the wage/rental ratio on a regional or provincial basis. This question relates to the regional schema presented in Chapter 3 where objective functions 3 and 4 can be achieved via the tax transfer process (which would include equalization) but where objective functions 6 and 7 would require the government to intervene on the allocation, as distinct from the distribution, front.

Economists for the most part would argue for handling regional disparity concerns via distributional policies (such as a negative income taxation for individuals and an equalization program for provinces) and would shy away from utilizing government policy to distort the allocative process on a regional or provincial basis. No doubt there may have to be some exceptions to this principle, but in general I would support the proposition that equalization be the principal vehicle for regional or provincial distribution and that the remainder of government policy refrain, wherever possible, from incorporating regional or provincial distortions with respect to resource allocation.

Equalization and Decentralization

It has become common to view the Rowell-Sirois recommendation for a system of national adjustment grants as the forerunner of the present system of equalization. There is a sense in which this is certainly true: equalization payments can be viewed as addressing the same issues as the national adjustment grants. Moreover, the wording of the new constitutional provision with respect to equalization is similar to the Rowell-Sirois phraseology.

However, there is also a sense in which equalization payments can be viewed as having taken on a life of their own, quite apart from Rowell-Sirois. One of the principal recommendations of the report was to centralize the collection of direct taxation. And under the exigencies of wartime economic management, personal and corporate income taxation were centralized at the federal level. In return, the provinces received "tax-rental" payments. Appendix Table A-1, which traces the history of the personal income tax arrangements in Canada, shows that the provinces were offered several options with respect to these tax rental payments. In terms of the phraseology employed earlier, it is correct to suggest that the vertical fiscal imbalance was addressed by transfers that followed the principle of equalization rather than the principle of derivation.

All this was changed dramatically when Quebec initiated its own personal income tax in 1954. In order to move toward more uniform treatment for all provinces, the federal government in 1957 offered all provinces given shares of the income taxes that arose within their boundaries. This system converted these transfers to the principle of derivation which, since it implied quite different per capita transfers across the provinces, generated a need for a program to restore horizontal balance. This was the rationale for the 1957 equalization program.

Whereas Rowell-Sirois recommended national adjustment grants as part of a package which would transfer all direct taxation to the federal level, the actual experience was such that Canada did not incorporate a separate equalization program as long as direct taxation remained under

Ottawa's control (although it is true that the federal-provincial transfers under the aegis of tax rental payments did incorporate equalizing features); moreover, Canada embarked on a formal equalization program only when responsibility for direct taxation began to be returned to the provinces.

While the existence of an equalization scheme will in general enhance provincial autonomy and, therefore, lead to a decentralization of powers, the characteristics of the Canadian equalization program were and are such that they have contributed to a particular type of decentralization — decentralization of the power to tax. The poorer provinces could be enticed to accept decentralization via increased provincial tax room only to the extent that they would share "fairly" in the process. Indeed, this is one of the reasons why the equalization standard in the early years was defined in terms of the yield of the two richest provinces, rather than the national average. It was only after the program was broadened to include tax sources other than the direct taxes that the national average standard became generally accepted. Moreover, this way of viewing equalization also provides a rationale for the unconditional nature of equalization payments: the revenues accruing to the richer provinces from their enhanced tax room can obviously be spent as these provinces wish, so that it was only natural that the resulting equalization flows to the poorer provinces should also be unconditional.

There is a further implication relating to equalization and the division of powers — that it is far too narrow a conception of equalization to be viewed as a program only for the poor or recipient provinces. What equalization provides the richer provinces is the ability to increase their fiscal autonomy by flexing their power to tax. Indeed, the existence of an equalization program designed to equalize provincial tax revenues to the national average (now the five-province) standard probably provided the rationale for the substantial post-1957 transfer to the provinces of tax points for personal and corporate taxation. Even though there is still a large cash transfer component to the EPF payments, this cash transfer portion would no doubt be much larger without the existence of an equalization program.

In this sense, then, the equalization program is probably a major factor in determining the manner in which the fiscal system in our federation has been decentralized.

Equalization in Action

The new equalization provision in the Constitution states that the role of equalization is to ensure that all provinces have sufficient revenues to provide reasonably comparable public services at reasonably comparable levels of taxation. While there has not been an attempt to define "reasonably comparable," Table 7-1 presents some evidence relating to the actual role that equalization plays in the finance of the various provinces.

Row 1 of the table contains estimates of the disparities across provinces in terms of their own-source revenues. P.E.I. has access to revenues from its own sources equal (on a per capita basis) to 55 percent of the national (all-province) average. Alberta's access is four times as great —217 percent of the national average. And if Alberta had tax rates at the P.E.I. level, this multiple would be somewhere between 5 and 6 times the P.E.I. access (from row 4, P.E.I.'s tax effort is 99 percent of the national average level whereas the comparable figure for Alberta is only 79 percent).

Equalization flows dramatically enhance revenue access for the recipient provinces. These figures appear in row 2 of Table 7-1. After equalization, P.E.I. has 83 percent of the national average revenue access. If one then includes other federal-provincial transfers (such as EPF and CAP transfers), the disparities shrink further. P.E.I. now has 96 percent of the all-province per capita revenue access (row 3). An interesting comparison is the group of have-not provinces plus Ontario — all except the three westernmost provinces. The range is relatively narrow —96 percent for P.E.I. to 87 percent for Ontario. Hence, in this context, equalization can be seen to be fulfilling its role of ensuring that all provinces have access to per capita revenues roughly equal to the national average level. Alberta is the only real outlier with an index of 186.

There are two other features of Table 7-1 that merit attention. First, Ontario has the lowest per capita revenue access of any province. From row 4, which presents indices of tax effort, it is clear that Ontario's low revenue situation is not due to a low tax effort (its tax-effort index is 100). This finding should not be surprising since this is why Ontario qualified for, but as noted above did not receive, equalization during the 1977–82 period. The entry in Table 7-A1 for 1981 deals with the "personal income override" which prevented Ontario from receiving equalization over this period.

Second, the last row of Table 7-1 focusses on per capita expenditure indices for fiscal year 1977–78. The disparities here are much narrower — from 82 for New Brunswick to 118 for Alberta. This relatively low figure for Alberta (compared to its revenue index) reflects the fact that a substantial portion of its energy revenues are deposited in its Heritage Fund and not taken into current expenditures.

Therefore, even though there are vast differences across provinces in access to own-source revenues, the federal-provincial transfer system (and, particularly equalization) rectifies this situation considerably. But whether the resulting indices of aggregate revenues, tax effort, and expenditures are such as to satisfy the "reasonably comparable" phraseology of the new equalization provision in the Constitution I leave to the legal minds.

TABLE 7-1 Provincial Disparity Indices, 1981–82, Percent of All-Province Per Capita Average

Row	Nfld.	P.E.I.	N.S.	N.B.	Que.	Ont.	Man.	Sask.	Alta.	B.C.	Total
1. Own-source revenue	59	55	66	66	78	94	79		217	111	100
2. Own-source revenue plus equalization	83	83	84	84	86	88	88	105	203	104	100
3. Own-source revenue plus all transfers	90	96	89	92	90	87	90	106	186	102	100
4. Tax effort (on own-source revenue)	102	99	84	86	121	100	97	104	79	102	100
5. Per capita government expenditures (1977–78)	88	96	86	82	108	94	99	103	118	100	100

Source: Courchene, 1984c, chap. 4.

Equalization in Other Federations

As noted earlier, the United States does not have a separate equalization program that compares to that in Canada. However, several years ago the United States did have conditional-grant programs which incorporated some equalizing features. Federal funds for construction of highways were allocated to the various states on the basis of their revenue raising abilities — states with less than the average per capita were allocated larger per capita grants. It is this sort of scheme that has on occasion been recommended for Canada in terms of the Canada Assistance Plan. For example, provinces with a welfare case load larger than the national per capita average would be provided with extra support. Thus, equalization need not by synonymous with unconditional grants.

The Australian approach to equalization is a combination of vertical and horizontal transfers.[3] The commonwealth transfers a fixed percentage (40 percent) of personal income tax revenues to the states. The per capita proportions that go to each state are a function of the revenue means (fiscal capacity) of the states as well as their expenditure needs. Thus the formula does not determine the total amount of the transfer (this is fixed at 40 percent of income tax revenues); rather the formula is utilized to determine the shares of this fixed pie that go to the various states. One unique feature of the Australian model is that the determination of the formula is left to a body called the Australian Grants Commission. Lest one get too excited about the possibility of importing this piece of institutional machinery into Canada, it should be pointed out that for the last two years the commonwealth government has not accepted the commission's recommendations for equalization, and, at the time of writing, the future of equalization in the Australian federation is not at all clear.

Equalization in the Federal Republic of Germany provides yet another model. The largest portion of revenues for both levels of government come from four shared taxes. Three of these (wage and assessed income taxes, other income taxes and the trade tax) are shared equally and the states' (or laender) shares depend on the local yield of these taxes — they are determined by the derivation principle. The fourth tax, the value-added tax, is shared 70:30 between the federal government and the laender. Of the states' share (the 30 percent), three-quarters is allocated on the basis of population and the remaining quarter is used to assist financially weak states. Hence, this part of the vertical-balance transfer does incorporate substantial equalization.

However, the Germans also have a formal equalization program. It takes the form of what in the Canadian context would be referred to as an interprovincial revenue-sharing pool. Specifically, rich laender contribute some of their revenues into a common pool and poor laender can draw from this pool.[4] This interlaender equalization approach is enshrined in the German Constitution.

Switzerland has no formal equalization program, but 30 percent of the personal income tax goes to the cantons (five-sixths of this is on the principle of derivation and the remaining sixth is distributed on the basis of population, modified somewhat by tax capacity). Some smaller taxes are allocated to the cantons on the basis of population. Overall, however, the concept of fiscal equalization is not pursued very far in Switzerland, with the result that the richest canton (in 1979) had access to total (after fiscal equalization) revenues on a per capita basis that was roughly four times that of the poorest canton (Nowotny, 1983).

It is apparent from this brief survey of other federations that the notion of equalizing fiscal revenues is pursued very unevenly across federations and that the mechanisms for achieving this equalization also vary widely. Indeed, it may not be particularly useful to focus, as we have in this chapter, on the distinction between vertical and horizontal balance. In principle, it is possible for a federation to achieve a relatively equal access to revenues by the constituent states in the absence of a formal equalization program. For example, vertical transfers (of, say, a major portion of a shared tax) which are geared to population and fiscal capacity rather than designed on the derivation principle are a close substitute for a formal equalization program. Hence, Canada's EPF transfers, which are distributed on an equal per capita basis, can also be viewed as part of overall fiscal equalization since the federal revenues used to finance this transfer would presumably be derived across provinces in a manner that relates closely to provincial per capita incomes.

Conclusion

By way of summary, the following observations appear appropriate:

- Some federations are willing to tolerate a good deal more in the way of horizontal (interprovincial) imbalance on the fiscal side than is the case for the Canadian federation.
- Even though I have argued that our equalization program has contributed to decentralization and to provincial autonomy, concern over interprovincial fiscal balance is not a sine qua non of decentralization. Apart from Canada, the two most decentralized federations (at least in the sense of having decentralized tax systems) — the United States and Switzerland — do not pay a great deal of attention to horizontal balance: the U.S. states have no formal equalization program, and the degree of horizontal imbalance among the Swiss cantons is considerably larger than that in other federations.
- We can mount a case for an equalization program on both equity and efficiency grounds. The presence of wide variations in net fiscal benefits (NFB) across provinces might be such as to induce migration in order to capture these fiscal benefits. An equalization program designed to minimize these NFBs across provinces might serve to

ensure that the migration decision is motivated more by market than by fiscal criteria. This result would enhance efficiency.

- Based on efficiency criteria alone, the appropriate equalization program would probably take the form of an interprovincial revenue-sharing pool — a direct transfer of monies from the high NFB to the low NFB provinces.
- Canada's recent approaches to equalization do not fit well in terms of the economic efficiency rationale.
- The equity case for equalization rests on the notion that in the presence of NFBs which differ across provinces horizontal equity would not obtain. An unconditional system of equalization payments may not be the only way to rectify the problem, but it represents one avenue that is consistent with the notion of a federal state.
- There may also be other ways to justify an equalization program. One of these is the "federalist" or "constitutional" rationale: If we are to have a real and not illusory federal system, the provinces should have access to sufficient funds to carry out those responsibilities constitutionally assigned to them. Another might be a "nationhood" rationale: Canadians have a right, by virtue of citizenship, to certain basic public goods and if these goods fall under the constitutional authority of the provinces, there should be funds sufficient for the provinces to supply these goods. Others may wish to subsume this rationale under the concept of equity.
- However, in terms of the historical evolution of equalization payments, it appears that they were designed to allow the provinces to acquire greater autonomy in terms of taxation. The event that triggered the return to the provinces of this tax autonomy was probably the establishment by Quebec of its own personal income tax.
- Viewed in this way, equalization payments are not simply a transfer to the poor provinces. Rather, they are part and parcel of the set of arrangements that has allowed all provinces greater fiscal autonomy.
- From this vantage point, it would appear that equalization payments are one of the keys to the postwar increase in decentralization and provincial autonomy. This may not imply causation, however. Indeed, the causation may go in the other direction — that the regional and cultural diversity of the federation was (and is) such that a move toward greater decentralization was essentially preordained, and equalization payments simply turned out to be the most obvious avenue for accommodating this shift of autonomy toward the provinces.
- Canada's system of equalization payments, along with the remainder of the federal-provincial transfer system, has reduced dramatically the horizontal fiscal disparity across the provinces. Whether the disparities that remain fall under the "reasonably comparable" phraseology of the new constitutional provision for equalization is probably a matter for the courts to decide.
- The fact that this equalization provision was enshrined 25 years after

Canada initiated the equalization program speaks well of the flexibility of our constitutional framework: the Constitution Act, 1867 (or the BNA Act) has allowed our federation to innovate in those areas where there was a need for new approaches or institutions.

- Finally, it seems to me that Canada should attempt to ensure that the equalization program incorporates the bulk of the regional or provincial transfers, i.e., there should not be a regional component in each and every federal policy. The equalization program should be the principal vehicle for the delivery of funds to the poorer provinces. More particularly, the federal government should shy away from building distributional considerations into its allocative policies.

Appendix

TABLE 7-A1 A Summary of Major Developments with Respect to Equalization

Date	Subject	Description of Amendments or Innovations	Comments
1867	BNA Act statutory subsidies	Payments to provinces in return for surrendering indirect taxes to Ottawa. The subsidies contained an element of equalization in that they were per capita grants up to a maximum population. They were revised on many occasions (e.g. Duncan Royal Commission, White Royal Commission) and were geared toward the notion of fiscal need. Still exist today, but are of no real financial significance now, whereas in 1867 they represented a substantial share of provincial revenues.	Important in that they allow the concept of equalization to be traced back to the BNA Act.
1940	National Adjustment Grants	Recommended in Rowell-Sirois Report. These grants were to be paid on the basis of fiscal need. Determined by evaluating provincial/local expenditure needs in relation to access to revenues.	Not implemented. However, the rationale for these grants — to enable provinces to provide national average levels of basic services at not unduly high tax rates — underlies the present-day formulations of equalization.
1957	First formal equalization program. Part of 1957–62 fiscal arrangements	Federal government agreed to bring per capita yields from the three standard taxes up to the average yield in the two wealthiest provinces. The revenue sources and tax rates were as follows: personal income taxes (10 percent), corporate income taxes (9 percent), succession duties (50 percent).	Equalization was restricted to the three "shared" taxes. The tax rates applied in calculating provincial revenues for equalization purposes were those that applied in the tax rental arrangements. Alberta fell into the category of a "have-not" province. Indeed, only the richest province (Ontario, at this time) did not receive payments. This was a necessary result of equalizing to the wealthiest two provinces.

TABLE 7-A1 (cont'd)

Date	Subject	Description of Amendments or Innovations	Comments
1958	Increased equalization for personal income tax	The provincial share of personal income taxes paid to the provinces increased from 10 to 13 percent. This entered the equalization formula.	Equalization was tied in closely with the tax arrangements, as one might expect.
1958–61	Atlantic Provinces Adjustment Grants and Newfoundland Additional Grants Act	Additional unconditional grants to the Atlantic provinces, rationalized on the basis of their low fiscal capacity.	The additional grants appear to have been modelled after Rowell-Sirois adjustment grants.
1962	1962–67 fiscal arrangements agreement	Personal income tax share rose to 16 percent, in accordance with the tax arrangements. Introduction of 50 percent of three-year average of provincial revenues and taxes from natural resources. Equalization standard reduced to the national average level.	First initiative to expand equalization beyond shared taxes. As compensation for movement down to national average, the Atlantic Provinces Adjustment Grant was increased from $25 million to $35 million. Alberta and British Columbia become "have" provinces as a result of the resource provision.
1962–67	Provinces acquired an increasing share of personal income tax	The share of personal income taxes allocated rose from 16 percent at the outset of the arrangements to 24 percent by 1967. This increasing proportion automatically entered the formula.	Consistent linking of the equalization program with the tax arrangements.
1964–65	Natural resource changes	In fiscal year 1964–65, the equalization standard once again became the two top provinces. Resources were pulled out of the formula, and provinces could receive equalization only to the extent that their per capita entitlements exceeded 50 percent of the amount by which their per capita resource revenues (three-year average) exceeded the national average level.	Equalization payments increased because the impact of equalizing to the two top provinces was worth more than the pulling of resource revenues from the formula. Alberta and British Columbia had positive equalization entitlements, but these were reduced to zero by the resource deduction provision.

1967	Introduction of the representative tax system of equalization (RNAS)	Sixteen revenue categories, each with its own base, equalized to national average level. Revenues that were eligible for equalization were based on provincial total revenues. Entitlements were summed over all sixteen categories. This total, if positive, represented the province's equalization. Negative overall entitlements were set equal to zero (i.e., funding was a federal responsibility, no province paid money into the scheme).	Characteristics of this type of program are spelled out in Chapters 4 and 5. Program was open-ended, driven by the degree of disparity in the revenue sources and by total provincial revenues. Underlying rationale cited for program was drawn from Rowell-Sirois Report. Attempted to be representative of taxing practices of provinces. Did not include revenues designated for local purposes.
1972	Program extended	Addition of three new tax sources brought total to 19. Revenues from these three sources (race track revenues, medical premiums, hospital premiums) were previously equalized under miscellaneous revenues.	Part of the "housekeeping" involved in keeping the system "representative."
1973–74	School-purpose taxes included	That proportion of property taxes levied for school purposes was incorporated in the program.	Potentially a major modification in that property taxes are viewed as a local rather than as a provincial tax.
1974–75	Energy revenue modification	Two sorts of energy revenues, "basic" and "additional." Basic revenues refer to those derived in 1973–74. Additional revenues are those generated above this level and attributable to the rise in prices rather than to an increase in output. Basic revenues equalized in full. Additional revenues equalized to extent of one-third.	Abandonment of concept of "full" equalization. Financial implications of not enacting this measure would have been a tripling of total payments and the inclusion of Ontario in the have-not category.

TABLE 7-A1 (cont'd)

Date	Subject	Description of Amendments or Innovations	Comments
1977	Equalization component of Fiscal Arrangements Act	Program expanded to 29 sources as a result of reclassification of revenues. Major changes in definitions of some tax bases. Only 50 percent of non-renewable resources eligible to enter the formula. Natural resources override provision meant that no more than one-third of total equalization could arise from resource revenues.	Postponed rather than solved problems created by mushrooming energy revenues. The 50 percent provision from 1977 onward was in fact a more generous treatment of energy resources than the "basic" and "additional" compromise devised in 1974. Federal government felt it was more consistent to treat all non-renewable resources in an identical fashion.
1981	Bill C-24	Two provisions: • withdrawal of sale of crown leases category from the program; • personal income override — no province eligible for equalization of its per capita personal income exceeded the national average level in the current and preceding two years.	The personal income override was made retroactive to fiscal year 1977–78, thereby confiscating over $1 billion of equalization due to Ontario. While one may agree with the spirit of the action, the personal income override is an arbitrary measure and does not fit well into the conceptual basis of the program, which has to do with fiscal capacities and not with personal incomes. This provision may lend support to a "macro" equalization program where the basis of fiscal deficiencies is calculated with respect to variables such as personal income.
1982	New tax source added	Under the National Energy Program, Ottawa returns half of oil export tax to the exporting provinces. It enters the formula.	Question becomes: should it enter as a separate category or be lumped in somewhere with existing revenues from energy? See conclusion.

| 1982 | 1982–87 fiscal arrangements. New Representative Five-Province Standard (RFPS) equalization program | Five provisions:
• New formula brings provincial revenues per capita up to the average per capita level of five provinces (Ont., Que., Man., Sask. and B.C.). Referred to as the representative five-province standard.
• Coverage extended to include municipal revenues and 100 percent of resource revenues.
• Beginning in 1983–84, equalization payments constrained by the rate of GNP growth.
• Provision guaranteeing a minimum level of payment for recipient provinces.
• A transitional payment incorporating minimums for a three-year period. | Removed the personal income override, the resource cap, the differential treatment of energy and non-energy resources, and extended the coverage to include all provincial and local revenues. Energy-related equalization will fall compared with the previous system because the five provinces comprising the RFPS are, on average, not energy rich. RFPS system replaces the original federal proposal for 1982 — the "Ontario standard." |
| 17 April, 1982 | Constitution Act, 1982 | A provision ensuring equalization is enshrined in Canada's new Constitution. | "Parliament and the government of Canada are committed to the principle of making equalization payments to ensure that provincial governments have sufficient revenues to provide reasonably comparable levels of public services at reasonably comparable levels of taxation." |

Source: Courchene, 1984c.

Chapter 8

Financial Markets and the Division of Powers

In this fourth part of this study I shall discuss selected aspects of allocative efficiency and the manner in which they interact with the division of powers. The two chapters in this section will focus, respectively, on financial markets and the Canadian economic union.

The present chapter focusses on the efficiency of and the division of powers with respect to the process of financial intermediation. Specifically, three related areas will be highlighted for special treatment:
1. the primary and secondary markets for equities;
2. the "four pillars" (banking, trusts, insurance and brokerage); and
3. pension funds.

The rationale for the three-fold approach to the financial intermediation area, rather than a single overview piece on the financial markets, is that it lends itself to addressing three separate issues. The focus of the first section dealing with the structure of the markets for equity capital is the differences that exist between Canada and the United States in the regulation of securities markets. In particular, should Canada follow the U.S. lead and establish a Canadian equivalent of the federal Securities and Exchange Commission? Emphasis is directed toward the various alternative constitutional approaches that Canada could take to the regulation and supervision of securities markets. These approaches are general in the sense that the analysis in this section can be applied to many of the subject areas in this monograph.

The second area deals with the major current concern in the financial intermediation area. Should Canada move to secure the existing boundaries for the traditional financial activities of banking, trusts, brokerage and insurance? Or should these barriers be allowed to wither away under pressure of cross-boundary activity? The interesting question in this regard is whether the present concerns are related more to the jurisdictional authority over these functions or whether the issues are really those of devising the appropriate policies irrespective of federal or provincial responsibility.

Finally, the pension area is of interest not only because the role of pensions is currently under intense review, but also because of the varying federal-provincial jurisdictional framework associated with different aspects of the overall pension system. The message of this section is that the institutional and constitutional framework has had an influence on the decision-making process in the pension area. The intriguing question, however, is whether this is good or bad and what lessons are to be derived for the future.

Securities Legislation

Provincial Dominance

The securities market is defined to include the stock exchanges, clearinghouses, brokers, underwriters, transfer agents and such institutions as the Canadian Depository for Securities. It is useful to distinguish between two types of markets (although they are obviously related) — primary (new-issue) markets and secondary (retrading) markets. Needless to say, it is critical to our economic future that such markets operate as efficiently as possible. And surely one prerequisite for achieving market efficiency is to ensure that the market is truly national in scope. Yet, compared to other federations such as the United States, the federal presence in regulating the Canadian securities markets is virtually nonexistent. Can the provinces be relied on to develop a national market? Do they have enough powers to do so? These are the questions and/or issues that have dominated much of the discussion associated with ensuring an efficient national securities market in Canada.

The approach I have taken to this topic is, first, to outline the arguments in favour of a larger federal presence; second, to focus on the alternative ways in which this might be implemented; and, third, to assess the potential benefits and costs of departing from the status quo. To anticipate the conclusion somewhat, it seems to me that this is one area where the provinces have done an admirable job, at least thus far. It is entirely appropriate for the federal government to keep an eye on the securities industry in terms, for instance, of ensuring that markets do not become balkanized, but the federal government's assumption of a direct regulatory role has the potential for doing as much harm as good.

The Status Quo
In a major three-volume study prepared under the auspices of the federal Department of Corporate and Consumer Affairs, Philip Anisman and

Peter Hogg comment on the dominance of the provinces in respect of securities legislation:

> The provinces have enacted securities legislation under their authority to legislate in relation to "Property and Civil Rights in the Province" which has been interpreted to include contracts, dealings with property and the regulation of businesses, trades and professions. Provincial power in relation to the securities market in particular has been generously interpreted by the courts. in 1932 the Privy Council upheld the Alberta Security Frauds Prevention Act, 1930, as a valid exercise of provincial jurisdiction intended to protect local investors from fraudulent practices and the case, now the leading decision in the field, has been broadly read so that in most instances in which a question concerning the validity of a securities act has arisen, the provincial legislation has been upheld. Judicial sympathy for provincial securities legislation is reflected even more dramatically in a number of decisions which held that no conflict exists between federal legislation and overlapping provisions in the securities acts.[1]

The authors go on to offer the observation that "the reluctance of the courts to strike down provincial securities legislation likely stems in part from the fact that there is no federal securities law so that a declaration of the invalidity of a provincial act or any of its provisions would create a potential gap in the existing regulatory scheme that might be exploited by the unscrupulous" (Anisman and Hogg, 1979, p. 145).

As part of the provincial regulatory influence over the securities area each province has some version of a securities act with a corresponding securities commission to administer the act. For example, in the province of Ontario the Ontario Securities Commission (OSC) administers the Ontario Securities Act. Moreover, much of the regulation in the securities area is in the nature of self-regulation. Among the self-regulated organizations (SROs) that fall under the umbrella of the OSC are the Toronto Stock Exchange (TSE), the Broker-Dealers Association of Ontario and the Ontario operations of the Investment Dealers Association of Canada (IDA). Each of these associations is vested with (self-) regulatory powers. The five stock exchanges in Canada (Toronto, Montreal, Winnipeg, Alberta and Vancouver) are governed by their respective provincial securities commissions.

The situation is very different in the United States. In 1934 Congress enacted the Securities Exchange Act which created the federal Securities and Exchange Commission (SEC) to oversee the securities industry. However, it was not until the Securities Reform Act of 1975 that the SEC was put on notice to direct and supervise the development of a national market system for securities (Anisman and Hogg, 1979, p. 141). It is this development, among others, that has motivated some analysts to recommend greater federal involvement in the Canadian securities industry.

The Nature of Securities Regulation

As the Royal Commission on Banking and Finance noted in 1964:

> The philosophy of securities regulation in Canada is based on two principles, full disclosure and the prevention of fraud. . . . The first is supported by securities and company legislation and the regulation of stock exchanges, while the second rests on the preventative and punitive powers of the securities laws and the federal Criminal Code as well as those of the by-laws and regulations of the self-regulating associations.(p. 345)

In terms of the mechanisms involved, John Todd, in a recent Ontario Economic Council publication, elaborates:

> To enforce the principle of full disclosure, provincial legislation relies on two general methods: registration and investigation. The first ensures that the Ontario Securities Commission (and its counterparts across Canada) has control over those selling securities to the public, and that those persons are properly qualified. Registration applies not only to the brokerage firm itself, but also to the salesmen employed by the firm.
>
> The OSC uses registration to ensure that the rules pertaining to full disclosure are adhered to. . . . The OSC has control over all TSE (Toronto Stock Exchange) by-laws that it considers to affect the public interest.
>
> The OSC is also empowered to investigate any complaint of wrongdoing. Although it does not have the power to fine or imprison, the OSC can suspend or cancel registration of a broker or brokerage house. The OSC can also order that trading in a particular security can be halted. These decisions are made when the . . . OSC perceives that the public interest is being harmed. (Todd, 1983, pp. 15–16)

Much more time could be devoted to spelling out the characteristics of securities regulation. However, the above will suffice since the object of the exercise is to ascertain whether the present regulatory environment is suited to developing efficient and national securities markets.

Because of the dominance of the TSE and the OSC, securities regulation has tended to be more national in scope than we might expect from a decentralized regulatory process. With some important exceptions, Ontario has normally taken the lead in setting the regulatory pattern, and the remaining provinces have tended to follow Ontario. As John Howard (writing in 1978) has noted:

> Following enactment of the Ontario Securities Act of 1966, there was once again a strong uniformity movement that produced relatively uniform securities laws in Ontario and the Western Provinces and a securities law in Quebec that adheres closely in principle to the Ontario act. In addition, spurred on by a renewed federal interest in the securities field, the provincial securities administrators have set up a quite formal organization — the Provincial Securities Administrators — to coordinate their policies and procedures with a view to simplifying compliance with the several provincial acts. The securities administrators have together produced a set of

uniform policy statements and have collaborated closely to develop a new Ontario Securities Bill, the most recent version of which was tabled in the Ontario legislature on February 28, 1978, and which is intended to be the model statute for all the provinces. (Howard, 1979, p. 1683)

Nonetheless, the existing network of regulation is not characterized by either complete uniformity or full harmonization. Many analysts believe that there can be no true national securities market unless there is more federal involvement. Even the Ontario Securities Commission put forth its CANSEC proposal (an acronym for "The Case for a National Securities Commission") in 1967 for a national presence in the regulation of the securities market. Commenting on this proposal, Howard makes the following observations:

> In its discussion paper on CANSEC the Ontario Securities Commission pointed out that with respect to securities market regulation in Canada the ideal system would embody uniform laws, uniform administration, a common data base and an expert staff to do policy analyses and research specific problems, to investigate problem cases and to administer the overall system. However, the discussion paper goes on to point out that the present Canadian system did not develop with ideal goals in mind but rather in response to different problems in different jurisdictions. Consequently the issue was characterized not as development of an altogether new system but coordination of existing systems to increase administrative efficiency and to develop a mechanism that will enable policy makers and administrators realistically to seek to achieve those ideal goals and so overcome the present dilemma of balkanized provincial regulation: on the one hand, only the larger provinces have the volume of securities business to justify both a sound act and the expenditure of substantial resources on effective administration. As a result the larger provinces — through sheer competence — necessarily attract the major business and thus tend to dominate the field. The major problem therefore in designing a Canada-wide securities regulation system is to reconcile centralized policy making with decentralized administration in a way that does not relegate any jurisdiction, federal or provincial, to an ineffective status. (p. 1690)

Arguments for a Federal Presence

The increasing interprovincial and international nature of the securities business, the spread of computerization which may eventually replace the trading floors of the stock exchanges with a Canada-wide automated trading system, and the inherent difficulty of applying provincial regulatory measures beyond provincial boundaries lead Anisman and Hogg to argue for an overarching federal role in the securities area. After citing numerous cases which have created problems for the provincial regulatory authorities, they conclude:

> It is clear, therefore, that the limitations on provincial jurisdiction not only cast doubt on the ability of the provincial commissions to enforce their own

acts in connection with interprovincial and international transactions but also on the ability of the provinces, even acting cooperatively, to enact a scheme that will satisfactorally regulate the entire securities market. It goes without saying that similar restrictions do not apply to the federal government's ability to legislate; indeed, it is clear that Parliament may enact legislation with extraterritorial impact. . . .

In summary, it is fair to say that limitations on provincial legislative jurisdiction may create serious impediments to pervasive regulation of the Canadian securities market by the provinces. Despite their having filled an otherwise regulatory void, particularly by cooperative efforts which have been accelerated in recent years, it appears that some form of federal legislation to ensure a comprehensive scheme of securities regulation in Canada is warranted. (Anisman and Hogg, 1979, pp. 150, 153)

Anisman and Hogg suggest that the federal government find constitutional support for entering the securities field from one or all of the following sources: trade and commerce power; section 92(10) or the "general advantage clause"; "peace, order and good government," and criminal law power. In terms of the deliberations of the Supreme Court, the recent decision with respect to *Multiple Access Ltd. v. McCutcheon*[2] indicated that at least one justice is favourably inclined toward federal securities legislation of some sort.[3]

Support for a federal presence also came from the Royal Commission on Banking and Finance (1964). Although they had some reservations about the operations of the SEC south of the border and recognized that much has been accomplished in terms of provincial co-operation, the commissioners concluded that "the job which remains to be done is likely to be accomplished most effectively if a federal agency takes the lead in setting high and uniform national standards" (p. 349).

In my analysis of securities markets, I have presented the range of arguments for a greater federal presence. Counter arguments can and do exist, but they will be dealt with later. For now I continue with the notion that federal regulation is necessary and turn to a rather general discussion of alternative ways in which this federal presence can be accommodated within the existing constitutional framework. The next section presents an overview of alternative federal-provincial roles in respect of securities regulation. Following this discussion the analysis will then focus on a few of the more concrete proposals for securities reform. The section will conclude with an assessment of whether or not Canada's experience with securities market regulation warrants much if any alteration of the existing institutional and constitutional fabric.

Alternative Federal-Provincial Arrangements

Table 8-1 presents 15 alternative models for regulating the securities industry. Model 1 gives all powers to the federal level. Models 2 through

14 progressively decentralize the regulatory authority culminating with model 15 which assigns all authority to the provinces. Interestingly enough, it is model 15 that reflects the current Canadian regulatory environment. This is in sharp contrast to the U.S. system which is typified by model 3, where all secondary market regulation is federal, and the individual states are restricted to variations in standards and in disclosure rules in the new issues markets. Moreover, as the table indicates, there was (in 1979, when the table was assembled) a move toward even greater centralization of authority in the United States (see model 2).

In discussing these options, John Howard essentially dismisses the pure versions of the "unitary systems" (federal dominance) as being infeasible in Canada for both constitutional and historical reasons. For example, provinces would surely have the constitutional right to control intraprovincial issues. Howard settles on model 6 as the only unitary prototype that has any probability of adoption and "it is only unitary in the sense that all administration is vested in one level of government, that is, the provincial level" (Howard, 1979, p. 1704). In terms of the pros and cons of this modified unitary approach, he notes:

Model 6 has several distinct advantages: it gives the federal government considerable influence over Canada-wide securities market policies with a minimum of administrative overlap and, as a corollary, preserves much provincial autonomy; it obviates compliance with two levels of regulation; it makes maximum use of experienced personnel, and it is flexible in the sense that it enables decentralized decision making in a manner that is sensitive to local conditions. The signal disadvantages of such a system are that federal influence may prove to be rather tenuous, particularly where federal policy is not congruent with provincial policy or administrative practice; that there is no strong incentive to develop uniform statutes and procedures, and that centralized information processing is improbable. Although a possible model, for these reasons it is unlikely to obtain much support. (p. 1704)

A second approach to regulation is a "dual" system. Model 10 is Howard's choice of a workable version of such a dual system. In terms of assessing its properties:

Model 10 has the advantages that it preserves both provincial and federal autonomy within their respective jurisdictions, but because it requires a separate federal commission inherent in it are two clear disadvantages. First, it institutionalizes a dual system and therefore creates few if any incentives to achieve uniformity of policies and administration. Second, and even more important, assuming a decentralized federal commission administered through regional offices, it does not make the efficient use of experienced regulators. In effect, it would superimpose another level of regulation on the existing system, except to the extent duplication of work could be avoided through the use of common disclosure standards and the use of techniques of notification and coordination to simplify the qualification of

TABLE 8-1 Models of Securities Market Regulatory System

Model Number	Federal Law		Concurrent Federal and Provincial Laws		Provincial Law	
	Primary	Secondary	Primary	Secondary	Primary	Secondary
1	All except intraprovincial issues	All				
2	All except intraprovincial issues but subject to added provincial substantive standards (proposed U.S. Federal Securities Code)	All				
3	All except intraprovincial issues but subject to added provincial substantive standards and disclosure rules (present U.S.)	All				
4			Federal law federal issuers foreign issuers interprovincial issues Provincial law intraprovincial issues	Federal law — all (except intraprovincial trades not made through an interprovincial system)		
5			Federal law federal issuers foreign issuers interprovincial issues Provincial law interprovincial issues intraprovincial issues	Federal law — all (except . . .)		

#	Law applicable	Applicable law
6	Same as 4 but federal law administered by provinces	Federal law — all (except . . .)
7	Same as 5 but federal law administered by provinces	Federal law — all (except . . .)
8	Either model 4, 5, 6, or 7	Provincial law — all

9	Federal law
	  federal issuers
	  foreign issuers
	  interprovincial issues
	Provincial law
	  intraprovincial issues
	Federal and provincial law (province of incorporation or head office)
		Federal law — all (except . . .)

10	Federal law and provincial law (province of incorporation or head office)
	  federal issuers
	  foreign issuers
	  interprovincial issues
	Provincial law
	  intraprovincial issues (even of federal or foreign corporation)
		Federal law — all (except . . .)

11	Either model 9 or 10	Provincial law — all
12	All	All

TABLE 8-1 (cont'd)

Model Number	Federal Law		Concurrent Federal and Provincial Laws		Provincial Law	
	Primary	Secondary	Primary	Secondary	Primary	Secondary
13			Joint commission that acknowledges federal jurisdiction over interprovincial trades			
14			Joint commission that does not so acknowledge (CANSEC)			
15					All (present Canada)	All (present Canada)

Source: Howard, 1979, Table 6. Reproduced with permission of the Minister of Supply and Services, Canada.

prospectuses. Judging from the almost unanimously hostile response to the partial two-level system proposed in part XV of the *Business Corporation Proposals*, published by Consumer and Corporate Affairs Canada in 1971, model 10 is not likely to find favor with the federal government, any provincial government, the securities firms, or the professional advisers of those firms. (pp. 1704–05)

The third approach is an "integrated approach." Howard focusses on model 13 as the prototype for this model of regulation:

The third alternative is the integrated system referred to as model 13, which assumes broad, federal legislative power and delegation from the federal Parliament and the several provincial legislatures of comprehensive regulation-making (i.e., legislative), adjudicative and administrative powers to a common regulatory commission. Model 13 would avoid creation of a two-tier, dual system; but it places the federal government in an awkward minority position from which it can extricate itself only with great difficulty, that is, by withdrawing from the integrated system and setting up an independent federal system. Such action would almost certainly result in a lengthy constitutional struggle to determine the respective legislative powers of the federal parliament and provincial legislatures and probably would not gain much public support. As a result, once it agrees to an integrated system the federal government will probably be, in the absence of any crisis, locked into that system. Nonetheless model 13 . . . has a number of desirable characteristics: it permits some federal and provincial autonomy; it tends strongly to statutory and administrative uniformity; it necessarily leads to a common system of information processing; it renders the duplication of facilities unnecessary; it permits more efficient use of experienced personnel, and it permits flexible, decentralized administration at little added cost. (p. 1705)

Table 8-2 summarizes the suggested advantages and disadvantages of the unitary, dual and integrated prototype for a federal presence in the securities area.

My personal view is that if, for whatever reason, the federal government does enter the area, then the integrated approach is the appropriate vehicle. Indeed, even within this approach there are several options. A decentralized version of an integrated approach is what the CANSEC proposal was all about (model 14 of Table 8-1). As Howard recognizes:

It is the requirement of a comprehensive federal securities act that distinguishes model 13 from the CANSEC proposal. The CANSEC proposal is directed at uniform administration of a narrow, supplemental federal law and several discrete provincial laws, whereas model 13 is directed at uniform administration of a uniform law with a substratum of provincial laws that preserves provincial autonomy with respect to intraprovincial transactions. (p. 1705)

In other words, the federal role under a CANSEC or "decentralized" version of an integrated approach would be principally one of building on

TABLE 8-2 Comparison of Models of a Regulatory System

Characteristics	Model 6		Model 10		Model 13	
	Advantages	Disadvantages	Advantages	Disadvantages	Advantages	Disadvantages
Federal autonomy	Yes but constrained	No administrative control except to withhold resources	Yes	Dual system	Yes but constrained	Minority position
Provincial autonomy	Yes but constrained	Federal superimposed at least in part *re* disclosure	Yes	Dual system	Yes but constrained	Threat of federal withdrawal
Political accountability	Yes	Responsibility diffused therefore accountability is attenuated	Yes	Dual system	No	Responsibility completely diffused
Uniform laws and procedures	No	Tends to a dual system	No	Dual system	No but tends to uniformity	Less local experimentation
Obviates duplication of regulation	Yes	Tenuous federal control	No	Dual system	Yes	Complicated system to approve change
Makes use of experienced regulators	Yes	Ontario and Quebec dominate	Yes at provincial level	No, particularly at regional offices	Yes	
Makes possible central information processing and overall systems analysis	No	Requires coordination of discrete provincial files	Yes	Yes, except intra-provincial operations	Yes	
Flexible — decentralized decision making and responsive to local conditions	Yes	Lack of uniformity of standards and procedures	Yes	Dual system of regional offices	Yes	
Flexible — efficient use of personnel, finances, capital assets	Yes	Ontario and Quebec dominate	No	Almost certain duplication	Yes	

Source: Howard, 1979, Table 9. Reproduced with permission of the Minister of Supply and Services, Canada.

the existing framework, providing a vehicle for more coordination and harmonization, and of filling in any legislative voids in the interprovincial network.

The series of background studies which contained the papers by Howard and by Anisman and Hogg is volume 3 of a major federally sponsored effort directed toward proposals for a securities market law for Canada. Volume 1 of the study actually contains, in draft form, a full-blown proposal for a Canada Securities Act. From my reading of the draft legislation it would appear to fall under model 4 of Table 8-1. The proposed federal legislation ranges across the entire securities field and incorporates a Canadian Securities Commission which would regulate all stock exchanges. While there is provision to accommodate various degrees of co-existence with the existing arrangements, these allowances are entirely at federal discretion. In the limit, the provinces could count only on maintaining jurisdiction over intraprovincial issues. This proposal represents the extreme case in terms of altering the existing (de facto) distribution of powers, and it may have many proponents.

Much of the above analysis assumed, explicitly or implicitly, that there ought to be a greater federal regulatory presence in the securities area. It is probably the case that if we were assigned the task of designing an institutional and legislative framework for a securities market in a federal nation, the existing Canadian approach would not spring early to mind. Why five separate stock exchanges? Why no federal securities act? And so on. It seems to me, however, that the appropriate issue to be addressed is whether the Canadian securities markets are working well.

Two Cheers for the Provinces

In an era in which the provinces are coming under increasing criticism for "province-building" (erecting barriers to the internal common market), the securities market area represents a sphere of economic activity where they appear to have performed quite admirably. This is not to say that the provinces' actions are motivated solely by national concerns. They probably are not. However, there are powerful forces at work in the system to ensure some considerable degree of harmonization. For example, the TSE is by far the largest stock exchange in the country. Hence the decisions of the TSE (and the OSC) will naturally have an important (inordinate?) influence on the regulations in other provinces, particularly the smaller ones. The options for these smaller provinces are limited: if they want to have a different set of regulations with respect to disclosure, they will have to build up a qualified staff of experts to deal with the differences in the regulatory system. For most provinces, these extra costs do not warrant moving away from Ontario legislation. However, suppose that the Saskatchewan securities commission, for example, does want to have more strict rules for disclosure. This decision is surely its right, and this right would presumably exist even if there were federal legislation. After all, the U.S. states have the option of state-specific disclosure rules. Thus, a federal presence, such as the SEC in the United States, is no guarantee of uniformity.

The open (international) nature of our securities markets also has a major impact on the existing Canadian regulatory environment. Since some company shares are listed on the NYSE as well as the TSE or the Montreal Exchange, what happens to the U.S. system tends to be considered quickly and seriously in Canada. Thus the unfixing of U.S. commission rates in 1975 was followed, albeit with a lag, by a similar deregulation of commissions in Canada in 1983. Given this openness, if the Canadian exchanges wish to maintain their position as major stock exchanges, it is essential that they remain competitive internationally. In turn, this ensures that the stock exchanges will strive to be competitive in the national as well as in the international context. A Canadian version of the SEC might attempt to ensure that Canadian-based companies could list their shares only on domestic exchanges. (Indeed, there have been some proposals to this effect.) Such a situation is hard to imagine (on both constitutional or competitive grounds) under the present system and in my view this is an important plus for the decentralized approach.

The competition between the various Canadian stock exchanges has had an important impact on the system. Those in favour of a federal presence in the securities area typically focus on some of the negative implications of this rivalry and, specifically, on the recent period where arbitrage between the Montreal and Toronto stock exchanges was forbidden. As Anisman and Hogg (1979) note:

> On occasion parochial interests have even become dominant to the detriment of the efficient functioning of the market. The prime example is the implementation of a policy in 1969 by the Quebec Securities Commission requiring orders received in Quebec to be filled on the Montreal or Canadian stock exchanges; the application of the policy as a basis for disciplining a registrant for executing a Quebec order on the Toronto Stock Exchange resulted in a retaliatory amendment to the Toronto Exchange's by-laws precluding arbitrage transactions by its members with the Quebec exchanges and thus served to some extent to balkanize the Canadian market. (p. 142)

This was indeed a retrograde step. It passed on to the investor the task of deciding which was the appropriate province in which to place a buy or sell order. As of 1977, arbitrage between the exchanges was again permitted. There are no doubt many other instances where the competition between exchanges can be viewed in a negative light. But there is little evidence that these sorts of practices in Canada are out of line with what occurs between exchanges in the United States under the umbrella of the SEC.

As important, however, are the positive implications arising from competition between the exchanges. Innovations can be implemented by one exchange and will spread across the system if the results are deemed to be positive. Examples are not hard to come by. The Montreal Stock Exchange has recently introduced a new facility in the international currency exchange area. With hookups to various international exchanges investors can now trade gold options on a 24-hour basis. Even more important is the MSE's move in the direction of establishing a specialist system of trading. These specialists are designated to trade solely for the purpose of stabilizing markets (i.e., they do not undertake agency trading). As a result the overall liquidity in the market has been improved, and frequently the MSE has better prices than the TSE, with the result that some trading is moving to Montreal. Needless to say, the TSE is monitoring these initiatives closely. For its part, the TSE has recently widened its coverage of futures trading. At the time of writing both exchanges are in the process of "internationalizing" markets by establishing even closer contacts and cross-listing with U.S. exchanges.

The likelihood is that these sorts of innovations will intensify as the Canadian exchanges vie with each other and with the U.S. exchanges. Innovation could, of course, take place within a Canadian version of an SEC, but is unlikely to proceed at the same pace. For one thing, the current decentralized approach tends to put an additional premium on developing efficient markets. Secondly, not all experimentation is likely to be successful. Hence, an argument can be made for a decentralized system in that any initiative will affect only part of the overall market. It would appear that an umbrella organization like a Canadian SEC (to which all exchanges would report) would tend if anything to strive for uniformity and inhibit innovation by individual exchanges.

It is important to re-emphasize the degree of interprovincial cooperation that is occurring under the existing decentralized system. One such example was in connection with the recent OSC decision to move away from fixed commissions. Naturally, the Ontario commissioners were present at the hearings; but so were the chairman and a commissioner from the Alberta Securities Commission, the superintendent of brokers for British Columbia, and the chairman of the Commission des valeurs mobilières du Québec. In addition, the counsel to the Quebec Commission also participated in the hearings. Hence, when the OSC finally comes up with a decision on a given matter, not only are the other provincial securities commissions normally fully aware of what is going on but they have often participated in a meaningful way in the decision-making process.

A similar outcome happened in connection with the recent Ontario initiative with respect to takeover policy. Here, however, the underlying issues were more serious. In the 1978 version of its securities legislation, Ontario incorporated the so-called "follow-up offer obligation" as part of its regulations with respect to takeovers. Some of the other provinces did not parallel this feature. Thus, the provision was proving problematical from several vantage points including the fact that it was, in effect, enforcing extraterritoriality in a policy area that was not generally accepted by the other provinces. This is precisely the sort of area where many commentators would argue that federal securities legislation would prove valuable. No doubt it might, but the existing system has also generated a response.

Pierre Lortie, president of the Montreal Stock Exchange, headed a Joint Industry Committee to look into this issue. Included were representatives of the four major exchanges (Toronto, Montreal, Alberta and Vancouver) as well as the IDA. Among the objectives of the committee was the "need for uniformity among the statutes regulating take-over bids in Canada" (Securities Industry Committee on Takeover Bids, 1983, p. iii). This committee's report was published in November 1983. While the recommendations of the committee are obviously important, they are not as instructive in the present context as the process itself. As the report noted:

> It is hoped that the Canadian Securities Administrators and legislatures will concur in the conclusion that, while the recommended framework may not suit everyone's preferences, it is the one that reconciles the competing objectives and is fair to all market participants. The Committee hopes that the Securities Administrators and legislators will move for prompt implementation of this framework, and that the federal government will amend the Canada Business Corporation Act where applicable. (p. 3)

If, as anticipated, the provinces do enact legislation in accordance with the recommendations, then the system will have demonstrated again that where harmonization is essential it can be achieved.

Therefore, the question of a major federal presence in the securities legislation area boils down to the issue of the manner in which such a move could enhance the efficiency of the existing securities market. (It should be noted that Ottawa is not entirely absent. Its corporation legislation has an important influence, and the criminal code is operative as well.) Some improvements are clearly in order and a federal role may provide the needed catalyst. However, there is also the downside risk to consider. The move will generate substantial uncertainty and will probably rekindle federal-provincial confrontation. There will likely be an increase in bureaucracy and perhaps a dual level of regulatory legislation. Moreover, there will be a very different set of pressures brought to bear on such an agency. For example, I would place even money that one of the first moves of a Canadian SEC would be, in the name of regional equality, to develop and fund a Maritimes stock exchange.

In short, I believe that there is little need for a national regulatory body. Even now, there is at least as much uniformity in Canada as there is in the United States in terms of the preparation of prospectuses. More-over, there is one important feature of the present system that is serving the nation well — the option for the federal government to move into the area if the provinces are lagging in either developing efficient markets or in not looking after the interests of investors. This alternative places a substantial pressure on the various provincial securities commissions to work together — precisely what we would want from a system.

To conclude, it is useful to have a provincial perspective on the operations of the present system of securities regulation. The following are the views of William Pidruchney (1983), chairman of the Alberta Securities Commission:

> The fact is that the federal government has some time ago done studies, drafted a model Act and so forth, and perhaps is ready, willing and able to take over the system. This is an ongoing concern although presently there's not been any particular pressure. I would simply like to make a case for this regulation being left in the jurisdiction of the provinces and territories of this country, as it currently is. . . . I think we start with the first proposition that I think you won't find too abhorrent, and that is that were certainly do not want a duplicitous system. We do not want a federal and a provincial or territorial system in place. That's the American experience where they have the S.E.C. and they have state regulation as well. That's too much regula-tion. I'm going to suggest to you that there is in fact a dynamism in diversity and the provinces and regions of this country are in fact very diverse. Each province in fact does have its own aspirations and it does have its needs, and I think it's entirely legitimate, not only legitimate but actually desirable, that these provincial aspirations and regional aspirations be pursued and met as best possible. And there are some other advantages. There is a freedom of choice to an issue who wishes to do business in a country wherein there are different jurisdictions. There's the advantage that, should a regulator decide to vary his course and to do something for him to test that option, and there's the opportunity for several jurisdictions to test several options all con-currently. There is the advantage of avoiding total disaster should a whole monolithic system, a unitary system, be derailed. And I'm suggesting that that has happened historically and could conceivably happen again. This way, disasters if they occur, are localized. There's a greater degree of specialization in all of the regions. Alberta, I think you'll concede, has probably specialized in oil and gas affairs, and oil and gas regulation. And that's logical and that's the type of expertise we need. We need more specialization rather than less. There's a counter-balancing that occurs when all of these regulators in their different modes come together and share their opinions and views. This system of course does lead to some variance and the fact that Quebec has varied in the question of who can be registered as brokers or as brokerage registrants has been raised today. I think this is entirely legitimate. I think it's important for us as members of the same national family to have a perspective on this. While there is a variance at the present time I think it's an interesting and a valid experiment and the effects of that experiment will be instructive to the rest of us. I think that logic and

commonsense always do prevail and that the regulators will eventually mainstream on whatever side of the fence they end up. But I think it's important to the structure of our country and to the operation of this country that people have this opportunity.

I would like to assure you of this, the Canadian Securities Administrators of all regions and provinces meet twice a year. And they meet expressly for the purpose of sharing views, establishing policies that are national or regional, and the point of the whole exercise is to ensure that enterprise and issuers doing business in this country have the opportunity to do business on a national basis without impedance, hindrance or obstacle. We've coined a little bit of a phrase that we say — compatability in all jurisdictions if not uniformity. And I say to you that's our promise to you. I say to the federal government — we have a good system, the system works, if it's not broken don't try to fix it. (pp. 84–85)

Even if Canadians were to adopt the position that the securities markets are performing well under the existing arrangements, there is still the likelihood that Ottawa could enter the regulatory scene because of the pressing range of issues and challenges related to overall financial intermediation, of which securities markets are only a part. To this "four pillars" issue I now turn.

The "Four Pillars" and the Division of Powers

The Four Pillars

The traditional Canadian approach to the financial intermediation industry was summarized recently by the OSC:

> Each of the major participants in Canada's financial system — the securities dealers, the banks, the trust companies and the insurance companies — has a core function. Public policy, as reflected in our laws, reserves to each group the performance of its core function. The Canadian financial system may therefore be described as a segregated system and the division of the system into four segments may metaphorically be referred to as the "four pillar" concept. (Ontario Securities Commission, 1983, p. ii)

While the market may be segregated into these four pillars, the jurisdictional overlay is not so neatly segregated. Banking falls under federal legislation by virtue of one or all of currency and coinage (section 91(14)); banking, incorporation of banks, and the issue of paper money (section 91(15)); and savings banks (section 91(16)). Trust companies are generally regulated by the provinces but can be incorporated under either federal or provincial charters. However, they qualify for deposit insurance which is regulated federally. Insurance companies come under provincial jurisdiction and, as we have seen, so does the regulation of the securities industry.

As the barriers between these four functions begin to wither away, the jurisdictional responsibilities correspondingly become progressively less clear and less obvious. Part of the confusion arises because there is no precise definition for "banking." Canada is not peculiar here: the United States has not defined banking either. If banking were defined as to ability to accept deposits for transfer by order, for example, then trust companies, credit unions and even brokerage houses would fall under federal jurisdiction. If the definition for banking were the ability to engage in commercial lending, as W.A. Kennett (1983, p. 14), the inspector general of banks recently defined the "core function" of banking, then again the federal government would have some control over trust companies. Moreover, unless the Supreme Court took an historical approach to interpreting section 91(16), which gives the federal government control over savings banks, it is difficult to see how such institutions as credit unions would not fall under federal jurisdiction. Trust companies, for example, originally came under "property and civil rights in the province" (section 92(13)) and "The Incorporation of Companies with Provincial Objects" (section 92(11)), respectively, for regulation and chartering. As they move into new areas, however, the degree to which they fall under provincial responsibility becomes increasingly questionable. Even now they are covered by federal deposit insurance.

Therefore, just as in the securities industry, we could make the claim that the federal government might well win a court challenge on the issue of federal-provincial regulatory responsibility for selected aspects of the overall financial intermediation industry. Hence, one obvious question to be addressed is whether the federal government ought to attempt to press its potential constitutional right in order to provide more federal direction to the industry. However, more so than in the securities industry, there is a major policy issue as distinct from a jurisdictional issue that must be sorted out first. Specifically, should the four-pillar concept be maintained or should the existing barriers be allowed to wither away further? This issue would have to be faced irrespective of which jurisdiction held sway. It may well be that a streamlining or reorientation of the division of powers would facilitate an appropriate decision with respect to the underlying policy issue; but this is far from clear. What may be the better approach is to come to terms with the policy dilemma first and only then to investigate what alterations, if any, in jurisdiction will facilitate the implementation of the chosen policy. This is, of course, consistent with schema in Chapter 3 which suggested that alternative overall policy goals may call for different federal-provincial implementation strategies.

It is this interaction between policy and jurisdiction that underlies the following analysis of the financial intermediation industry. At the outset it should be obvious that the discussion will only cover the tip of the iceberg. The literature both in Canada and elsewhere on this issue has mushroomed into a veritable flood, and it is unlikely that it has yet crested. The analysis begins with the recent decision that has unleashed this torrent of literature and concern — the OSC's decision with respect to discount brokering.

The GLIS Decision[4]

On April 1, 1983, brokerage commission fees were deregulated. Almost immediately the Toronto Dominion Bank announced its Greenline Investor Service (GLIS). Historically, the banks have been able to accommodate customers wishing to trade in equities. Section 190(4)(b) of the Bank and Banking Law Revision Act, 1980, continues to permit a bank to act as agent for equities provided that the actual purchase or sale is effected by a broker. The rationale for this service was, and is, to provide security market access to persons in rural areas who have no other convenient access to a broker. The banks did not actively market this service.

GLIS changed all this. The TD Bank decided that the access to brokerage execution services at discount rates enabled it to package and market an investor service where it would act as agent in conjunction with the services of a discount broker, Equity Trading Inc. The TD Bank argued that this service was fully within the letter and the spirit of both the Bank Act and the Ontario Securities Act. In terms of the Bank Act, the offer was consistent with section 190(4)(b) referred to above. In terms of the Ontario Securities Act, the TD Bank relied on section 34(1)(11) which provides:

> Subject to the Regulations, registration is not required in respect of the following trades:
> 11. The execution of an unsolicited order to purchase or sell through a registered dealer by a bank to which the Bank Act (Canada) applies or a trust company registered under the Loan and Trust Corporations Act as agent by such a person or company and the trade by such person or company in placing the unsolicited order with the bank or trust company.

The exemption is known as the "unsolicited trade exemption."

The arguments against allowing GLIS to proceed were many and varied: the acceptance of GLIS would be in violation of the four-pillars concept; the "unsolicited trade exemption" applied to chartered banks' traditional investment services, but the marketing of GLIS hardly fits the definition of "unsolicited"; competition would decrease because the awesome geographical and financial size of the chartered banks would eventually overwhelm the securities industry; a regulatory void would be created because investors who obtain discount brokerage through financial institutions would be denied the benefits of the "suitability rule,"[5] since the rule is not applicable to financial institutions when relying on the unsolicited trade exemption from Securities Act registration; and so on. In addition, of course, there is a jurisdictional problem since provincial securities commissions (in this case the OSC) are engaging in the regulation of federally chartered and regulated banks.

In spite of these arguments, the OSC endorsed GLIS. There are two aspects of its decision that are of particular interest, and they will be dealt with in turn. First, in order to provide a framework upon which it could base a decision, the OSC had to come to grips with the precise nature of the issue. The framework that it adopted is not only interesting but, in my view, the correct one. There is no substitute for the commission's own words:

> The commission determined that the test that it should apply in considering the implications of discount access services should be based on what is perhaps the fundamental principle of any free society: namely the presumption that any action is permissible unless it can be demonstrated to be contrary to the public interest. Thus the question before the Commission was: "Is the offering of discount services by financial institutions prejudicial to the public interest?" rather than "Are such services in the public interest?" The use of this test reflects the Commissions's belief *that free market forces should generally determine the availability of a service and that the four pillars concept is an exception from this view dictated by particular circumstances*. The Commission was not therefore concerned with protecting one segment of the financial system from competition from another as a matter of principle: Rather it sought to determine whether any breaking down of the separation of the investment banking and commercial banking segments of the system resulting from discount access services would prejudice the healthy functioning of the capital markets in Canada.
>
> In addition, the public interest requires the Commission to determine whether the offering of discount access services by financial institutions would have an adverse impact upon investor protection so essential to the healthy functioning of our capital markets.[6]

Second, in spite of this general test that the OSC decided to apply to the GLIS proposal, the OSC did finally come down on the side of respecting the four pillars. It was how the commission identified the core function of the securities industry that was intriguing. Rather than associating the securities core with overall brokerage, the commission designated underwritings, or the new-issue function, as the securities core. Underwriting would be the exclusive preserve of securities dealers. Discount brokerage is not an integral part of the new-issue process and, hence, the GLIS proposal was accepted. Again, the commission's words merit note:

> On a functional basis then, what is the impact of the discount broker upon the performance of the new issue function? The discount broker simply provides an execution service. The discount broker does not solicit purchases and sales of securities. (In this context we are using the work "solicit" to include providing advice in respect of a purchase or sale of a specific security.) Discount brokerage is only related very indirectly to the

core function of the securities industry. It is not an integral part of the new issue process. It is related indirectly in the sense that it contributes to the liquidity of the secondary market which is essential to the new issue business. On the other hand full service brokerage is more directly related to this business because the full service broker is an important part of the distribution network relied upon by the securities dealer engaged in new issue financing. Although we would not characterize full service brokerage as the core function of the securities industry we do consider it to be essential to and supportive of the new issue business. Full service brokerage provides one of the bases for the customer contacts which are necessary for the placement of securities which is inherent in the new issue business. (pp. 30–31)

In rendering its decision the commission made two final points that have significance both for the GLIS experiment and for the general issue of maintaining the compartmentalization of the financial intermediation sector. First:

The regulation of the Canadian segregated financial system is of course complicated by its multi-jurisdictional nature. We support this multi-jurisdictional regulation on the basis that it is more sensitive and responsive to the needs of various activities and regions. Because of the many jurisdictions involved and because the pressures put on one segment by another segment will not go away, we believe that there is a need for all regulators of participants in the financial system to meet, on a regular basis, to develop a compatible approach to resolving the pressures on the conventional organization of our financial system. (p. 72)

Toward this end, it is instructive to note that securities administrators from Quebec, Manitoba, Saskatchewan, Alberta and British Columbia participated in part of the OSC hearings on Greenline. Second, and as a link to the general discussion of the increasing encroachment upon the four pillars that follows, the commission noted that "the segregation of the investment banking and commercial banking segments of our financial system can be preserved and that the effects of the domino theory will not materialize. However, if the Canadian financial system integrates, we are confident that the integration will not result from the banks providing discount access services" (p. 70).

It may be that too much space has been devoted to the Greenline decision, given that this initiative is only one of the many areas where the financial system is "integrating," to utilize the OSC's term. However, it represents somewhat of a milestone in the sense that a "determination" was made by a regulatory commission that it was acceptable. Of perhaps even more significance is the fact that in the wake of this decision the federal government struck a "blue-ribbon committee" of industry representatives to advise Ottawa with respect to the approach it should take to regulating the financial sector. I shall return to this jurisdictional issue later. For the present, it is instructive to focus on the many other cross-boundary activities that threaten the four-pillar concept.

Eroding the Four Pillars

Canadians have read with considerable interest the apparent rapid integration of the U.S. financial sector — how the cash management account of Merrill Lynch has enabled this brokerage firm to lay claim to being, effectively, the first nationwide bank, a position not attainable by any commercial bank by virtue of the 1927 McFadden Act (which limits the ability of the banks to branch interstate), and how Sears-Roebuck with its thrift, securities, insurance and real-estate activities has become a "one-stop financial supermarket" and indeed a "one-stop everything" if one throws in its traditional line of products. What may not be so obvious to the average Canadian, but what is most assuredly all-too-obvious to those directly involved, is that Canada is moving in the same direction. Outlining some of these recent innovations is the purpose of the section.[7]

Integration of the financial system is not entirely new. Some would claim that it began when the chartered banks were allowed to become major players in the mortgage area. For their part the banks might claim that it was the ability (although still limited) of the trust companies to engage in commercial lending. What is new, however, is the pace at which the integration is proceeding. With the trust companies now granted access to the clearing system (the Canadian Payments System) and with both the banks and trust companies competing with round-the-clock ATMs (Automated Teller Machines), the distinction for the transacting consumer between these two types of institutions is fading rapidly. But they are subject to very different sorts of regulations. Banks must be widely held, but trust companies need not be. Banks are prohibited from entering into the trusteeship function, but trust companies have at least a toe into the commercial lending area. Another difference is that there is a ten-year sunset clause to banking regulation so that there is a periodic reassessment of the role of banks in the economy — an important part of which is to update the regulatory environment. For several years now both trust companies and insurance companies have been pushing for an overall review of their regulatory environment. To date, these efforts have been in vain, except for the recent proposals of the Ontario Ministry of Consumer and Commercial Relations which were motivated more by the Crown-Seaway-Greymac debacle than by an attempt to reassess the role of trust companies within the context of a rapidly changing financial intermediation industry.

Insurance companies are potentially under the most pressure for rationalization, since their traditional methods of selling insurance are becoming incredibly expensive. A simple flyer enclosed with Chargex, Amex, or Mastercard bills represents one viable alternative. It would be hard to argue that the consumer would not be better off. A few regulatory changes are all that prevents this further aspect of financial integration. Under these and other forces, many insurance companies have been acting to both solidify and expand their operations. For example, since there is no restriction on the ability of an insurance company's acquiring a substantial share position in a trust company, this is one route that is open. Manufacturers' Life now has a 25 percent share of Canada Trust. Trilon Financial, an arm of Brascan, has both London Life and Royal Trust under is wing. Power Corporation has the Investors Group which controls Great West Life Assurance Co. and Montreal Trustco. These are the beginnings of a new corporate form — the financial service conglomerate. However, in terms of bringing financial services to the people, as it were, none of these organizations has an edge on Eaton-Bay financial services which, following Sears-Roebuck, offers both trust and insurance facilities.

The Merrill Lynch approach in the United States is also being carried over to Canada. Many brokerage houses already have a foot in the deposit-taking business by paying interest on cash deposited by their clients. Now, Merrill Lynch of Canada has openly indicated that it is considering introducing a plan similar to U.S. Merrill's cash management account. Other brokerage houses are sure to follow suit, particularly since cash management accounts are not only lucrative but represent an effective way of counteracting the banks' invasion of the securities industry.

No doubt analysts more familiar with the inner workings of the financial system could extend these examples several-fold and could indicate other ways in which the four pillars are eroding. But the above description is probably sufficient to indicate that this erosion is both ongoing and escalating.

The policy questions that arise are many and varied. Can the four pillars be maintained? Should they be maintained? Should the focus of regulations switch from regulating institutions to regulating functions? What would best serve the interests of the consumer? What are the likely implications of maintaining the current regulatory framework? Would a more unified framework (presumably with an overarching federal role) lead to a more competitive financial system? And so on. In focussing briefly on some of these issues, it is important to address them in terms of some underlying philosophy or approach. The one I have adopted is that Canada's financial system has in general served us well and in many areas is world class. The overall approach to the sector should be one of maintaining excellence and ensuring that the system encourages the development of world-class institutions.

Policy Alternatives

Can the Four Pillars be Maintained?
The combination of rapidly advancing technology and the pressure of consumer demand would seem to indicate clearly that the status quo

with respect to the four pillars is untenable. Consider the security firms. They are now moving toward full computerization, including information about their clients' overall financial status and needs and head-office research on economic forecasts and available financial options. The ability to bring these data up on a terminal screen immediately will mean that these firms will find themselves with too much "power" to be willing to confine themselves to the sale of securities. The securities firms also feel constrained in another way. The current Canadian ownership rules imply that they cannot merge or easily associate with overseas firms in order to provide domestic clients with access to international capital market options. Thus, both technology and the drive to satisfy their clients' needs will ensure that the major brokerage firms will continue to chip away at the fringes of the four pillars and will mount increasing pressure for regulatory reform.[8]

The only way that I can foresee the maintenance of the present four-pillar concept is for the federal government to take over the regulation of the entire financial system and to enforce rigidly the regulations — regulations which would have to include some degree of protection from foreign competition. The federal government will probably not attempt this regulation, but it appears to be the only way of maintaining any degree of compartmentalization.

Put differently, the current regulatory environment will virtually guarantee further financial integration — a result of the decentralized and competitive nature of the system. Consider Quebec, for example. With a number of indigenous financial institutions such as the caisses populaires and certain life insurance companies, the province is anxious to give these companies an advantage over federal and other provincial companies (Panabaker, 1983, p. 40). Moreover, some non-brokerage financial institutions (e.g., Royal Trust) are registering with the Quebec Securities Commission as limited brokers. This permits them to advertise their stock brokerage business and to give advice. Eventually, they may apply to the Montreal Stock Exchange for membership, which at least one knowledgeable official of the TSE believes would be granted (Friedland, undated, p. 6). This is but one example of how a decentralized system can lead not only to increased deregulation but to pressure on the self-regulating organizations (in this case the TSE) to meet the competition.

This difference in approach to regulation was confirmed recently by Peter Dey (1983), the chairman of the Ontario Securities Commission:

[T]he Commission (the OSC) expressed its willingness to exercise its powers so long as the segregated system is public policy in Ontario to preserve the protected functions of the securities industry. The Ontario position is to be contrasted with the position of the Quebec Commission which is determined not to exercise its powers to preserve the segregated system and, I understand, has taken the position that it will register financial institutions to carry on any aspect of the securities business provided the institution is fit for registration and is empowered by its governing legislation to engage in the securities business. (p. 48)

In short, the pressures for financial integration arising from the emerging technology and the demands of consumers are probably aided by the decentralized nature of the current regulatory environment. This is not necessarily bad. Indeed, in my view, a considerable degree of further financial integration is not only inevitable but desirable. The issue is whether Canada will be dragged into this integration or whether it is possible, perhaps by adept use of the regulatory process, to have some influence on how the integration will proceed.

Regulating Institutions versus Regulating Functions

Much of the current regulatory framework focusses on institutions and in many cases on registering individuals within these institutions. An alternative approach would be to regulate functions or markets and to allow a broad range of institutions to operate in these markets provided that each of them meets the criteria set out for the market in question. This is generally referred to as the functional approach to regulation of the financial markets, and one of its chief proponents is the Economic Council of Canada in its 1976 report, *Efficiency and Regulation.*

Regulation by function would presumably imply that a given institution would be subject to both federal and provincial regulation, depending on the particular market. For example, to the extent that a provincially incorporated trust company engaged in banking (assuming that an acceptable definition for banking is incorporated in legislation) it would be subject to federal regulation. Likewise, a federally chartered bank doing insurance or brokerage business would be subject to provincial regulation. The thrust of regulation in each of these areas would be to develop efficient markets and to protect the consumer interest. Even under this regulatory framework, some compartmentalization of activities may be necessary. The long-standing concern relating to the conflict of interest that can arise between the banking and trust function would have to be sorted out satisfactorily before we would want to integrate the banking and trust functions.[9] I shall return to the question of regulation by function after focussing on a few other aspects of the regulatory process.

Consumer Protection

With the Crown-Seaway-Greymac debacle still fresh in peoples' minds, the Ontario Ministry of Consumer and Commercial Relations (1983) has issued a white paper on the regulation of trust companies in Ontario. The proposals have received a mixed review. They imply vastly expanded powers for the regulators (and will require a corresponding expansion of the regulatory staff). One aspect of the proposal is that the initial capital requirements for establishing trust companies will be raised from the present $1 million to $10 million. It is possible that this will tend to keep some of the "unscrupulous" out of the trust business. More likely, in the view of Seymour Friedland (undated), "all this will do is restrict entry into the industry to those who are very rich as opposed to those who are moderately rich. No moral philosopher has ever claimed that there are more scoundrels in the $1–$9.99 million class than in the class with $10 million" (pp. 14–15).

Friedland goes on to point out that part of the problem associated with protecting the consumer relates to the existing framework and, in particular, to the role of the Canadian Deposit Insurance Corporation. Specifically, the CDIC provides a single level of coverage at one premium:

> More coverage should be available for those institutions that wish it — which could be attractive to large depositors. And the premium should reflect the level of risk that the institution represents. Actuaries should be able to handle this. This should be an incentive for institutions to shape up and, if the penalty premiums are publicized, would inform customers about the soundness of the institution, somewhat like a credit rating. (p. 15)

Indeed, we can take this further. The combination of the allowance of dominant shareholders for trust companies, the existence of single premium deposit insurance, and the provision for the allocation of a portion of trust company assets into real estate can provide an open invitation for abusing the system. The recent move to raise the coverage of deposit insurance to the $60,000 level means that a trust company can attract additional depositors to increase its leverage in the real estate area. If the investment falls through, the depositors are protected. If it succeeds, the windfall accrues in large measure to the principal share-holder. This is not to say that the trust companies are managed by a group of persons likely to engage in this sort of activity. The opposite is almost assuredly the case. However, the point remains that the incentives in the system are such that, if an owner is so inclined, the way is open for this type of action.

Thus, in terms of ensuring greater consumer protection, it is not obvious that the preferable route is to pile on a further level of regulation. There are some features of the existing system that might well merit restructuring. The two that received attention here were the operations of the federal deposit insurance and the provision that trust companies, unlike banks, need not be widely held. No doubt other aspects are worthy of reconsideration as well.

The Level Playing Field

There is a good deal of concern that, if wholesale financial integration became the order of the day, the chartered banks would simply swallow up some of the other financial institutions. For example, allowing the banks to enter the securities business may lead them to buy up the existing brokerage firms. There may be some likelihood that this will indeed occur although the experience from Britain suggests that the banks are as likely to start up their own securities firms if they wish to enter this market. But some considerable reorganization of the financial intermediation system is probably in the cards in any event. To counter the dominance of the chartered banks, other players might be allowed a head start. This is where divided regulatory jurisdiction may be an advantage: the provinces could deregulate now, with some certainty that the federal government will not reopen the banking legislation until 1990, when it must again be reviewed. In any event, the conception of Gulliver and the Lilliputians freewheeling on the so-called "level playing field" is a concern to participants and regulators alike.

Competition and Internationalization

Perhaps the most important force in the drive toward the blurring of boundaries in the financial sector arises from competitive pressures. On the push side, as it were, firms are driven to new areas in order to cover the costs of their distribution networks and technological upgrading. On the pull side, the markets for equities are becoming increasingly internationalized — to such an extent that we can now meaningfully talk about a global market for equities. To become competitive in this increasingly internationalized market may at the same time be to run afoul of internal regulatory requirements. In this context the Canadian model, which is essentially a functional separation approach, may be too restrictive. One alternative model — regulation by function — may appear more inviting, but it probably runs up against the existing divided jurisdiction problem. For example, solvency concerns will always remain important and, at base, solvency relates to the institution generally and not to its separate functions. Pierre Lortie offers another concern related to the erosion of the four-pillars approach. Under a regulation-by-function approach, what happens when a firm runs into trouble? It could trigger a systemic reaction. In order to prevent this result, there would have to be some regulatory body that is able to take control of the entire organization and not just an "arm" or a "leg." In turn, does this not suggest an umbrella regulatory agency to embrace all functions?[10]

In short, these concerns bring us back to the central issue raised in Chapter 3, that there is a close interrelationship between the division of powers and the overall policy goal. In this case, the existing regulatory jurisdiction is likely to have an influence on how the financial industry will develop. It may even be that the pressures for change in this industry are such that the evolving structures will not be consistent with the existing regulatory approach. At the same time, the existing framework may not allow the various sectors to evolve in a manner consistent with ensuring that Canada's financial institutions remain world class. If we were to provide a blueprint for the "ideal" financial system of the future this may entail, as a companion requirement, a reassignment of regulatory powers in order to achieve this ideal financial structure.

Summary

By way of summary, the following points appear worthy of emphasis:

- Financial integration is proceeding quite quickly.
- The pressures of expanding technology, consumer demand and the internationalization of financial markets imply that more integration is inevitable.
- Regulation of the financial sector as it becomes more integrated is going to be considerably more difficult.
- The existing regulatory framework is already fairly complicated in the sense that it is multi-jurisdictional. Indeed, some institutions like trust companies can be chartered at either the federal and provincial level, and they are also subject to regulations from both levels of government.
- The competition between jurisdictions at the provincial level likely implies that, in certain areas at least, the most lenient jurisdiction will set the standard which other jurisdictions may be forced to meet. In this sense, the existing regulatory framework may determine the eventual structure of the financial sector.
- However, this may not be the "ideal" financial market structure, in light of the changing international and competitive nature of financial markets.

In terms of the thrust of this monograph, the central question is whether or not an alternative division of powers will improve economic management of the area. I submit that the answer to this question is far from clear. On the one hand, a more unified regulatory framework will allow a decision, once made, to be implemented more easily than is the case with a multi-jurisdiction framework. On the other hand, a unified federal presence could, if it wished, enforce to a far greater extent than is possible now a continued compartmentalization of the financial sector. Since my prejudices are in the direction of further integration, I would find this troublesome.

Overall, I think the critical problem in this area is a policy problem, not a jurisdictional problem. It seems a bit premature to attempt to reassign jurisdictional responsibility without first deciding on the appropriate policy. Once the latter becomes clear, it is likely that the jurisdictional concerns will sort themselves out. As a final comment, I would suggest that the Canadian financial markets have developed very well for a country with only 20-odd million people. Many of our institutions are world-class. Maintaining this excellence where we now have it and encouraging it in the remainder of the sector would seem to be the appropriate underlying objective for any rethinking or reorganization with respect to the four pillars. If maintaining the four pillars means that Canadian financial institutions will, in say 10 years, be relegated to second-class institutions in terms of where the industry is headed south of the border and, as well, be hampered in their ability to compete internationally, then it is surely not in the consumer or national interest to continue with the present protectionist arrangement with respect to the financial intermediation sector.

Pensions

Introduction

Pensions and the industry that has developed around them have from time to time been referred to as the fifth pillar of finance. The regulation of the pension industry is subject to every bit as much federal-provincial overlap as are some of the other pillars. However, the "fifth-pillar" label is misleading, since the institutions associated with each of the four pillars are for the most part also active participants in the overall pension industry. Indeed, one might say that the pension industry is "integrated." Nonetheless, because of the tremendous growth in pension assets, the complicated federal-provincial jurisdiction, and the recent proposals to overhaul the pension system, the area is worthy of discussion in terms of the objectives of this monograph — to investigate alternative divisions of power and their implications for economic management of the federation.

The first part of this section will focus on the structure of the overall pension system. This will be followed by a discussion of federal-provincial responsibilities with respect to pensions. Part of the analysis will focus on the implications of the existing pension jurisdiction and how it has influenced policy-making with respect to pensions. The final substantive section deals with Bill S-31, The Corporate Shareholding Limitation Act, which highlights one of the many problems associated with pensions. While this piece of legislation relates as much to the maintenance of an internal common market as it does to pension regulation, I have decided to deal with it in the context of pensions rather than in Chapter 9 on the internal common market.

An Overview of the Pension System[11]

Table 8-3 presents an overview of the existing pension system. Since the table is essentially self-contained and contains more information than is needed for the task at hand, the following discussion will focus only on the key features.

The rows labelled 1 and 2 of the table constitute the private pension system. In terms of employer-sponsored pension plans, normally referred to as occupational plans, two general types dominate — defined benefit plans and money purchase plans. The bulk of Canadians with occupational pensions belong to the defined-benefit type. In defined benefit plans each year of contributions normally entitles the employee to one unit of benefit. There are several ways in which these years of service, or units of benefit, can be related to the eventual pension entitlement. They include:

- *final average (or final earnings) plans*, which apply the unit of benefit credited for each year to the members' average earnings for a specified number of years, say five, just before retirement;

TABLE 8-3 An Overview of Existing Pension Arrangements

	Who Contributes?	Who Benefits?
1. Occupational Plans		
A. Defined Benefit	• both employers and employees in contributory plans, only employers in non-contributory plans	• retiring employees who were with the firm long enough to be vested • surviving spouses in plans with survivor benefits
B. Money Purchase	• both employers and employees	• same as above
2. RRSPs	• individuals contribute to own or spousal plans • contributions are tax deductible up to a limit	• individuals can withdraw funds from plans before or after retirement
3. Old-Age Security (OAS)	• federal government, out of general revenues	• all Canadians aged 65 +
4. Guaranteed Income Supplement (GIS)	• federal government, out of general revenues	• low-income residents aged 65 +
5. GAINS[a]	• Ontario government, out of general revenues	• Ontario residents aged 65 + with low incomes
6. Elderly Tax Exemptions[b]	• federal and provincial governments, out of general revenues	• Canadians, aged 65 +, with income high enough to be taxpayers
7. CPP/QPP	• employers and employees pay special CPP/QPP contributions • current rate is 3.6%, evenly split	• those 65 +, or disabled, who have paid sufficient CPP/QPP premiums • surviving spouses of CPP/QPP contributors

TABLE 8-3 (cont'd)

	How Are Benefits Determined?	Nature of the Contractual Agreement
1. Occupational Plans		
A. Defined Benefit	• specified formula (e.g., final-average earnings, career average, flat benefit plans)	• explicit contract between employers and employees, often part of overall compensation package
B. Money Purchase	• function of past contributions plus accumulated earnings • pensioner can select various types of annuities	• same as above
2. RRSPs	• same as money purchase plans	• between RRSP owner and financial institution holding the fund; otherwise self-administered
3. Old-Age Security (OAS)	• flat benefits, fixed by federal legislation • indexed quarterly to CPI	• no formal contractual relationship • strong implicit or social contract
4. Guaranteed Income Supplement (GIS)	• maximum benefits fixed by federal legislation • benefits differentiated between single and married units • income tested (50% tax back) • indexed to CPI	• same as above
5. GAINS[a]	• maximum benefit fixed by provincial legislation • benefits differentiated by single and married units, latter are indexed • income tested (50% tax back)	• same as above
6. Elderly Tax Exemptions[b]	• benefit depends on claimant's marginal tax rate; higher marginal rate, larger benefits • exemptions are indexed	• none
7. CPP/QPP	• specified benefit formula, determined more by earnings than contributions • indexed quarterly	• no formal contractual arrangement although the public perception is one of contributing to retirement income

TABLE 8-3 (cont'd)

	Who Administers and Controls the Plan?	Other Characteristics
1. Occupational Plans		
A. Defined Benefit	• generally the employer • some public sector plans tend not to be funded in the actuarial sense[c]	• benefits basically are a function of earnings profile, not contributions
B. Money Purchase	• generally the employer, although often an employee has some say over how his/her funds are invested	• benefits basically determined by contributions and fund performance, not by earnings profile
2. RRSPs	• individual or institution, although inflow of new funds is controlled by individual	• same as money purchase plans • maximum contribution rates have not been indexed
3. Old-Age Security (OAS)	• no plan or fund	• basically an intergenerational transfer • universal program, not dependent on work experience
4. Guaranteed Income Supplement (GIS)	• as above	• CPP/QPP benefits are viewed as part of income in terms of being subject to the 50% tax back
5. GAINS[a]	• same as above	• 50% tax back rate • GAINS benefits are "stacked" with GIS so that overall tax-back rate is 100%
6. Elderly Tax Exemptions[b]	• same as above	
7. CPP/QPP	• joint federal-provincial plan • surplus CP contributions invested in provincial securities • QPP also invests in private assets	• until fund matures, current contributors receive a substantial subsidy relative to future contributors

Source: Ontario Economic Council, 1983a, Table 1.

a. Guaranteed Annual Income System. This program operates only in Ontario. Most other provinces have alternative schemes.

b. This relates to the age exemptions. The $1,000 pension exemption would be characterized similarly, although it is not indexed. The various provincial tax credits for the elderly are excluded from the table, as are such things as free health care, etc.

c. A better distinction between public-sector pension funds is whether they fall under the category of trusteed funds and, therefore, are similar to private-sector funds or whether they are consolidated revenue funds, which are not "funded." For Ontario, the former would include the teachers' superannuation funds and OMERS (Ontario Municipal Employees Retirement System). These are essentially funded plans.

- *best earnings plans*, which apply the benefit credited each year to the members' average earnings for a specified period of highest earnings, e.g., the highest five of the last ten years of service;
- *career average plans*, which apply the unit of benefit credited each year to the members' earnings in that year; and
- *flat benefit plans*, which specify a dollar amount of pension to be credited for each year of service.

Money purchase plans specify the annual contribution of the employer and employee. They do not define the pension benefits, which are determined by the amounts contributed and by the investment performance of the pension fund.

A significant feature of all pension plans is that contributions (both employer and employee) are treated as a deduction for tax purposes. Moreover, accretions to pension assets associated with investment returns under a money purchase plan or increased entitlements under a defined benefit plan are also eligible for tax deferral until these funds are taken into retirement income. In terms of other important features of occupational plans the following excerpt from the OEC position paper is instructive:

> [S]everal further concepts need to be introduced. Contributions to a pension are said to be locked in if they cannot be withdrawn after a certain date. Normally, locking-in occurs once an employee has attained a certain age or completed a certain period of service. A pension is said to be vested if on termination of employment an employee has a right to his accrued pension. Normally, the employee acquires the right to the employer's past contributions as well. Typically, vesting is associated with locking-in. Thus, vested benefits usually take the form of a deferred annuity commencing at retirement age. Statutory vesting occurs when the employee meets the age and/or service conditions set out in the pension benefits legislation (in Ontario, currently age 45 and 10 years of service). A pension is said to be portable when an individual, on severing employment, can take the pension with him to his new employment or convert it into an RRSP. (Ontario Economic Council, 1983a, pp. 32–34)

The issues relating to occupational pension plans that are playing a major role in the current debate are increasing coverage; increasing portability; and moving toward earlier vesting.

RRSPs (registered retirement savings plans) are usually viewed as part of the private pension system. They have the same tax privileges as a registered pension plan, and they are available for annual contributions from individuals without occupational pension plans of up to 20 percent of income or $5,500, whichever is lower. Members of an occupational plan are limited to an annual RRSP contribution of $3,500 less the employee contributions for that year. RRSPs can be self-administered or managed by a financial institution. Essentially, they are individually owned money purchase plans. RRSPs differ from vested occupational plans in that the former are not locked in: they can be drawn into taxable income at any time.

The public pension system consists of a variety of instruments and arrangements, as outlined in rows 3 through 7 of Table 8-3. Old-age security (OAS) is the universal federal old-age pension. The guaranteed income supplement (GIS) is the federal income-tested top-up to OAS. Many provinces also have income-tested benefits for the elderly. Row 5 of Table 8-3 details the characteristics of Ontario's supplementary benefit to the elderly (GAINS). Row 7 of Table 8-3 focusses on the Canada and Quebec Pension Plans. The CPP/QPP is a compulsory program for all Canadian workers which is roughly similar to a defined benefit plan; it is funded in part by a payroll tax of 3.6 percent, split evenly between employee and employer.

In 1982 expenditures under the public pension system amounted to roughly $11 billion. Slightly over one-half of these benefits were in the form of OAS payments and slightly under one-quarter in each of GIS and CPP.

It is clear that the overall pension plan system extends well beyond the confines of what we would normally refer to as the financial sector. However, it is equally clear that the pension system absorbs an enormous amount of personal savings. Moreover, the manner in which the pension system is organized has dramatic implications on capital markets. Table 8-4 focusses on certain capital market aspects of the present pension system. As of 1981, pension fund assets totalled $137 billion. In terms of asset holdings, occupational plans in the non-government sector had 60 percent of their assets invested in debt instruments and 40 percent in ownership-type assets. In the CPP 100 percent of assets were invested in non-marketable government debt (provincial bond issues at concessionary rates). In spite of the fact that the accumulated assets of pension funds were, as noted above, $137 billion, the accumulated liabilities arising form the operations of the CPP, QPP, and some under-funded government occupational plans were even larger — $142 billion. What this means in practice is that the contribution rates will soon have to be raised in order to provide for these unfunded liabilities. In technical terms, the CPP and QPP will soon be put on a "pay-as-you-go basis" — contribution rates will rise in order to fund the benefit payouts. This is, of course, the manner in which the present OAS system is financed. In effect it is an intergenerational transfer from the young to the old, and in terms of the claims on the future generations (the last column in Table 8–4) the amounts involved for the OAS are again at least as large as the total shown in the table.

Pensions and the Division of Powers

While it is probably correct to say that the regulation of occupational pensions is a shared field, the responsibility for establishing pension standards governing such plans rests with the provinces. These stan-

TABLE 8-4 1981 Pension Fund Asset Distribution (Based on Values Rounded to the Nearest $Billion)

	Debt Type Assets (%)				Ownership Type Assets (%) (stocks and real estate)	Overall Amount $billions	Claims on Future Generations
	Non-Govt.	Govt. Market-able	Govt. Non-Market-able	Total	Total		
Employer Plans							
Private sector	40	20	0	60	40	30	0
Public sector I[a]	35	31	17	83	17	29	0
Public sector II[b]	0	0	100	100	0	27	12
Universal Plans							
CPP	0	0	100	100	0	20	95
QPP	0	83	0	83	17	6	35
RRSPs	84	4	0	88	12	25	0
Total						137	142

Source: Ontario Economic Council, 1983a, Table 1.
a. Trusteed plans (Crown corporations, health and educational, provincial and municipal).
b. Consolidated revenue plans (most federal government plans).

dards deal with such issues as vesting, portability, solvency, investment and disclosure. Most provinces now have legislation covering the regulation of private pension plans, usually in the form of pension benefits standards acts. There are several avenues through which the federal government also influences the private pension system. First, under the federal Pension Benefits Standards Act, Ottawa regulates pensions in those sectors of the economy that fall under its jurisdiction, such as banking and interprovincial transportation. Second, pension plans in provinces which have not as yet enacted pension legislation must conform to the federal regulations. Third, the federal government (under the provisions of the federal Income Tax Act) establishes guidelines for plans seeking to qualify for the tax deductibility of contributions and for the exemption of investment income.

As the Ontario Economic Council (1983a) has pointed out, this joint responsibility creates a tension between pressures for change and pressures for uniformity of pension regulation across the country.[12] While the provinces are free to alter their own pension regulations as they see fit, their ability to do so in practice is considerably constrained:

> For one thing the mobility of labour and capital across the country creates pressures for broadly similar standards. For another, businesses that operate on a nationwide basis strenuously oppose regional variations in pension standards that would create administrative complications for their own plans. (Ontario Economic Council, 1983a, p. 202)

It is interesting to contrast this situation with that for securities markets. A move by the Montreal Stock Exchange to allow trust companies to have the privileges of brokers would encourage the shift of trust company activity to Montreal and at the same time place intense pressure on the OSC and the TSE to follow suit. However, an innovating move in the pension reform area by Quebec, say to require immediate vesting of occupational plans, would cause employers to shy away from the provinces, thereby placing strong pressures on Quebec to fall back in line with the other province. This being the case, reform in the pension area (where reform is defined as increasing portability, shortening the period for vesting, and the like) probably requires some federal initiative or a concerted move on the part of the key provinces. In other words, the fragmented jurisdiction in the pension area tends to lead to institutional paralysis.

The provinces helped in 1974 by creating the Canadian Association of Pension Supervisory Authorities (CAPSA), which has contributed to harmonization across provinces and provided a lead in pension reform. However, the principal catalyst in the current move toward pension reform was the Parliamentary Committee on Pension Reform which conducted hearings across the country and produced its report in the fall of 1983. While there will always be disagreement about the details of various reform measures that are needed in several areas, it is apparent that there is a genuine consensus with respect to some aspects of pension reform. Yet a decentralized regulatory system might have a very difficult time initiating such measures.

RRSPs and RPAs

RRSPs are probably best viewed as a federal instrument, deriving from the powers of the Income Tax Act. Hence, the dollar limits of RRSPs, their withdrawal features, their spousal aspects are all defined in the income tax legislation. The proposed Registered Pension Account (RPA), discussed in former finance minister Marc Lalonde's 1984 budget and previously in the report of the parliamentary pension committee, would obtain its constitutional grounding from the Income Tax Act. The provinces with their pension regulatory function would presumably have some say as to the types of institutions that would oversee these accounts, the characteristics of the RPA portfolios as they related to solvency issues, and the manner in which RPAs would interface with existing occupational plans. Nonetheless, the RPA (which is essentially an RRSP into which both employers and employees can contribute) does represent a novel pension device and one through which the federal government should be able to exercise considerable influence over the existing pension arrangements.

There is one constitutional wrinkle that must not be overlooked, however. The provinces also have a constitutional right to be in the income tax area. As stressed on many previous occasions, Quebec has its own personal income tax. Hence, this province would have to enact its own RPA (and, indeed, its own RRSP) provisions in order that the treatment would apply to the provincial tax sphere. Two recent initiatives from the province of Quebec bring home this very point. The first relates to the Quebec Stock Savings Plan which allows taxpayers to deduct up to $15,000 for provincial tax purposes for purchases of new issues of Quebec-based companies. This feature will be dealt with in more detail in Chapter 9 on the internal common market, since the characteristics of the program are such that it represents an impediment to the free flow of capital across provincial boundaries. For present purposes, however, the essential point is that the tax treatment accorded this investment is similar to that accorded RRSPs, in the sense that the stock purchase price is deductible. Indeed, it is more generous, since it is never taxed, i.e., it is more like a RHOSP (registered home ownership savings plan). The second point is more speculative. It relates to a recent newspaper article to the effect that the forthcoming Quebec white paper on taxation may recommend a move to an expenditure tax for the province. The characteristics of an expenditure tax is that all (or most) savings will be treated like RRSPs or pension contributions — i.e., they are deductible for tax purposes. Under such a system, pension contributions no longer receive special tax treatment and if pension contributions are "locked in" they may end up being rather poor substitutes for other types of savings which would not be locked in.

CPP/QPP

By far the most complicated pension system from a jurisdictional point of view is the Canada Pension Plan.[13] While the CPP was created by an act of the federal Parliament, any amendments to the CPP must be approved by two-thirds of the provinces with at least two-thirds of the population. This sets up a series of multiple vetoes over the CPP, as noted in Chapter 6. First, the federal government can block any changes to the plan; it would simply refuse to amend the act. Second, any four provinces can block a proposed amendment. Third, because Ontario has one-third of the population it has a veto on any CPP changes. Finally, and certainly somewhat anomalously, the province of Quebec is included in the rules governing amendments to the CPP, despite having its own public pension system (the QPP). Thus Quebec and one other province (to make up one-third of the population) can veto any CPP amendment even though the other eight provinces and the federal government might be in favour of the change. These provisions were embodied in the legislated framework for the CPP/QPP. The provinces' powers with respect to the CPP actually extend beyond those listed above. The act setting up the CPP allows any province to opt out of the CPP and to establish its own plan. Only Quebec has exercised this option.

The characteristics of the CPP/QPP have no doubt had a substantial influence on the way that the pension system has developed over the years. As Banting has pointed out, the federal Guaranteed Income Supplement (GIS) was introduced as a transitional component of old-age support in order to act as a bridge between the level of income that the then current elderly would get in comparison with the amount they would receive when the CPP matured. The expectation was the GIS would be phased out as the CPP matured. The opposite has happened. Partly because of the institutional and political barriers to change associated with the CPP and occupational plans and partly because of the features of GIS (e.g., its ability to target income), GIS is now more appropriately viewed as an alternative (a barrier) to certain changes in both the CPP and occupational plans.

There are two further items that should be noted in the context of the jurisdictional characteristics of pensions. First, it may be the case that a generous interpretation of section 121 of the Constitution or the mobility provisions of the new Charter of Rights and Freedoms would transfer some increased control over pensions to the federal government, or at least force further restrictions on the provinces' actions in this area. For example, the absence of full portability of occupational plans may inhibit labour mobility sufficiently that the courts would require some alterations in powers or in the existing legislation. The second is related: Would an alternative division of powers with respect to pensions be preferable? In my view the answer is far from clear. What is clear is that we would likely have a different pension system today if there were a different allocation of responsibilities. For example, many observers believed that the federal government wanted to double the CPP (or establish a new CPP) with initial contributions well in excess of initial payouts so as to generate a "fund" which could then be taken into the current budgetary and spending process. It is probably true that the existing pension arrangements made this difficult, if not impossible, to accomplish. Is this a bad thing?

On the positive side, the country has just gone through a multi-year intensive debate on pensions and their role in the economy. One of the surprising features of this process is that it has led to a broad consensus with respect to many aspects of pension reform, and as a result our pension system will undergo substantial improvement over the next few years. To this extent, at any rate, the country has been able to overcome the inertia in the system that arose from the jurisdictional overlap. It is not obvious that the measures that will result are inferior to those that would have arisen under an altered division of powers.

In general, however, a type of institutional or constitutional determinism may exist in some policy areas: the types of policies and processes available for the job at hand are constrained by the framework within which decisions must be taken. Banting (1984) makes the point quite cogently in terms of the pension area:

> The decision rules which govern any reform process are critical to the kinds of decisions which emerge from it. The rules which determine the way in which authority is shared, and the formal procedures through which policy must be formulated, act as a set of constraints on decision makers. Such constraints are never neutral. They inevitably condition the ability of different interests to influence policy decisions smoothing the way for some and raising obstacles for others. They make some outcomes more difficult to achieve, and others easier. (p. 189)

While not attempting to dispute this claim, we should expect policy formulating to be somewhat more complicated in a federation than in a unitary state. Moreover, some of the major achievements of our federation, such as the institution of federal-provincial conferences and perhaps even the equalization program, may well have their rational in finding avenues for sorting our policy-making in the context of divided jurisdiction.

The concluding section of this discussions of pensions focusses on the problem that has arisen in connection with the actions of the Caisse de dépots, the investment arm of the QPP.

Bill S-31

The Role of the Caisse

With the rapid growth of pension assets, several public and private sector pension funds have amassed large pools of capital. Quebec's Caisse de dépots et placement is probably the largest such fund. It was established by the Lesage Government in 1965 to invest and administer the assets of the QPP. It now receives deposits from other sources including the Government and Public Employees Payment Plan and the Quebec government's automobile insurance plan (Tupper, 1983, p. 5). Illustrative of the Caisse's prowess is the following:

> [C]urrent assets [are] slightly more than $16 billion. Of this total, $3.5 billion are invested in the common stocks of Canadian corporations. The Caisse's portfolio now boasts holdings in such major firms as Alcan Ltd. ($271 million), Bell Canada ($244 million), Canadian Pacific Ltd. ($258 million) and Domtar Inc. ($88 million). By industrial sector, the Caisse has invested $704.8 million, $547.7 million, $375.4 million and $263.5 million in financial institutions, mining and metals, oil and natural gas, and transportation respectively. (Tupper, 1983, p. 5)

In spite of these holdings, the regulations governing the Caisse do not allow equity investments to exceed 30 percent of the common stock of a single firm or, cumulatively, 30 percent of the total assets of the Caisse. These regulations are not very different from those in place in the other provinces governing the investment portfolios of pension funds. For example, Ontario's Pension Benefit Act, which applies to occupational plans, stipulates that no one investment can constitute more than 10 percent of the total fund value and that no fund can hold more than 30 percent of the common shares of a single corporation.

At this juncture it is instructive to focus on the Alberta Heritage Savings Trust Fund (AHSTF). While it is not a pension fund in the traditional sense, it does nonetheless serve as a "rainy day" fund for Alberta. The assets of the Heritage Fund are currently in the range of $11 billion. Recently, the Alberta government established a Commercial Investment Division for the AHSTF which will allow it to invest in corporate stock with a view to enhancing the yield of the fund. The regulations pertaining to this commercial investment division stipulate that "the investment in equities is being undertaken using a passive, balanced approach with stock holdings representing a broad range of Canadian industrial sectors and public companies" (Alberta Heritage Savings Trust Fund, 1982). To ensure that the AHSTF will remain a "passive" investor the legislation will not allow the fund to acquire more than 5 percent of the shares outstanding in any company. In this respect it differs from the Caisse and from other pension funds as well. However, Heritage Fund assets can be used to make investments that will strengthen or diversify the economy of Alberta while providing a reasonable (not necessarily a market) rate of return. There is no limit on the percent of the overall portfolio that can be used for this purpose. Hence, the potential does exist for the Heritage Fund to be an instrument of provincial development policy, even to the point of engaging in pro-Alberta (beggar-thy-neighbour) activities. The criticism levelled against the Caisse is exactly the same: from its original role as a passive investor of pension assets, the Caisse is seen by many as moving from this "trustee role" to take an active role in corporate management in industries deemed to be in the interest of the province.

Two recent initiatives by the Caisse have fostered this concern:

> The first controversy stems from the Caisse's view that Crown corporations are not subject to federal and provincial company law and securities legislation unless they are specifically mentioned therein. Much to Ottawa's chagrin, the Quebec Superior Court supported the Caisse's argument when it ruled in August 1982 that the Caisse was indeed immune from certain provisions of the Canada Business Corporations Act. After this decision the federal government was alarmed by its diminished capacity to scrutinize certain of the Caisse's activities. Similarly, the Caisse's position that it need not follow Ontario law governing "insider trading" led the Ontario Securities Commission to ban it from trading in Ontario. Such debates focussed attention on the hitherto neglected question of the applicability of securities legislation and company law to Crown agencies. A second source of concern is the Caisse's view that it should now have representation on the boards of those corporations in which it has a major stake. In this vein, the Caisse has recently sought and won seats on the boards of eleven major corporations including Noranda, Domtar, Gas Metropolitan, and Provigo. (Tupper, 1983, pp. 6–7)

The event that triggered federal action with respect to the Caisse was its intention to increase its share position in Canadian Pacific beyond 10 percent and to have representation on CP's board of directors. On November 4, 1982, the Senate of Canada introduced Bill S-31, the Corporate Shareholding Limitation Act.

Details of Bill S-31

The important provisions of Bill S-31 can be summarized as follows:

- No provincial government can hold more than 10 percent of the voting shares of any transportation company involved in interprovincial or international energy pipelines, railways, shipping, trucking, bus companies and commodity pipelines.
- The legislation is not retroactive, so that Ontario's investment in Suncor and Alberta's PWA purchase, for example, do not come under the law. However, if a provincial agency which already holds 10 percent of shares attempts to increase its holdings, it loses the right to vote any of its shares.

- If a provincial agency owns less than 10 percent of a company's shares as of November 3, 1982, and thereafter increases its holdings beyond 10 percent it will only be able to vote those shares held before November 3. More importantly, if a provincial agency acquires its shares after November 3, 1982, it cannot vote the shares.

Although it was the Caisse that triggered this legislation, the provisions of the bill apply to any provincial agency and not just pension funds. One of the underlying reasons for the legislation is related to the division of powers. Interprovincial transportation falls in the federal domain. Hence the provinces cannot regulate interprovincial or international transportation. However, the federal government felt that the provinces (specifically Quebec, via the Caisse) might attempt to bypass the Constitution by influencing interprovincial transportation via the ownership route. A second federal concern related to the free flow of goods and services across provincial boundaries. Ownership might be used to induce corporations to favour provincial interests, and thereby balkanize the internal common market. More generally, Ottawa was also fearful of a growing provincial ownership presence in the economy.

While these issues are obviously related, they can be dealt with separately. The ownership concern refers basically to the degree of equity ownership that can or should be held by provincial governments. But why not include the federal government here as well? Ottawa has embarked on a series of ownership ventures — Petro-Canada, Canadair, de Havilland, and the Canada Development Corporation (CDC), not to mention the bail-out of Chrysler, Massey-Ferguson and Dome. In what sense is provincial socialism, as it were, more problematical than federal socialism? No doubt we can make a case that it might be, particularly if the intent is to coerce companies to meet the needs of a specific province or region at the expense of other provinces or regions. I do not want to focus on this point here. It will be dealt with in Chapter 9 in the context of the internal common market as but one more example of the recent federal initiatives to constrain the provinces and at the same time ensure that none of the restraints are binding on itself. There is, however, one aspect of this private sector/public sector trade-off that should be raised. This relates to section 125 of the Constitution which in effect states that the Crown cannot tax the Crown. In practice it implies that there is an incentive for public sector ownership of industry, since taxes to the other level of government are not required. Thus, if a province acquires ownership of an enterprise, Ottawa will no longer get its share of the profits. This certainly holds if the company is overseen by a minister and it may hold as well for ownership at greater arm's length. In my view, there is a need to rethink section 125. In effect, it represents an incentive for public ownership. It seems to me that rents, interest and profits should be treated in a similar fashion whether they accrue in the private or public sectors. It is interesting to note that the recent Parliamentary Task Force on Federal-Provincial Fiscal Arrangements (1981) also registered its concern with respect to this issue:

> Should provincial or federal Crown corporations become more common, governments may at some point have to consider the application of section 125 of the BNA Act. An amendment to the Constitution permitting taxation of Crown corporations may be appropriate. Alternatively, the federal and provincial governments could argue for reciprocal taxation of Crown corporations. No doubt both courses of action would be highly controversial. Nevertheless, the implications of a potentially large expansion in the number of Crown corporations would seem to be a matter for federal-provincial and public discussion. (p. 192)

I heartily endorse this view. Not only does this existing framework have the potential for influencing the allocation of capital, it also corroborates an underlying message of the study: that there are indeed policy areas where the existing division of powers can influence economic activity.

To return to the issue at hand — the role of pension funds in the capital markets — the prevailing attitude with respect to pension investments is that the pension funds ought to be passive participants, overseeing a trustee relationship rather than embarking on an ownership and management relationship. It may well be that the 30 percent limit for ownership of widely held enterprise is too high in the sense that 30 percent may imply control of the company. Several solutions are possible here. One is to reduce the ownership and voting limits for publicly held companies for all pension funds, private and public. Another is to allow 30 percent ownership but to restrict voting to 10 percent, again to be applied to all pension funds. One of the problems with Bill S-31 is that it focusses the issue too narrowly — to control the investment policy of the Caisse but not that of other pension funds appears to me to be inappropriate.

The other underlying rationale for Bill S-31 has to do with the constitutional implications — provinces short-circuiting the Constitution via ownership in those areas that fall under federal control. A more even-handed approach might be to include a provision which would also limit Ottawa's ability to obtain control of enterprises that function within the provinces' constitutional ambit. The appropriate mechanism here might be a federal-provincial code of economic conduct with respect to the functioning of the internal common market. This and alternative approaches to securing the internal common market will be dealt with in Chapter 9.

Bill S-31 died on the order paper. It may or may not be resurrected. If it is, it will surely be in a different form, since some of the implications of the earlier bill were peculiar, to say the least. For example, if a business enterprise were to purchase an interprovincial transportation company this would pre-empt any move by a provincial agency from acquiring voting shares in the company, even if the main business of the company was not in the transportation area. More importantly, underlying Bill S-31 were several very critical issues that deserve a hearing in their own right rather than being forced into the narrow framework of the bill. Among these are:

- What ought to be the balance between public and private ownership of enterprise in the economy? Bill S-31 implied that expanding provincial ownership is unacceptable presumably because provinces as share-holders will not take the national interest into account, but that central government ownership is fully acceptable. This is too narrow a con-ception of the problem which, it seems to me, ought to focus on the desirability of expanding the role of government at any level in the economic management of the economy. The obvious next step might be to design acceptable criteria for public participation whether fed-eral or provincial. Included in this process should be an investigation of provisions like section 125 which gives public participation prefer-ential treatment vis-à-vis private sector ownership. This subject will not be addressed in any detail in this study although Chapter 9 will present some evidence relating to how the constitutions of some other federalisms put limits on the role of government in the economy.
- As pension fund assets accumulate, there is a growing issue relating to the degree of financial control that these funds should be able to wield. (The newly proposed pension device, the RPA, may serve to diffuse the power of these funds since this new account is designed to be administered by the employee. Indeed, over the long term it may well serve to involve most Canadians in an equity role in the enterprises of the economy.) Bill S-31 was very inadequate in this regard since it was, in effect, singling out only the Caisse among pension funds for restric-tive treatment. Any limitation on the degree of financial control by pension funds ought to apply across the board to federal, provincial and private funds.
- The issue of circumventing federal constitutional authority by means of direct ownership is more complex. To the extent that the purpose in such ownership is to subvert the workings of the internal common market, then one way of handling the problem is via a code of federal-provincial conduct (see Chapter 9) or, alternatively, entrenching a common market provision in the Constitution. To the extent that the purpose of voting participation and representation on the boards of such companies is to have a say in national transportation policy, the issue is even more complicated. Obviously the federal government must preserve this sphere of influence. However, Ottawa seldom

thinks twice about utilizing its expenditure power to influence, let alone dictate, provincial policies with respect to responsibilities that are, constitutionally, in the domain of the provinces.

What is clear, it seems to me, is that Bill S-31 was inappropriate in the sense that it may have generated precisely the wrong sorts of reactions from several provinces: the AHSTF may be induced to invest in a wide range of equities in anticipation of a further bout of restrictive federal legislation. While the issues underlying the bill were important and remain so, Bill S-31 itself simply did not provide the appropriate context within which these issues could be addressed.

Conclusion

The purpose of this chapter was to focus on the operation of the financial markets in terms of whether or not an alternative division of powers would facilitate both efficiency and economic management. The most intriguing feature of the market for securities, both primary and secondary, is just how different the Canadian situation is from that in the United States. Our system is essentially decentralized; theirs is close to being entirely centralized. Obviously, both systems are viable. The question is whether or not Canada would be better served if we moved closer to the U.S. system. it is probably true that the Supreme Court would accept a greater federal presence. The up-side of such a move might be greater harmonization and a regulatory system that would be able to fill the "voids" that result because the provinces cannot legislate extraprovincially. The down-side effects might be a restriction on regional diversity (since the regional economies are very different, and some of the regional economies are very different, and some of the regional stock markets reflect the industrial composition of the region), a two-tier layer of regulations, and a rekindling of federal-provincial rivalry. In addition, the possibility would exist under federal legislation for the country to turn inwards and restrict the transnational listing of shares. This latter event would be most unlikely to occur under the present decentralized regulatory system.

On balance, I come down in favour of retaining the status quo, partly because the system has worked reasonably well. The fact that Ottawa will always be around to exercise its role if things go awry provides an important lever over the actions of the various regulatory agencies. The decentralized structure ensures that innovation and competition, both domestic and international, will characterize the system. The recognition that the federal government has the constitutional power to intervene tends to ensure that the provincial regulators strive toward harmonization of regulation wherever possible.

The second part of the chapter focussed more broadly on the structure of the financial intermediation sector in Canada. Traditionally, the regulation of this sector adhered (and essentially still does) to the notion that the four pillars ought to remain intact or compartmentalized. It seems to me that technology is quickly rendering this approach passé. Moreover, consumers will demand that the system integrates. The real issue is not if these regulatory walls crumble, but how they crumble. The argument for enhanced federal control in this area is that it might expedite any decision with respect to the way in which the system should integrate. The down-side cost of a greater federal presence is not very different from the potential cost of an increased federal role in the securities area — only with federal control will it be possible to maintain the compartmentalization of the pillars. However, I do not think that the federal government would take such a protectionist approach.

My conclusion with respect to the four pillars is that the time has come for a joint federal-provincial commission to devise the guidelines by which the system will be allowed to integrate. In my view, the functional approach holds the most promise, one where markets, not institutions, are regulated. However, only when Canada has come to grips with this policy issue does it make sense to question whether it is the provinces or Ottawa that should increase their regulatory authority. The underlying goal should not be to protect vested interests but rather to ensure that in the 1990s Canada will be in the marketplace with world-class financial institutions.

There are at least two lessons to be derived from the above analysis of the pension industry. The first is that the institutional and political regulatory environments may influence the types of policy decisions that result. This is a general observation that no doubt applies in a more global context. Put differently, there may be an institutional and constitutional determinism that obtains across a wide range of policy-making. I have no doubt that this is true over the short run, but I suspect that market forces dominate over the intermediate and long run. Nonetheless, the analysis of pensions suggests that the existing division of powers does influence the types of policy choices that are available in the short term.

The second lesson deriving from the analysis of pensions relates to Bill S-31 and the attempt by the Senate of Canada to restrain the activities of the Caisse. The issue at stake is very complicated, but, at the risk of gross oversimplification, I shall make a few points. First, it is appropriate to be concerned with the role of pension funds in terms of their ability to dictate the direction of the economy. I find no problem with ensuring that such funds act as "trustee" rather than "manager" in terms of equity investment, nor with regulations that would limit the ability of pension funds to vote no more than 10 percent of their holdings in any corporation. But this must apply to all pension funds and not just the Caisse, as happened with Bill S-31. Second, it is important that measures be instituted to ensure that governments (federal or provincial) cannot distort the free flow of goods, services and factors across provincial boundaries. If the motive of the Caisse in acquiring greater voting participation in CP was to influence corporate policy in the direction of serving Quebec's interests, then this is to be deplored. The question is one of how best to regulate such violations to the internal common market. Various alternatives will be suggested in Chapter 9. While the federal government might be allowed some leeway in this area, it is important to recognize that Ottawa too can distort the interprovincial flows of goods and factors. Hence, a code of economic conduct must also include some limitations on the freedom of Ottawa to embark on regionally protective policies.

The third issue that arises in connection with the actions of the Caisse and the implications of Bill S-31 relates to the role of the public sector in the management or control of enterprise. We need to reconsider section 125 of the Constitution, which provides an incentive for public rather than private ownership of enterprise. One approach would involve incorporating a provision for the economic rights of individuals in the Charter of Rights and Freedoms.

Finally, and more generally, it may well be that we are prone to put too much emphasis on both the set of regulations and who does the regulating. I believe that there is a certain inevitability as to what the structure of the financial system will be like in the 1990s. It will have more to do with the computer revolution, with the demands of consumers, and with the evolution of the financial industry internationally than it will with the particular set of regulations Canada puts in place today or whether these regulations are federal or provincial. This is long-run economic determinism, as distinct from the institutional or constitutional determinism that I argued earlier might hold sway over the short term. In this perspective, the dominant factor will be whether the nation as a whole maintains an overall economic climate that is inviting and exciting as a place to innovate and do business.

Chapter 9

The Canadian Economic Union

Earlier chapters have made reference on occasion to the concept of a Canadian economic union (CEU) or an internal common market (ICM). For example, in Chapter 5 on fiscal policy, the "code of good tax conduct" was a CEU-type recommendation in the sense that it limited provincial tax systems from becoming instruments of "province-building." In Chapter 6 on social policy, the concern that interprovincial migrants not be subjected to long residency requirements to qualify for services such as a health or social assistance was also a recommendation for enhancing the CEU.

The purpose of this chapter[1] is to focus in considerably more detail on the CEU issue. In the minds of most Canadians the term CEU has become synonymous with interprovincial barriers to mobility. Part of the analysis that follows will attempt to place these high-profile barriers in the broader (and more appropriate) context of the whole range of issues, economic as well as political, that are associated with the CEU.

Any consideration of a Canadian economic union also concerns the division of powers. Analysts frequently point out that the pursuit of a full-blown internal common market is likely to be very centralizing in the sense that almost anything that the provinces do can be construed as an impediment or barrier to the free flow of goods or factors. This is especially true if the instrumentality for securing the CEU is an increase in a federal head of power, such as the "trade and commerce" power, section 91(2). However, it is important to recognize that a full-blown CEU can also be very decentralizing (in the sense of giving powers to citizens) if the economic union is secured via an iron-clad bill of "economic rights." Perhaps it is inappropriate to refer to his situation as decentralizing, since even though power is transferred to the people the ultimate arbiter is the Supreme Court (a federal institution). In any event, in this case both levels of government would be constrained, and the transfer of powers would be away from governments and toward the people.

Indeed, it is this very interaction between a CEU and the division of powers that has made the CEU such a contentious issue. The appropriate way to proceed with respect to ensuring a CEU might well be to attempt to disentangle the two concepts: to decide on the division of powers issue on its own merits and then to attempt to enhance the extent and scope of the CEU.

The chapter proceeds as follows. The section outlining the economic and political arguments for a CEU is followed by a section which identifies and classifies some of these internal market barriers. The next section focusses on some of the underlying economic issues as they relate to the CEU. Concepts like the theory of the second best and the openness of the economy are brought to bear on the rationale for and severity of ICM distortions. The following sections try to estimate the costs of CEU barriers and the interaction between the CEU and the division of powers. The recent constitutional debates and the attempt to enshrine the CEU in the Constitution are dealt with in some detail. Included in the analysis is a brief description of the economic union provisions in other federal constitutions. Despite the apparent failure of the initiative to enshrine the CEU in the Constitution, the next section shows that the existing constitutional provisions may yet come to be applied in a way that enhances the CEU. The final section focusses on some non-constitutional ways of freeing the internal common market, with emphasis on federal-provincial pacts or compacts. The conclusion summarizes the chapter and ends with a compromise proposal for approaching the CEU issue.

It is useful to define what is meant by an economic union. The federal government's "pink paper," *Securing the Economic Union in the Constitution*, contains the following definition:

> An economic union is an entity within which goods, services, labour, capital and enterprise can move freely, that is, without being subject to fiscal and other institutional barriers, and which is endowed with institutions capable of harmonizing the broad internal policies which affect economic development and of implementing common policies with regard to the entity's external economic relations. (Chrétien, 1980, p. 1)

While this is an acceptable definition for a Canadian economic union, the principal emphasis in this chapter will be on the mobility aspects of the definition, with lesser emphasis on harmonization and almost no reference at all to external economic relations.

Economic and Political Rationales

The Economic Rationale

The economic arguments for a CEU are, on the surface, quite straightforward. Canada already has one of the smallest domestic markets in the industrialized world. To fragment the market by erecting barriers to goods and factor mobility and/or by engaging in protectionist policies at the provincial or federal level is to run the serious risk of generating substantial inefficiency and undermining our international competitiveness. These costs relate essentially to the inability to reap the gains from the division of labour and the specialization of production as the market becomes more fragmented. Specifically, the federal background paper includes the following as part of the costs of fragmentation:

- higher supply costs, fragmentation and stunted growth for firms, and diseconomies of scale which enhance import penetration and reduce international competitiveness of domestic production;
- diversion of trade to foreign suppliers, when fragmentation results in neither in-province or out-of-province suppliers being able to service provincial markets on a competitive basis;
- lower incomes and fewer employment opportunities for residents of all provinces;
- higher burdens upon national and provincial taxpayers, due to higher cost of public procurement and lower tax yields. (Chrétien, 1980, pp. 5–6; Safarian, 1974, Part I)

In other words, the economic rationale has to do with increasing the size of the national economic pie. While most of the remainder of this chapter will focus on internal barriers and how they might or might not affect the size of the pie, there is one important aspect that merits immediate discussion: the way in which a CEU relates to the economic theory of federalism.

The idea behind the economic theory of federalism is that if citizens of different provinces have different preferences for public goods, a decentralized form of government offers the potential for greater economic welfare by providing a range of locally produced public goods that reflects these varying preferences. Put somewhat differently, welfare will not be maximized if, in the face of varying regional preferences, all public goods are provided centrally. Subnational governments are viewed as providing alternative bundles of public services and citizens can choose their province of residence ("voting by foot," as it were) in accordance with their preferences for these various bundles. This introduces into the government sphere some of the flexibility and competition that characterizes the operation of decentralized markets. The experimentation and innovation that will inevitably result from the decentralized supply of these bundles of public goods and services "may thus promote both static and dynamic efficiency in the provision of public goods and services" (Oates, 1972, p. 12).

How can we reconcile an internal common market with the economic theory of federalism? At one extreme, they are probably incompatible. Richard Musgrave recognized this long ago:

The very purpose of fiscal federalism . . . inevitably leads to differences in the levels of taxation and public services. The resulting differentiation in tax levels may interfere with the most efficient allocation of resources and location of industry for the region [nation] as a whole; such is the cost of political subdivision. (Musgrave, 1959, pp. 179–80)

The point at issue is that if citizens' preferences do vary provincially, then maximizing national output (through, for example, reaping economies of scale in the production of centrally provided public goods) would result in a fall in welfare. In other words, maximizing the welfare of citizens, which must be at the heart of the economic theory of federalism, need not imply maximizing national output (Melvin, 1983). While this is an important theoretical point that must be kept in mind, the bulk of the analysis, particularly in those sections focussing on the costs of barriers, will be cast in terms of output or efficiency.

The Political Rationale

There are also powerful political arguments in support of an internal common market:

To be a citizen of Canada must be a dynamic reality rather than a static abstraction, a reality that extends beyond the realm of political and legal institutions to the vital aspects of one's material existence. . . . To the extent compatible with federalism, this basic equality of all citizens must apply to economic affairs, under provincial law as well as under federal law. Wherever they may have been born or have chosen to reside in the country, Canadians should be free to take up residence, to acquire and hold property, to gain a livelihood, to invest their savings, to sell their products and purchase their supplies in any province or territory of Canada, provided they abide by the laws of general application of that province or territory. (Chrétien, 1980, p. 2)

Or, in the same vein, "the freest possible access to the national market should be inherent to Canadian citizenship" (p. 2).

Even though I shall later argue that some of the common market distortions, such as the National Energy Program and the tariff, generate costs, in terms of lost national output, that dwarf provincial purchasing preferences and the like, it is nonetheless true that these "visible" provincial barriers are the focus of the political arguments for a CEU.

Political Legitimacy
Moreover, if, following Prichard and Benedickson (1983), we consider the notion of "political legitimacy," it is again the provincial and not the federal barriers which become the object of concern. Provincially erected barriers are more pernicious, the argument goes, because the out-of-province residents who are discriminated against have no forum in

which to register their complaints. Nor are the provincially elected officials accountable to these injured third parties.

In contrast, Prichard and Benedickson note, "federal interventions, despite any apparent defects, possess a presumptive legitimacy derived from the political process which generated them: they were adopted by the federal government acting within its constitutional authority and potentially accountable to the entire electorate" (p. 49). However, it is not entirely clear what to make of this notion. Even Prichard and Benedickson point out that the current regional disaffection with the federal government and the gross imbalances in the regional representation of federal parties in Parliament tend to undermine the concept somewhat. In what follows, I shall basically ignore this issue, though I do not dismiss it.

Identifying Internal Common Market Distortions

The framework I have adopted (but which is by no means value-free) is that a CEU distortion is defined as a policy or program that violates regional Pareto-optimality — i.e., any policy which alters the terms-of-trade, the labour-leisure trade-off, the wage-rental ratio and the like on a regional basis comes under the umbrella of a distortion. Thus, a distortion or a CEU barrier or impediment will reduce national output and efficiency (with the earlier caveat in mind with respect to welfare). In some sense this loads the dice against barriers, since the focus is on their economic costs and not on any benefits that Canadians may associate with these policies. Nonetheless, this is the only way to proceed, since in order to assess the economic costs of the various distortions we need a benchmark, and any other benchmark would be less general and more arbitrary. However, many of the policies that are identified below as CEU distortions are near and dear to the hearts of many Canadians. The thrust of the analysis is not to argue that these policies are inappropriate (after all, they are the result of political decisions) but rather to recognize that they have costs and to compare their costs to other barriers.

Federal Barriers

There are, of course, several ways to classify these distortions. One approach is to distinguish between those policies which are distorting in their effect and those which are distorting in their intent. Others have referred to these policies as "implicit" and "explicit" barriers, respectively. While Canada's tariff policy may not qualify as an explicit barrier (although to the extent that overall commercial policy embodies quotas and tariffs to protect regional industries it could be viewed as an explicit barrier), the effect of the tariff is surely to distort internal trade patterns. Likewise, the National Energy Program has the effect of transferring resource rents from the treasuries of the energy-producing provinces to consuming Canadians and in the process distorts relative prices.

However, some federal policies clearly fall in the "explicit" barrier category. For example, the regional benefits under unemployment insurance and the seasonal UI benefits for fishermen were clearly intended to alter factor prices at the regional level.

There is a further set of CEU distortions that tend to be viewed as provincial barriers but which, when looked at closely, could equally well be associated with the federal government: the various marketing boards which have an influence on interprovincial trade. A Supreme Court decision in the 1950s restricted marketing boards to intraprovincial trade. However, in 1957 the federal government amended the Agricultural Products Marketing Act in such a manner that it could authorize provincial boards to impose the equivalent of indirect taxes. Are these provincial barriers? Or should they be viewed as federally authorized barriers, since they can exist only because Ottawa passed the enabling legislation? The same reservation applies to the maze of provincial trucking regulations which owe their existence to federal enabling legislation.

Provincial Barriers

The Canadian public, however, has come to associate internal market barriers with the policies of provincial governments. Several high-profile disputes have alerted Canadians to the rise of these internal barriers — Newfoundland's hiring preferences for its residents for off-shore energy jobs; Quebec's regulations relating to out-of-province construction workers; Ontario's choice of an Ontario-based firm over Bombardier for a major contract a few years ago even though Bombardier had the lowest bid. The list could go on, but since several extensive classifications of these barriers already exist, little is accomplished in reproducing them once again (Trebilcock et al., 1983; Chrétien, 1980; Maxwell and Pestieau, 1980). Of more interest are some of the lower profile, but potentially more serious, areas where impediments appear to be on the rise.

One of these areas relates to taxation. Chapter 5 presented the details of the shared federal-provincial personal income tax system for all provinces but Quebec and the shared corporate system for all provinces except Quebec, Ontario and Alberta. Included in the discussion were the three provisions the federal government has laid down for agreeing to collect provincial tax credits, whether corporate or personal. For present purposes the key provision is the one requiring that a proposed tax credit not jeopardize the functioning of the Canadian economic union. This provision came to the fore in 1979 when Quebec introduced its

"Stock Savings Plan," which allowed Quebec residents to deduct, in computing their provincial taxable income, up to $15,000 for purchases of new shares of Quebec-based companies. The discriminatory aspect of this plan is that it applies only to Quebec residents and only to Quebec-based firms. When other provinces attempted to follow Quebec's lead and to implement similar provisions via the tax credit route, Ottawa refused to collect them on the grounds that they violated the letter and the spirit of the tax collection agreements. Were this sort of provision to spread across all provinces, the net result might be a serious fragmentation of the national market for capital (on the assumption that the market for capital is a national rather than an international one, a point which will be raised later) in the sense that Canadians would in effect have an incentive to purchase equities of firms based in their own province. Quebec is free to mount such programs because it has its own separate personal income tax, and because there is no constitutional provision guaranteeing an internal common market. One possible implication, however, is that several more provinces may opt for their own personal income tax systems. This concern was presumably part of the rationale for the heightened federal interest in pursuing a constitutional provision with respect to a domestic common market.

A second area that has generated concern with respect to the preservation of a CEU relates to the existence of substantial pools of capital in the hands of the various provinces. The heritage funds of the western provinces, particularly the Alberta Heritage Savings Trust Fund, and Quebec's Caisse de dépots are obvious examples. The spectre of having the assets of these funds deployed for industrializing or diversifying a provincial economy (for "province-building") by drawing industry away from other regions via subsidies or tax holidays, or by assuming a controlling position on the board of directors of various companies, probably also served to put the issue of a CEU high on the 1980–82 constitutional agenda.

Relatedly, the existence of section 125 of the Constitution which states, effectively, that one level of government cannot tax the other level runs counter to the notion of a CEU. There is an incentive for government ownership vis-à-vis private ownership, since profits (or, more generally, factor incomes) accruing to one level of government are not normally subject to taxation by the other level. For example, the $1 billion or so of potential interest income that could accrue annually to the Alberta Heritage Fund would effectively escape taxation. Not surprisingly, this infringement on the economic rights of Canadians did not loom large in the 1980–82 constitutional deliberations, but it is an important part of the overall issue.

While this general identification or classification of barriers might appear to be straightforward, the following section focusses on some of the many conceptual problems associated with measuring their impact.

Economics and the Economic Union

The Theory of Second Best

Principal among the complications associated with assessing the costs of internal market barriers is what economists refer to as the "theory of the second best." With several distortions already in the system, it cannot in general be proven that the introduction of yet another barrier or distortion will make things worse. For example, suppose that there exists some policy, such as the tariff, which alters the terms of trade for a province. If the province responds by mounting an explicit CEU barrier which has the impact of restoring the original terms of trade, the presumption would be that this distortion would increase national output. Needless to say, the implications of this theorem can be very substantial for any exercise that attempts to assign "costs" to existing barriers. Moreover, it may also help explain why some barriers exist — as defensive mechanisms initiated by provinces to protect them against the impacts of other distortions.

The point can be put in more general terms. Canada can be viewed as a "ten-nation" customs union in which, in principle at least, there are no internal barriers but there is a common external tariff. Since the common external tariff is a distortion, there can be no presumption that zero barriers between the ten regions is optimal. The conditions under which this would be the case are quite restrictive.

One specific area where this issue arises is with respect to equalization payments. Equalization flows reduce the tax-price of public goods and services in recipient provinces, thereby inhibiting outmigration. What is not clear, however, is whether this is efficiency retarding or efficiency enhancing. The traditional view of the effect of equalization was that it ran counter to efficiency and regional adjustment. The more recent view is that equalization flows are needed to slow down outmigration which would otherwise be triggered by the existence of net fiscal benefits in the energy-rich provinces. Both arguments are correct on their own assumptions, so that the issue is largely an empirical one. What would appear to be clear, however, is that the actual equalization program (as distinct from a program which would be designed along the lines of the efficiency concerns) has little claim to be efficiency enhancing (Courchene, 1984c, chap. 3).

The Implications of a Small Open Economy

Capital Markets are International

The manner in which we approach the cost of barriers alters considerably depending on what we assume about the openness of the economy.

The first implication relates to the degree that capital markets can be viewed as international rather than national in scope.[2]

Consider, once again, Quebec's stock savings plan. If capital markets are essentially domestic in nature, then the impact of this program will be to draw capital away from other provinces and toward Quebec (in the sense that Quebec residents will be less likely to invest their savings elsewhere in the country). However, to the extent the capital market is international, capital will not be drawn away from other provinces but rather from the rest of the world. Thus, ascertaining the degree to which capital markets are domestic or international in nature is critical to assessing the costs of any "barriers" to the flows of capital.

Mobility and Barriers

More generally, Gérard Bélanger of Université Laval has long argued that the openness of the provincial economics is such that it is very difficult for a province to export the costs of any ICM distortions to other provinces. Under the assumption (and, to a large extent, the reality) that factors are mobile, it is probable that the costs of any barriers will ultimately be borne by the initiating provinces. In this sense the internal common market is, in part, self-policing. Ontario cannot afford to get too far off-side Michigan in terms of its policies or else both labour and capital will flow south. And so on.

What follows from this situation is that provinces will have a greater incentive to mount barriers if factor mobility is low. In turn, this suggests that Quebec can take, and to some degree has taken, advantage of the fact that language differences render its population less mobile than is the case for other provinces. But even this province is finding that its policies cannot get too far out of line with what is happening elsewhere. The recent Quebec white paper on taxation indicates that this province is considering bringing its tax policies more in line with those in Ontario: the white paper recommends reversing the recent emphasis on income taxation and putting more weight on consumption taxation, the net result (and intended result) being to align Quebec's taxation more with Ontario's system.

A further important implication, noted by Jean-Luc Migué and Gérard Bélanger, is that should Ottawa move to close off the international economy (via tariffs, quotas, the NEP), this then provides both the incentive and the ability for the provinces to mount discriminatory barriers they might not otherwise initiate were it not for the federal action. One recent example is Alberta's attempt to cut off feed stocks to the refinery in Sarnia. Were world prices (or at least U.S. prices) prevailing in Canada this would be a meaningless initiative on Alberta' part: Petrosar would simply get feed stocks elsewhere. But with the domestic economy cordonned off by the NEP, Alberta suddenly found itself able to flex its discriminatory muscle.

Interregional Integration and the CEU

The idea behind the CEU is to ensure that the domestic market becomes more unified in the sense, for example, that the markets for labour become more national. On the surface, this might imply that if all barriers were removed, there would be an increase in the flows of goods and factors between Canada's provinces and regions. In some areas, certainly, the elimination of provincial purchasing preferences would generate greater interprovincial trade.

As a general proposition, however, there is no presumption that a full-blown economic union would lead to greater interregional flows of goods. In Macdonald's 1879 National Policy, for example, the tariff served to close the Canadian economy to import penetration while the development of the transcontinental railway facilitated east-west trade. If by a CEU we have in mind the removal of all internal barriers including such policies as tariffs and transportation subsidies, then trade flows may well move north-south rather than east-west.

This point deserves emphasis. As James Melvin points out, there are two types of costs associated with such a policy.[3] Consumers lose because domestic prices would rise to the level of the foreign price plus the tariff. As a partial offset, the revenue from the tariff accrues to the government. Suppose, however, that the tariff was increased to the level where it became "profitable" for these goods to be supplied not from foreigners but from other regions of the country. Thus, trade now switches from being north-south to being east-west. Alternatively, at the same tariff levels, we could subsidize transportation which would have the same impact. Interregional trade flows would then be larger; but the previous tariff revenue from imported goods would be lost and, in effect, converted into transportation costs. This is a deadweight loss in the sense that these transportation costs would not have been required if the Canadian economy were more open — i.e., free of all common market distortions.

This situation poses a perplexing problem in estimating the costs of internal barriers. Typically, we take the existing interregional and inter-provincial flows and attempt to estimate the costs ("triangles") of these barriers. However, exactly what is being measured here is unclear, since some of the existing flows may themselves be a "distortion," resulting from the turning inward of the Canadian economy.

The purpose here is not to say that Canada ought to abolish all tariffs or all transportation subsidies. Rather, it is to gain perspective on the magnitude of the costs of some of the higher profile barriers such as provincial purchasing preferences. After all, from the economic vantage point, the rationale for pursuing an internal common market is to increase the size of national output. In this light, it is appropriate to compare the likely benefits that would arise from removing provincial barriers with the benefits that would arise from opening the Canadian economy internationally. As I shall argue later, Canada is likely to be involved in a negative-sum game if we free up the domestic market while at the same time we build walls around our national economy.

People Prosperity versus Place Prosperity

We could approach the issue of economic integration by focussing on what I have elsewhere called the "integration continuum" (Courchene, 1983). At one end of the spectrum there would be autarkic nation states (no integration) and at the other end unitary states, with the spectrum filled in by free trade areas, customs unions, confederations, federations and the like. This is a valuable perspective from which to focus on the gains from pursuing further integration, and it is the approach taken by Ivan Bernier and Nicolas Roy (1985) in their research on the CEU. They make the following interesting observation: in the move from autarky to, say, a free-trade association, the gains from integration are such that each region (or country) profits, but further up the integration spectrum (e.g., by enhancing the CEU) citizens may gain at the expense of regions. This is an important issue in the Canadian context because much of our concern for interregional equity in the popular mind is defined in terms of the prosperity of individual provinces.

To pursue this point further, it is instructive to focus on certain aspects of the interregional or interprovincial adjustment process.[4] Because the provinces belong to a common currency area (the Canadian dollar area) where exchange rates between them are not only fixed but set equal to unity, adjustment via exchange rates movements is not possible. In turn, this places greater emphasis on wage and price flexibility across provinces. However, the existence of nationwide pay scales for certain federal jobs, the tendency for nationwide bargaining or at least nationwide wage patterning, and provincial minimum wage legislation tend to limit the degree to which wage are flexible provincially. Hence, when adversity strikes a particular region, the result is to generate unemployment and to place greater pressure on outmigration than would be the case were there greater wage flexibility. Since outmigration is unacceptable to these provinces, there are equally strong pressures for the central government to take action to limit the outmigration. In my view, the regional-benefit aspects of unemployment insurance can be viewed as Ottawa's response to these provincial population concerns: indeed, these regionally extended benefits are frequently referred to in the Ottawa corridors as part of the "stay option" to maintain regional populations.

Most analysts would include these regional benefits as one of the federal CEU barriers. Yet it is important to recognize that they have arisen in part because there is insufficient wage and price flexibility in the provincial economies which, in turn, reflects to some degree federal wage policies. In this sense the regional aspects of UI transfers can be viewed as a defensive action on the federal government's part to prevent the working out of the implications arising from the rest of its policies. This reaction is similar to certain provincial barriers that represent defensive provincial actions in order to offset the implications of other federal or provincial policies.

The essential point arising from this analysis is that the trade-off between people prosperity versus place property may become more severe by removing the "up-front" or "high-profile" barriers but leaving in place the larger underlying distortions which alter regional comparative advantage. Economists would, by the nature of their discipline, put more emphasis on people than on place. But in the larger arena of Canadian public policy the implications of this trade-off become more important. This argument lends further substance to earlier suggestions that we cannot treat provincial barriers in isolation from the underlying distortions, many of which are frequently not viewed by the public as CEU distortions.

Federalism as a Degenerate Case of Economic Union

The notion that federalism is a "degenerate case" of economic union has pervaded much of the thinking with respect to internal barriers. There are two aspects to this hypothesis. First, there is the suggestion (not always implicit) that anything the provinces do fragments the economic union whereas Ottawa's policies are, almost by definition, in the "national interest." The second aspect, this time more implicit than explicit, is that unitary states are paragons of virtue when it comes to internal barriers.

In my opinion both these views are wrong, or at least the burden of proof ought to lie with those who make the claims. The above analysis attempted to demonstrate the weakness of the first argument, and the brief review of the empirical estimates of the costs of internal barriers in the next section will substantiate this further. As far as the second argument is concerned, there is no policy in the Canadian federation that inhibits labour mobility as much as the policies of the local housing authorities in the United Kingdom. Moreover, Britain's policies toward regions, including its system of differentiated regional employment premiums and its differential regional development grants, are arguably more distorting than the combined regional policies of both government levels in Canada. Therefore, it is difficult to make a case that there is a direct association between federalism and the fragmentation of the internal economic union. Indeed, in Chapter 10 I shall focus on the concept of "balance" in the various federations where the emphasis will be on the mechanisms that exist in various federations to hold the two levels of government in check.

Recapitulation

Rather than attempting to summarize the above analysis, I will simply reproduce a section of the Saskatchewan response to the initial federal proposals circulated during the 1980 constitutional debates. These federal proposals themselves appear in a set of tables later in the chapter. However, the Saskatchewan response, or that portion reproduced below, is self-contained. Moreover, like much of the above analysis, it attempts to place the high-profile provincial barriers in the larger perspective of those underlying federal and provincial policies which have substantial implications for the regional and provincial allocation of economic activity but which in the popular mind tend not to fall in the category of barriers to the CEU:

> Surely the levels of corporate, personal and other taxes in any province have a far greater impact on the mobility of resources than some of the barriers such as purchasing policy that are apparently under attack.
>
> Surely, the national tariff and transportation policies have an immeasurably greater impact on relative prices, rates of return and ultimately the location choice for capital and labour.
>
> We see the federal aim being taken at the explicit barriers that obviously impede movements among the provinces. The "big" economic levers such as tax rates, tariff and transportation policies, would not be brought into question. But, these major economic levers are precisely the forces having the greatest impact on the mobility of resources and products in Canada. And, the richest provinces have the greatest capacity to use such instruments to attract business away from other provinces. The only defence available to a small province may be to take action which creates barriers to protect their competitive position within the economic union — and these would be struck down instantly by the proposed section 121 [see Table 9-2 below]. (Romanow, 1980)

Estimates of the Economic Costs of Internal Barriers

John Whalley (1983a, 1983b) and Michael Trebilcock et al. (1983, chap. 4–6) have recently completed a "first pass" at quantifying some aspects of the costs of CEU barriers. They define as a barrier any policy which results in resources being allocated either within or between provinces in such a way as to reduce national real income. They also distinguish between explicit and implicit distortions where the latter would encompass policies like the tariff and the NEP. The background material for their estimates consists of the various distortions as well as the available data relating to interprovincial flows of goods, services, capital and people.

Their general conclusion is that the economic significance of interprovincial barriers to trade has been overplayed in recent policy debates. For example, they estimate that only $3 billion of the $43 billion of interprovincial trade falls within those categories designated as embodying major discriminatory policies. Under the assumption that these distortions are of the order of 10 percent, the annual cost of federal and provincial barriers comes out to considerably less than 1 percent of GNP. Moreover, of this total, the cost of federal distortions (essentially of the implicit variety) exceeds that of provincial distortions.

More recently, Richard Harris and David Cox (1984) have estimated the gains to Canadian multilateral free trade (*external* trade) to be in the order of 8 to 10 percent of GNP. While there are substantial differences in the manner in which Harris and Cox measure the costs of barriers (in their case, tariffs), it is likely that more gains are to be had from pursuing freer trade at the international level than from pursuing internal free trade. This does not mean that Canada should not move in the direction of ensuring greater mobility of goods and factors internally, but it does suggest that this pursuit should not be at the expense of balkanizing international trade.

The thrust of the chapter thus far is that the costs of our internal barriers are probably not high — at least for the "static costs." In my view, however, focussing only on the static costs underestimates the true costs of internal barriers. It does not take account of resources deployed to obtain preferences or to maintain the existing barriers (i.e., it ignores the costs of lobbying or rent-seeking). It also ignores any dynamic costs associated with fragmentation. For example, because the market is fragmented, firms may be of less-than-optimal size (this scale-economy effect is, in part at least, what leads to the larger set of gains in the Harris and Cox estimation procedure). Protection can lead to complacency — firms need not be efficient in order to obtain contracts if governments treat them preferentially. There is less reward for innovative behaviour if non-tariff barriers prevent access to larger markets. These sorts of costs tend to be ignored or at least underplayed by techniques that focus on the estimates of static costs. Finally, much of the concern about the CEU centres on what might happen in the future if there are no provisions put in place now to prevent further balkanization. It may well be that measurements of these more comprehensive costs will still generate small estimates. Nonetheless, it seems that concerns relating to the CEU are warranted and, further, that there is a case to set in place some mechanisms for ensuring maximum freedom of mobility across provincial boundaries for goods, labour and capital. This is even stronger if the political arguments for a CEU are considered.

In the remainder of the chapter I shall focus on the various ways in which the Canadian economic union might be enhanced, beginning with the 1980–82 federal attempt to enshrine the CEU in the Constitution.

Securing the CEU in the Constitution

The 1980–82 Experience

In the federal background document three avenues for enshrining the CEU in the Constitution were proposed:

(i) entrenching in the Constitution the mobility rights of citizens, as well as their right to gain a livelihood and acquire property in any province, regardless of their provinces of residence or previous residence and subject to laws of general application;

(ii) placing limitations upon the ability of governments to use their legislative and executive powers to impede economic mobility by way of general provisions, through the revision and expansion of Section 121 of the BNA Act;

(iii) broadening federal powers so that they may encompass all matters that are necessary for economic integration, thus ensuring that the relevant laws and regulations will apply uniformly throughout Canada, or that the "test" of the public interest will be brought to bear upon derogation from uniformity. (Chrétien, 1980, pp. 29–30)

The first of these three approaches would take the form of a charter of "economic rights" to go along with the Canadian Charter of Rights and Freedoms. The second avenue would strengthen section 121 of the Constitution (often referred to as the "free-trade provision") which currently reads: "All articles of Growth, Produce, or Manufacture of any one of the Provinces shall, from and after the Union, be admitted free into each of the other provinces." This provision has been interpreted by the courts to be a "free border" clause for goods and not much more. For example, it has not been interpreted to apply to capital or to services. The third avenue for enshrining a CEU would be via strengthened federal powers and, in particular, via an expanded section 91(2), the federal trade and commerce power.

The degree to which these three provisions are incorporated in the constitutions of various federations appears in Table 9-1. The table is adapted from an excellent comparative study of economic mobility in several federations by John Hayes (1982).

Tables 9-2, 9-3 and 9-4 present more detailed information relating to the three avenues for enshrining a CEU in the Canadian Constitution. The first part of each table reproduces the situation as of 1980. The second panel focusses on the initial federal proposals (summer, 1980), and the third panel of each table presents the changes incorporated in the Constitution Act, 1982. Elsewhere I have commented in detail on these tables (Courchene, 1984d). For present purposes it is sufficient to make a few points:

• While the federal background document argued that there are "compelling reasons for securing in the Constitution the operational rules of our

TABLE 9-1 Comparison of Constitutional Provisions

	Scope of mobility rights for individuals	(1) Scope of free trade guarantee (2) Whether federal authority is bound by the guarantee.	Scope of powers directly affecting trade and mobility	Scope of federal powers indirectly affecting mobility. (1) Compared with Canada (2) Examples
United States	Moderate	(Exclusive federal interstate jurisdiction is equivalent to a guarantee, so far as the states only are concerned.)	Exclusive federal powers over interstate trade extend well into intrastate. State trade powers largely confined to "police" regulations.	(1) Wider (2) Labour, securities, conditional grants.
Switzerland	Wide	(1) Wide (2) In principle, yes; but there is broad authority to override the guarantee.	No inter-intra distinction. Concurrent, with federal paramountcy. Wider federal powers than in Canada. State trade powers largely confined to "police" regulations.	(1) Wider (2) Civil law, labour, social security.
Australia	Moderate	(1) Wide (2) Yes, e.g., agricultural marketing and nationalization	Interstate: concurrent, with federal paramountcy. Wider federal powers than in Canada. State trade. Intrastate: exclusively state jurisdiction. No inter-intra distinction.	(1) Somewhat wider (2) Corporations, industrial disputes, treaties, conditional grants.
Germany	Wide	(Exclusive federal jurisdiction is equivalent to a guarantee, so far as the states only are concerned.)	Exclusive federal authority, much wider than in Canada.	(1) Much wider (2) The economy, labour, civil law, securities.
Canada	Rights of moderate scope are planned.	(1) Narrow; supplemented by narrow exclusive federal trade jurisdiction. (2) Yes	Exclusively federal, but narrowly interpreted. Courts have reserved intraprovincial authority for the provinces.	

Source: Hayes, 1982. Adapted.

TABLE 9-2 The Free Trade Provision

1.	BNA Act	*Section 121*: All articles of Growth, Produce or Manufacture of any one of the Provinces shall, from and after the Union, be admitted free into each of the other Provinces.
2.	Initial Federal Proposals	*Section 121(1)*: Canada is constituted an economic union within which all persons may move without discrimination based on province or territory of residence or former residence and within which all goods, services and capital may move without discrimination based on province or territory of origin or entry into Canada or of destination or export from Canada. (2) Neither Canada nor a province shall by law or practice discriminate in a manner that contravenes the principle expressed in subsection (1). (3) Subsection (2) does not render invalid a law of Parliament or a legislature enacted in the interests of public safety, order, health or morals. (4) Subsection (2) does not render invalid a law of Parliament enacted (a) in accordance with the principles of equalization and regional development recognized in section — , or (b) in relation to a matter that is declared by Parliament in the enactment to be of an overriding national interest. (5) Subsection (2) does not render invalid a law of a legislature enacted in relation to the reduction of substantial economic disparities between regions wholly within a province that does not discriminate to a greater degree against persons resident or formerly resident outside the province or against goods, services or capital from outside the province than it does against persons resident or goods, services or capital from a region within the province. (6) Nothing in subsection (3), (4), or (5) renders valid a law of Parliament or a legislature that impedes the admission free into any province of goods, services or capital orginating in or imported into any other province or territory. (7) Nothing in this section confers any legislative authority on Parliament or a legislature.
3.	Constitution Act, 1982	No change to original BNA Act

Source: The Federal proposal is taken from the Government of Saskatchwan, "Powers over the Economy: An Analysis of Federal Proposals," Document 800-14/029, First Ministers' Conference on the Constitution, Ottawa, September 8–12, 1980.

economic union and for ensuring that both orders of government abide by these rules" (Chrétien, 1980, p. 29), the federal proposals (as elaborated in the tables) essentially restrict only the provinces. This is clear in terms of the federal trade and commerce power (Table 9-3), since an increase in

TABLE 9-3 The Trade and Commerce Power

1. BNA Act	*Section 91*: ". . . it is hereby declared that . . . the exclusive LegislativeAuthority of the Parliament of Canada extends to all Matters coming within the Classes of Subjects next herein-after enumerated; that is to say . . " 2. The Regulation of Trade and Commerce.
2. Initial Federal Proposals	*Section 91*: Add to section 91 the following heads of jurisdiction immediately following head 91.2: 2.1 Competition 2.2 The establishment of product standards throughout Canada (2) Add to section 91 the following new subsections: (2) For greater certainty, "regulation of trade and commerce" in subsection (1) includes the regulation of trade and commerce in goods, services and capital. (3) The authority conferred on Parliament by heads 91 (2.1) and 91 (2.2)does not render invalid a law enacted by a legislature that is not in conflict with a law of Parliament enacted under either of those heads.
3. Constitution Act, 1982	Original BNA Act wording remains.

Source: See Table 9-2.

federal powers cannot bind the federal government. In principle an economic Bill of Rights or a broad application of section 121, the free-trade provision, would impact equally on both levels of government. However, subsection 4(b) of Table 9-2 (relating to the free-trade provision) essentially allows Ottawa to do anything it wants by stating that the provision does not apply to any matter that is declared by Parliament (not the Courts) to be in the national interest. The same subsection appears in the Economic Rights Provision (Table 9-4).

- Thus, the federal attempt to enshrine a CEU in the Constitution was put in the context of a dramatic centralization of powers in the federation. This may have been part of a grand federal plan. Elsewhere I have suggested that it was Ottawa's backing off on these initial proposals that brought several provinces "on side" in respect to the final constitutional package (Courchene, 1984d).
- What eventually became enshrined in the Constitution Act, 1982, is the right for several provinces to fragment the CEU. As Tables 9-2 and 9-3 indicate, there were no changes in either the free-trade provision or the trade and commerce power, respectively — i.e., the Constitu-

TABLE 9-4 An Economic Rights Provision

1. BNA Act	None
2. Initial Federal Proposals	(1) Every citizen of Canada has the right to enter, remain in and leave Canada. (2) Everyone in Canada has the right (a) to move to and take up residence in any province; and (b) to acquire and hold property in, and pursue the gaining of a livelihood in, any province. (3) The rights specified in subsection (2) are subject to (a) any laws or practices of general application in force in a province other than those that discriminate among persons primarily on the basis of province of present or previous residence, and, (b) any other laws referred to in subsections (4) or (5) of section 121 of the *British North America Act*.
3. Constitution Act, 1982	Section 6 of the Canadian Charter of Rights and Freedoms: *Mobility Rights* 6. (1) Every citizen of Canada has the right to enter, remain in and leave Canada. (2) Every citizen of Canada and every person who has the status of a permanent resident has the right (a) to move to and take up residence in any province; and (b) to pursue the gaining of a livelihod in any province. (3) The rights specified in subsection (2) are subject to (a) any laws or practices of general application in force in a province other than those that discriminate among persons primarily on the basis of province of present or previous residence; and (b) any laws providing for reasonable residency requirements as a qualification for the receipt of publicly provided social services. (4) Subsections (2) and (3) do not preclude any law, program or activity that has as its object the amelioration in a province of conditions of individuals in that province who are socially or economically disadvantaged if the rate of employment in that province is below the rate of employment in Canada.

Source: See Table 9-2.

tion Act, 1982, simply duplicates the words of the BNA Act, or more correctly is silent on these issues so that the previous provisions apply. In terms of an economic rights provision, the Constitution Act, 1982, does incorporate mobility rights. However, as section 6(4) indicates (see Table 9-4) there is now a provision enshrined in the Canadian Charter of Rights and Freedoms that gives high-unemployment provinces the constitutional right to mount barriers to the free mobility of labour. In addition, elsewhere in the new Constitution the provinces were given the right to levy indirect taxes with respect to their resources. Both of these measures run counter to the notion of a CEU.

- This incredible turnaround in terms of enshrining a CEU in the Constitution would appear to lend substance to the argument that the original federal proposals were part of the bargaining process that were traded away to achieve the larger objective of enacting the overall constitutional package.
- Having thus failed to secure the CEU in the Constitution but still maintaining concern over the issue, it is perhaps not surprising that the full name of the present royal commission is the Royal Commission on the Economic Union and Development Prospects for Canada.

Despite the fact that the CEU has not been enshrined in the Constitution, the desire for enhanced mobility across the country has been firmly planted among Canadians. In part, the issue becomes one of seeking alternative ways to enhance the CEU. Prior to focussing on some of these alternatives it is important to recognize that the existing Constitution might yet become the vehicle for securing an enhanced domestic common market. To this I now turn.

Some Constitutional CEU "Sleepers"

The Trade and Commerce Power

Writing in 1980, Bushnell made the following comments with respect to the powers attributed by the courts to section 91(2), the trade and commerce power:

> The legislative authority given by the Constitution to the Dominion to regulate trade and commerce has always been recognized to be expansive due to the extremely wide terms used — trade and commerce. Indeed the Supreme Court of Canada in its early decisions saw this power to be just what it appeared to be from the words used — the full, complete, and unrestricted power to regulate business. But this wide view of Dominion authority was short lived and in 1881 the Judicial Committee of the Privy Council made the decision to restrict the power in order to preserve the autonomy of the provinces. This rationale for the curtailment of the potential Dominion legislative power inherent in the constitutional provision has never been doubted, and as late as 1951 the Judicial Committee could assert

that *"trade and commerce" had to be limited in order to preserve from serious curtailment, if not virtual extinction, the degree of autonomy which, as appears from the scheme of the act as a whole, the provinces were intended to possess.*[5]

The U.S. trade and commerce power appears quite similar. Nonetheless, over time a substantial number of powers have been judicially ascribed to the U.S. commerce clause to the extent that it has become the embodiment of an internal market provision. Part of the difference has been that the U.S. commerce clause did not run up against the long list of exclusive state (or provincial) powers that we find in section 92 of the BNA Act.

The essential point is that the accumulation of power in the interpretation of the U.S. commerce clause occurred basically in this century. Likewise, in several recent Canadian cases (e.g., Cigol), section 91(2) appears to be in an ascendent phase. If we believe that the Supreme Court is influenced to some degree at least by the economic needs of the day (and if we argue that an internal common market falls in this category), then it is entirely possible that section 91(2) will emerge as an important instrument in securing a CEU. This would, of course, satisfy Ottawa in the extreme, since a federal head of power such as 91(2) cannot be binding on the federal government.

Section 121[6]

Analysts frequently point to the fact that section 121 has been interpreted very narrowly, yet there is not much judicial interpretation associated with this provision. One probable reason is that very early on the courts ruled that section 121 applied equally to both levels of government, an interpretation which must have dampened federal enthusiasm for this provision. Indeed, in the federal background document reference is made to a roughly equivalent provision in the Australian constitution which has on several occasions prevented the Australian central government from nationalizing banks, taking over airlines and the like. The fact that the initial federal proposal with respect to section 121 (Table 9-2 above) contained a generous federal "escape clause" indicated that Ottawa did not want to find itself in the Australian bind.

This is an intriguing turn of events. The section 91(2) route to a CEU was blocked by the courts because a full exercise of this power would wipe out all provincial authority (see above quotation from Bushnell). And the section 121 route was bypassed (at least by the federal authorities) because it would have meant curtailing federal as well as provincial powers. Clearly, therefore, the federal concern over a CEU has been and still is related closely to the issue of the division of powers — i.e., the desire is to control provincial barriers, not to eliminate all barriers.

Individual Rights

Judicial interpretation of the mobility section of the Canadian Charter of Rights and Freedoms is just beginning so that it is too early to speculate on whether this provision will make a significant contribution to enhancing the CEU. However, there is another aspect of the charter that may be even more important when it comes into force:

> 15.(1) Every individual is equal before and under the law and has the right to the equal protection of the law and equal benefit of the law without discrimination and, in particular, without discrimination based on race, national and ethnic origin, colour, religion, sex, age or mental or physical ability.
>
> (2) Subsection (1) does not preclude any law, program or activity that has as its object the amelioration of conditions of the disadvantaged because of race, national or ethnic origin, colour, religion, sex, age or mental or physical ability.

At face value this appears to be a provision that prevents discrimination but allows for affirmative action programs on behalf of the disadvantaged. However, the 14th Amendment of the U.S. constitution (the "equal protection" provision) has been used as a means of securing individual economic rights. There is a difference in that the 14th Amendment includes a reference to property. Nonetheless, it is within the realm of possibility that the equal protection provision of section 15 of the charter could cause trouble for federal legislation (such as regional UI provisions) which differentiates between otherwise identically situated persons on the basis of region or province.

More generally, the charter is an entirely new concept for Canadians. For the first time in our history, there are certain areas where no government can legislate. In a very real sense we are being Americanized or republicanized. To the extent that Canadians take the charter to heart, they may attempt to restrict the actions of government in the economic sphere as well. Already, some attempt (confused in its execution) has been made to add property rights to the mobility clause. If this effort is eventually successful, it might provide a solid basis for a CEU based on citizen economic rights and one which would be binding on both levels of government, unless overruled by other sections of the Constitution.

Summary

Even though it is probably fair to say that the federal attempt to enshrine a CEU in the Constitution was not very successful, there is some, perhaps considerable scope for the existing provisions to be interpreted or reinterpreted in ways which will enhance the internal common market. However, most of the thinking with respect to he CEU has now begun to take the form of arrangements that would exist outside of the

Constitution. For example, in *Challenges and Choices*, the Royal Commission raises the possibility of a GATT-type arrangement internally for securing the CEU. The next section focusses on one variant of this approach.

Alternative Approaches to Securing a CEU

Is the Constitution the most appropriate vehicle for ensuring an internal common market? The United States has much stronger internal common market guarantees in its constitution than we have in ours, largely because of the broad powers accorded by the courts to the interstate commerce clause. Nonetheless most, if not all, of the states engage in preferential purchasing, and many now require in-state value added in order to qualify for government purchases. Moreover, despite these broader constitutional guarantees, the U.S. courts have allowed California's unitary tax which permits California to tax a share of a corporation's world rather than California profits. Canada has no such constitutional guarantees, but the issue of a unitary tax has not surfaced because of a federal-provincial pact on the definition of income for corporate tax purposes. These sorts of concerns lead to a general questioning of whether there might not be preferable ways of ensuring an internal common market.

In a recent publication from the Ontario Economic Council, Richard Simeon (1984) outlines three alternatives to policing an internal common market:

- judicial enforcement of rights of citizens and restrictions on government;
- making the federal government the guarantor and policeman;
- some kind of intergovernmental process.

In terms of a judicial (or constitutional) policeman, Simeon cites as the advantages the fact that any resolutions will be final and authoritative, that it will provide a stable planning framework, and that it will allow private organizations and citizens to initiate actions thereby ensuring that the rights of individuals rather than government will prevail. However, he feels that the disadvantages of this approach would exceed the benefits: the courts have to be specific in their judgements, so that they cannot ensure compromise and trade-offs; they are ill-suited to weighing the "bads" of barriers with the "goods" of other goals, and so on. This reservation coincides with the Saskatchewan response to the initial federal proposals: that the courts are ill-equipped to make the "complicated trade-offs between often conflicting economic objectives of responsible governments" (Romanow, 1980). Saskatchewan's preferred approach is a variant of Simeon's third proposal (to be outlined below). Having the federal government as the policeman is essentially a variant of Table 9-3 where Ottawa would receive its authority via an expanded version of section 91(2) of the Constitution. As Simeon points out, this role could evolve into an open invitation to federal power, with no logical stopping place, and it could therefore be inconsistent with the classical federal model.

Simeon's preferred method is policing through intergovernmental co-operation. More formally:

- The preamble to the Constitution should strongly state the commitment to the maintenance and extension of the Canadian economic market.
- The Constitution should stress mechanisms to achieve the goals stated in the preamble, rather than state those goals in very precise terms.
- Primary responsibility for maintaining the internal common market should not be given to any level of government, or to the courts.
- The Constitution should establish a federal-provincial mechanism for more continuous intergovernmental interaction on the economy, including not only protection against internal trade barriers, but also discussion of the relationship between federal and provincial economic policies and of ways they can be more fully co-ordinated. (Simeon, 1984)

The federal-provincial body involved in this proposal might be a standing committee of a new house of the provinces, or it could be made responsible to the first ministers' conference or given an independent existence. Whatever the precise institutional framework, the essence of the proposal is to "make the eleven governments collectively responsible for preserving the common market, and to give the resulting federal-provincial body the power, under the Constitution, to formally overrule serious transgressions."

A somewhat similar proposal was contained in the recent Ontario Economic Council consensus report (1983) on whether or not Ontario should establish its own independent personal income tax. In particular, the council recommended the establishment of an interprovincial or, preferably, a federal-provincial "code of economic conduct":

We are encouraged by the fact that at one point or another during the constitutional debates most or all the provinces declared themselves in favour of the internal common market. We do not presume to be able to suggest an appropriate structure or design for such a committee. However, we would argue strongly that its mandate should encompass much more than the matter of ensuring that the taxation system does not fragment the internal economic union. Matters such as expenditure and purchasing policies as well as regulatory measures, at both levels of government, should be incorporated under the umbrella of any such arrangement. (p. 160)

To round out the discussion of the various arrangements that might be utilized to enhance economic mobility within the nation, it is important to devote some time to the mechanism that is currently most heavily relied upon — the federal spending power as exercised through the various conditional grant programs. In return for receiving federal cash transfers for areas such as health and social assistance the provinces must, for example, ensure that interprovincial migrants have access to these programs with a minimum residency period. For health services there are further requirements — such as universal access and comprehensiveness of coverage — that allow Canadians to move between provinces without fear of losing access to these services. Adequate alternative mechanisms for safeguarding portability and access would have to be put in place before I would recommend that Ottawa withdraw from its current role in this regard.

Conclusion

The overall purpose of this monograph is to focus on economic management and the division of powers. Perhaps no single policy area has as much impact on both of these areas as does the pursuit of a Canadian economic union. In summarizing the analysis of this chapter, the emphasis will initially be on the implications for economic performance and later on the division of powers. The chapter ends with a compromise proposal for addressing the CEU.

In terms of the impact of barriers on the performance of the economy, the following observations seem appropriate:

- The provinces are not alone in erecting ICM barriers. Indeed, if we take a broad view of barriers where the focus is on effect rather than intent, then the federal barriers generate much larger output costs than do provincial barriers.
- Relatedly, some provincial barriers are probably best viewed as defensive mechanisms against some of the larger underlying distortions like the tariff or the NEP.
- The more open the Canadian economy, the less will be the incentive for the provinces to erect barriers. The obvious corollary is that if the federal government closes off the economy internationally, the provinces then have both the incentive and the ability to impede mobility of goods and factors.
- Not all internal barriers can or should be removed. In some cases the economic cost of the barriers is trivial, and it is simply not worth the cost to attempt to remove them. Even in those countries that have sweeping ICM provisions in their constitutions, barriers still exist — presumably because it is too costly to remove them.

- Federalism is not a degenerate case of economic union. This notion was implicit in much of the federal government's position. The provinces do an admirable job in some areas (e.g., the regulation of the securities markets). Moreover, some unitary states fragment the internal market. For example, there is nothing in our federation that inhibits mobility to the degree that housing policy does in the United Kingdom.
- Finally, Canada's internal market is simply too small for a domestic common market to be an end of and by itself. In particular, to free up the domestic market while at the same time embarking on protectionist measures at a national level is surely a negative-sum economic game. Of the various broader perspectives that we might adopt with respect to a CEU, the openness of the Canadian economy and its dependence on world trade suggest the following: Secure those aspects of the internal economic union that will facilitate increased Canadian penetration in world markets.[7]

In terms of the relationship between a CEU and the division of powers, the following points merit emphasis:

- In the limit, the pursuit of a CEU can be a very centralizing element. Indeed, elsewhere I have argued that the introduction by Ottawa of the CEU into the 1980 constitutional debates was a brilliant manoeuvre (Courchene, 1984d). Rather than jockeying for more powers, the provinces suddenly realized that the impact of the CEU might well be to undermine substantially their set of existing powers. In this way the CEU, and particularly the manner in which Ottawa backed off from its original proposals, may have played a role in securing the constitutional accord. The basic point in all this is that a large part of the reason why the CEU is such a contentious issue relates to the dramatic impact it might have on the division of powers.
- Securing a CEU by means of a strong charter of economic rights would transfer powers away from both levels of government and toward Canadians. While I am personally in favour of a stronger set of citizen economic rights, it is important that such an instrument not emasculate either level of government. However, it is probably equally important that Ottawa's hands be bound somewhat, particularly since federal distortions are as costly as provincial ones.
- There may yet be considerable scope for the existing constitutional provisions to carve out a stronger domestic economic union.
- Drawing from the experience of other federations, it is not obvious that a constitutional provision is the preferred way to proceed in terms of enhancing the CEU. A federal-provincial instrumentality, drawing authority from, say, the preamble to the constitution, is an alternative approach that merits consideration.

A Compromise Proposal

I want to end this chapter with a proposal that changes the perspective on the CEU issue. I am in favour of enhancing the CEU. However, it seems to me that the ongoing debate is substantially off-track. Not only is the public's focus principally on provincial barriers, but the rhetoric is not conducive to rational dialogue. Words like "balkanization," "beggar-thy-neighbour," "province building," and "fragmentation" load the dice in an unfortunate way — unfortunate because as Canadians we have accomplished a great deal in terms of ensuring a free domestic market. We have one of the most decentralized federations in the world, and yet we are still harmonized in our internal policies. Compared to the Swiss we have a highly uniform, although essentially equally decentralized, taxation system. We have an agreement among all governments for allocating corporate profits across provinces and, hence, do not get into the U.S. mess of a "unitary" tax. We have eliminated or minimized residency requirements for access to the various social programs. We do not have out-of-province tuition fees, and so on. Moreover, in some areas like securities markets where there is no federal regulatory presence the provinces have largely met the challenge of ensuring that this market is both efficient and national.

It is important to note that none of these feature has been directly secured via the constitutional route. Rather, they are either the result of federal-provincial agreements or, in many cases, the result of the exercise of the federal spending power — e.g., to obtain shared-cost funds the provinces have to abide by certain provisions, some of which serve the CEU.

Phrased differently, it seems to me that it is appropriate to become more positive with respect to our accomplishments on the CEU front and to zero in on a few more critical areas where progress is needed. Toward this end, let me offer the following proposal:[8]

- While the relationship between the CEU and the division of powers appears on occasion to be hopelessly intertwined, they can, in principle, be conceptually distinct. I propose that they be separated in the following manner. Let us determine first the appropriate division of powers between Ottawa and the provinces. Then, for this given division of powers (which could be the status quo) let us attempt to enhance the CEU.

- To ensure progress, this enhancement of the internal common market should be directed at specific areas. Pension portability, both occupational and interprovincial, is an obvious candidate. So might be some sort of code of tax conduct for both levels of government. The precise way in which these goals are accomplished is not as important as that they be accomplished. In this regard it is important to note that arrangements to enhance the internal economic union need not be central: the provinces may well be able to put in place schemes that are perfectly adequate.

Were we to make significant progress in these two areas over the next few years we would indeed have gone a considerable way toward ensuring an adequate CEU. And with the will and ability to succeed behind us, other areas for inclusion will suggest themselves. This may not be the theoretically "neat" solution to the CEU, but it does have the advantage that it places the issue in a far less divisive atmosphere and that our past successes on the CEU front were of this nature.

Chapter 10

Conclusions and Implications

Part I (chapters 2 and 3) of the monograph provided a range of frameworks for viewing the interaction between economic management and the division of powers. Parts II (chapters 4 and 5), III (chapters 6 and 7), and IV (chapters 8 and 9) focussed on selected policy issues in the general areas of stabilization, distribution and allocation. The purpose of this final chapter is to attempt to pull together the various strands of the analysis in the hope of providing some useful conclusions and implications.

In one sense, however, there is no need for a conclusion: each of the individual chapters contained a set of summary points related to the issue in question. To be sure, a reiteration of these summaries would serve as a conclusion, but it would not add anything to the analysis.

In another sense, a conclusion that attempts to generalize from the preceding analysis may be inappropriate because the selection of topics was not only quite arbitrary but far from exhaustive. For example, little or no attention was directed to energy policy and more particularly to the fact that energy royalties from Crown lands accrue to the provinces. One could mount an argument that this feature of the Constitution circumscribed the nature of Canada's approach to energy policy. If the royalties accrued to Ottawa (i.e., if there was no internal distribution problem), is it likely that Canada would have gone to world energy prices much sooner? Indeed, in a recent paper Richard Simeon (1985) has argued that the cleavage in federal-provincial relations in the 1970s was a regional cleavage — energy in the West and language and "sovereignty" in Quebec — so much so that frequently the very processes and institutions of federal-provincial relations came under question. In his view, federalism of the 1980s is likely to be very different, dominated by the politics and economics of fiscal restraint.

Thus, the issue becomes one of whether we can generalize from the small sample of policy areas covered in this analysis or whether each policy area has its own set of unique problems and must be considered in isolation. The truth, I suspect, lies somewhere in the middle.

In spite of both of these valid concerns, I shall attempt to draw some general propositions from the foregoing analysis. Specifically, the first section of this final chapter will focus selectively on the above results to provide a kaleidoscope of the structure and processes of Canadian federalism. The next section will then address the centralization/decentralization issue as it is practised in other federations. The emphasis here will be on the notion of the "balance" that is struck in each federation. The study ends with a few general implications relating to the interaction between economic management and the division of powers. In particular, it argues that to the extent that new arrangements are appropriate they are likely to take the form of an "economic constitution" rather than a new "Constitution Act."

Economic Management and the Distribution of Powers

What is striking about the manner in which the Canadian federation approaches the allocation of powers is the incredibly rich variety of arrangements that currently exist, even with respect to the limited number of policy areas that were dealt with in this study. This is most evident in the income security area where the arrangements encompass the three "classical" approaches to structuring a federalism: unilateralism or the separation-of-powers approach (as reflected in old-age security (OAS) and guaranteed income supplement (GIS) for Ottawa and programs like Ontario's guaranteed annual income system (GAINS) for the provinces); co-operative federalism (as reflected in the workings of the Canada Assistance Plan); and intrastate federalism, multiple vetoes, or the system of checks and balances (as reflected in the operations of the Canada Pension Plan). While this variety is not typical of all policy areas, it is nonetheless illustrative of the difficulty of approaching the division of powers from a *single* conceptual framework. It would be equally difficult, and perhaps even foolhardy, to attempt to redesign the division of powers from any one conceptual framework.

Further to this point, the analysis suggests that the institutions and structures of our federation appear to be continually evolving in order to meet the needs of the time. Even a selected survey of some of the ways in which process and structure have evolved reveals this diversity and dynamism:

• Some powers have been transferred by constitutional amendment

from the provinces to Ottawa (e.g., unemployment insurance, old-age pensions).
- Some powers have been transferred from Ottawa to the provinces (e.g., the federal enabling legislation which has allowed the provinces to establish marketing boards that interfere with interprovincial trade).
- Some new institutions have been created which, while not enshrined in the Constitution, nonetheless derive their existence from parallel sets of legislation at both levels of government (e.g., the Canada Pension Plan).
- New institutions and structures have developed that do not have either a legislative or constitutional framework but which clearly have become an integral component of the practice, if not the art, of Canadian federalism (e.g., executive federalism and the first ministers' conference).
- Other institutions and/or programs have emerged which have become so much a part of the practice of federalism that they have been enshrined in the Constitution (e.g., equalization).
- More important than any of these specific items is the fact that over the past 40 years the framework of the BNA Act has permitted the system to centralize dramatically in wartime; to create national programs in the socio-economic areas in the 1960s; to move toward considerable decentralization in the mid-1970s; and perhaps to begin another round of centralization in the 1980s. The principal instrumentality in most of this change was the federal-provincial transfer system and the exercise of the federal spending power. However, the provinces too have taken initiatives that have led to some of these changes (e.g., the establishment of a separate personal income tax in Quebec in 1954).

In addition to these initiatives, which tend to be associated with changes in the structure (either de facto or de jure) of federalism, the review of the various policy areas reveals a wide range of practices or processes that lend further support to the variety of arrangements permitted or encouraged by the existing constitutional framework:

- In the area of securities legislation the federal government probably has the constitutional right to become a major regulatory player. Thus far, however, it has deferred to the provincial regulatory authorities.
- Federal-provincial agreements have frequently been developed in areas where there is a constitutional void or where constitutional authority is unclear. One example of this relates to the securing of the Canadian economic union where, at least in comparison with some other federations, our Constitution does not appear to provide much help. Yet the generally accepted formula for allocating the profits of multi-province businesses across the various jurisdictions implies that in terms of this aspect of tax harmonization we are better off than, say,

the Swiss and the U.S. federations where, ironically, they do have stronger constitutional provisions for ensuring a domestic economic union.

- This leads to the more general point that, for certain policy issues, there may be avenues other than constitutional amendment or enshrinement that on occasion may be the preferred route to take.

To be sure, the above series of observations may cast a particularly rosy hue on the evolution of the division of powers. It is not meant to minimize the many problems on the constitutional front but rather to emphasize that there are many avenues that can be utilized to rectify problems which arise. Although it might appear that the evolution is in some sense "optimal," this is not my intention. For example, the federal enabling legislation for provincial marketing boards is, in my opinion, a retrograde measure.

Apart from these concerns, the above summary is deficient in yet another way — its focus is principally (and deliberately) on structure and practice and not on economic management. What do the preceding chapters have to say about the division of powers from the perspective of economics? Again, it seems appropriate to proceed in point form:

- The optimal assignment of powers will in all likelihood depend on the overall economic goals pursued by the federation. A change in the nature of the economic policy objectives will probably call for a corresponding change in the division of powers (either de jure or de facto).
- In any federation, there will always be some things that each level of government is prohibited from doing. However, this is not an important issue if the pursuit of these particular objectives does not make economic sense. For example, the provinces do not have a direct role in the conduct of monetary policy (i.e., monetary policy is not regionalized). This ought to be of no concern, since economic theory and practice indicate that monetary policy ought to be centralized.
- Relatedly, there are powers that can be exercised only in certain circumstances. Wage and price controls are a good example: Ottawa has the authority to enact such controls in an emergency but not in the ordinary course of events. From my economic perspective, this situation does not warrant redress since "in the normal course of events" it is hard to argue for a system of controls.
- There are often alternative ways to accomplish any policy goal. While some of these may run afoul of the Constitution, others are likely to be intra vires. Economists refer to this as the principle of effective market classification or the optimal policy instrument calculus. With respect to the wage and price control example, the federal government has the power to impose wage controls on its own employees and on those sectors falling under federal jurisdiction (e.g., transportation). Sim-

ilarly, the provinces can follow suit if they wish. Since the private sector can be counted on to respond to economic conditions, this is probably all that is warranted in terms of the powers to implement controls. However, there are other instances where it seems clear that the wrong policy instrument was utilized. The regional aspects of unemployment insurance as well as the special UI provisions for fishermen would probably fall into this category. If the role of UI is seen principally as a distributional role, then an instrument more suited to distribution is to be preferred. If it is an anti-migration policy, again the federal government should have tackled the problem (rigid wage rates across provinces) rather than the symptom (unemployment). In general, economic analysis would suggest that distributional instruments should be used to tackle distributional problems. Unemployment insurance can be viewed as tampering with resource allocation in order to handle a distributional problem.

- If one level of federal government is assigned the responsibility for achieving a particular objective, then the constitutional arrangements should ensure that it has the ability to address this objective in the optimal manner.
- Underlying all these comments is the more important requirement that the federation be able to adjust its structures and processes to accommodate the required economic adjustment. The comfortable economic niche in which Canada found itself during the decade of the 1960s has clearly vanished. The nations that will succeed in the 1990s are those that can allocate or reallocate resources with speed and efficiency to the sunrise industries. This is especially true for the small open economies like Canada. Hence, the constitutional framework must be capable of adapting to altered economic circumstances. Thus, the particular structure of powers at any point in time is probably not as important as the ability of this structure to accommodate new economic goals. In this sense, process is every bit as critical as structure.
- There is another reason why process may dominate structure. In our increasingly interdependent world, the role of government has likewise become more pervasive. A given assignment of powers no longer guarantees one level of government full freedom to act with respect to, say, sphere X since actions by the other level of government elsewhere in the complex system will surely rebound back on policy area X.
- In tandem, these concerns have led me in the direction of endorsing Carl Friedrich's notion of federalism (which, although it appeared earlier, merits repetition): ". . . federalism should not be seen only as a static pattern or design, characterized by a particular and precisely fixed division of powers between government levels. Federalism is also and perhaps primarily the process . . . of adopting joint policies and making joint decisions on joint problems."[1]

This emphasis on federalism as a process takes on added weight in light of the variety of structures in federal countries, to which I now turn.

Cross-Federation Comparisons[2]

Substantial portions of several of the above chapters focussed on the manner in which other federations have dealt with the particular policy issues under discussion. In general, these examples offered little in the way of practical guidance precisely because of the variety of ways in which other federations addressed any given policy issue. This suggests either that there is no unique, ideal structure or process to be associated with most policy areas or that, for each policy area, we ought to focus principally on those federations faced with a similar "environment" for the policy area in question.

Toward this latter end, one comparison that would initially appear to be particularly revealing is that between Canada and Australia, the only other industrialized federation with a British-type parliamentary system. As noted above, Australia can be viewed as falling, along with Canada, in the "interstate federalism" category: some of the processes developed by the Australians (e.g., executive federalism) also exist in Canada. However, as Richard Bird notes:

> [H]ad Australia not been established initially as a federal country, it seems most unlikely that it would be one today. Of all the countries examined [basically, the five referred to in the present monograph plus Austria] its fiscal policies are by far the most centralized . . . the impulse toward uniformity in this homogeneous country . . . runs deep.

The German federation is also highly centralized, even to the point where the constitution does not permit differential tax rates on the major shared taxes. Although the various states or laender do have some input into federal policies, the German federation is decentralized principally in the sense that there is decentralized implementation of national legislation. We could argue that this is more consistent with a unitary state with a structure of local governments than with the notion of federalism that is characteristic of, say, Canada and Switzerland. Even so, there may be a good deal that we can learn from the German experience, particularly in those policy areas where Canada goes some way toward the joint implementation model. To quote Bird again:

> Despite our up-and-down experience with using the federal spending power to slip (or bludgeon) a federal presence into the designated functions of the provinces, it may not be beyond the human mind to work out at least some limited "joint" tasks in Canada — "joint" in the sense of involving federal financing but provincial execution of essentially provincial expenditures, all subject to agreement by both sides on a basis of equality. Such an approach might prove valuable in such fields as higher education, health care, and

technical retraining — in all of which both federal and provincial interests are obvious.

In other words, we do not have to adopt the German institutional framework (intrastate federalism et al.) in order to see virtue in having some of our processes of federalism imitate those in the German federation.

In terms of the degree of decentralization, the Swiss and U.S. federations may provide more in the way of a role model. The diversity in these two federations leads Bird to two intriguing insights with respect to the operation of the Canadian system. With respect to the United States, he observes that "the U.S. system suggests how much more diversity in many respects — for instance, in local tax systems — can be tolerated than is generally considered to be the case in Canada." Even more insightful are his reflections on the Swiss model:

> [A]lthough Switzerland hardly offers readily transferable solutions to Canada's problems, a close look at its experience may provide the most illuminating of all possible comparisons for Canadians, in part because it suggests that some of the problems and solutions currently discussed in Canada may, when viewed from a different perspective, reverse their positions. As in a well-known optical illusion, when looked at in a slightly different way, background may become foreground and the foreground background — or problems (such as, say, tax diversity) may become solutions while solutions (such as tax harmonization) may become problems!

The Notion of "Balance" in a Federation

More generally, it seems that each federation has gone through a process of internal "co-existence." In some cases this co-existence was forced upon the system by the constitution itself. For example, the Australian Commonwealth found that it was prevented by the constitution from nationalizing airlines and banks and from creating national marketing boards. It eventually found a way around these restrictions by utilizing to the fullest its power to make grants to the states and by creating new institutions like the Australian Loan Council. In other federations, the co-existence is essentially directed "against" the constitution. For example, in the Swiss case the internal market provision in its constitution is such that the federal government has authority to harmonize the fiscal system and to put an end to the so-called tax jungle. But the cultural, historical and political (local democracy) traditions of the Swiss not only have prevented this from occurring but, as noted in the quotation from Nowotny in Chapter 1, the issue of the potential inefficiency arising from the tax jungle is not even widely discussed, except outside of Switzerland.

In other words, there is a "balance" that appears to have developed in each federation — a balance between centralization and decentralization, between the role of citizens and the role of governments, between uniformity and diversity, and so on. As any review of cross-federation approaches will demonstrate, this balance is struck at different places for different policies for different countries, and the balance is clearly time-dependent. Moreover, the nature of the balance operating in one federation in comparison with another can be much more than the positioning of the "fulcrum" in the two countries. Consider the internal common market issue. The Canadian government was quite correct to point out (in the constitutional discussions in 1980) that the Canadian provinces have more freedom to enact policies that may fragment the internal common market than is the case for the states of most other federations. However, what it did not point out (or at least did not emphasize) was that this was also true of the Canadian government: the federal governments of other federations tend to be more constrained by their constitutions in terms of implementing policies that give preference to one region or one state over other regions or states. Hence, there will be more regionally distortive policies in Canada implemented by *both* levels of government than we would find, say, in Australia. But the process is not explosive (although some may argue that it has gone too far), since each level of government in Canada has the power to escalate and, therefore, to generate dead-weight loss. This, too, is balance, albeit a balance that may be typically Canadian in the sense that it is probably born more of the particular economic geography of the provinces than of ideology.

There is a second element to any notion of balance that is probably important — that while the formal constitution is typically an important determinant of these trade-offs, there are other factors that will, almost of necessity, come into play. This was clearly evident in the example of Switzerland and its approach (or lack of approach) to tax harmonization. In turn, this suggests that the notion of balance is supported not only by the structure but also by the processes of the federation.

Several implications follow from this notion of balance. First of all, it tends to provide a different perspective from which to view certain features of federalism. Consider, for example, the "opting-out provision" in our fiscal arrangements, a feature that is probably unique to the Canadian federation. No doubt, it represents to many an undesirable feature of our federal structure. It is well recognized that opting out allows Quebec more flexibility on its fiscal side than would otherwise be the case. However, what is not so well recognized is that opting out also permits the remaining nine provinces to have a more harmonized (and perhaps more centralized!) fiscal structure than would otherwise be possible. Thus, in striking the balance between harmony and diversity, and perhaps between centralization and decentralization as well, the opting-out provision allows at the same time more diversity (for Quebec) and more harmony (for the remaining nine provinces) than would be the case if all provinces were made to toe some common intermediate line.

A second implication of this focus on balance is that changes in the formal constitution may not be the only, or the most appropriate, manner by which to usher in any desired changes. In some areas, like securities regulation, the federal government can (constitutionally) play a major role, but it has decided thus far to leave securities regulation to the provinces. Hence, in this area changes in the de facto division of powers will likely arise because of perceived economic or political needs. Much the same is likely to characterize other areas as well. It is largely for this reason that I suggested in Chapter 9 that the way to enhance the internal common market may not be via a wholesale alteration in the balance of the federation (e.g., by an enlarged trade and commerce power) but rather by a specific focus on those aspects of the existing arrangements that stand most in the way of securing greater domestic economic integration.

The problem with a dramatic shift in the formal distribution of powers is that it will almost assuredly set in motion a veritable chain reaction of adjustments on the part of both levels of government until some new "balance" is restored. Moreover, it is far from clear that the final outcome will be predictable. This does not mean that dramatic changes are necessarily to be avoided. What it does mean, however, is that any such constitutional change will eventually have to be filtered through the political, economic, cultural and geographical compromises inherent in the federation in order that a new set of structures and processes replace the old.

In this context, it is instructive to devote some time to the one element of the new Constitution that clearly has altered the traditional balance in the Canadian federation — the Canadian Charter of Rights and Freedoms. Surely this Charter will bring about dramatic changes in the practice of federalism in Canada. For one thing, it will "republicanize" the federation in the sense that it represents a move away from parliamentary democracy: there are now some things with respect to which no parliament can legislate. Moreover, as the Canadian public becomes more accustomed to the role of a bill of rights, my guess is that they will move to expand its application. For example, a move to include private property in the bill of rights (i.e., to move it more in the direction of an economic bill of rights) may well represent one way to secure an internal common market. However, the implications of securing a Canadian economic union via a bill of economic rights are vastly different from securing it, for example, via enlarging a federal head of power. The result would be a "decentralization" of powers, but it would represent a transfer of power to citizens (and to the courts) and away from both levels of government. Should this occur, it will have substantial implications for the governments' role in the economy, particulary on the allocation front (e.g., regional policy). It will take decades, rather than years, for the federation to generate a new "balance" in the wake of such a development. Nonetheless, I, for one, would welcome such an extension of the charter.

Toward an Economic Constitution

Finally, I want to return to a central theme of this study and focus once more on what economics and economic management might tell us about constitutional redesign. Unfortunately, apart from some obvious areas like monetary policy, I think the answer is "not much" (or at least not as much as I had anticipated prior to embarking on this study). Experience elsewhere indicates that both centralized and decentralized federations can be effective on the economic front. Moreover, if Canadians wish to decentralize further, this change need not imply constitutional redesign. Among the alternative options open are:

- legislative changes within the existing constitutional framework (e.g., the CPP experience);
- an increase in the proportion of provincial revenues that arise from own-source taxation as distinct from federal transfers;
- an increase in the proportion of federal transfers to the provinces that are unconditional; and
- an increase in the range of policy areas on which the provinces must be consulted (e.g., allowing provincial input into appointments for national bodies).

Nonetheless, there are several areas where economics suggests that new arrangements may be appropriate. Basically, however, most of these can be treated under the rubric of a new economic constitution rather than a new Constitution Act.

Toward this goal of providing an economic constitution for Canada, let me suggest the following items. First, there ought to be a recognition and indeed a commitment that it is desirable to enhance the Canadian economic union. I have suggested that the preferable route to follow here may be a federal-province "code of economic conduct" rather than a formal change in the constitutional allocation of powers. Whatever the mechanisms, however, there is need for a reorientation of policy in several areas. One approach that would appear to have merit is to attempt to enhance those aspects of the internal common market that will facilitate our ability to penetrate foreign markets. For example, portability of pensions and portability of social services across provinces will enhance labour mobility resource allocation. If the provinces are unwilling or unable to guarantee these mobility rights, then Ottawa should enforce them via its expenditure power (as a condition for federal-provincial transfers). A similar recommendation applies to the markets for capital. In Chapter 8 I argued in favour of retaining provincial control over the regulation of the securities market. However, if the provinces become embroiled in a beggar-thy-neighbour approach to regulating the capital markets, Ottawa can and should step in to ensure that the national market for capital is not balkanized. Therefore, enhancing the ability of goods, services, labour and capital to move free and freely within the federation is the first component of an economic constitution. An important corollary is that any such enhanced domestic integration should not be accompanied by decreasing international integration. One of the principal conclusions of the internal economic union chapter was that the costs of impediments on the international front exceeded those on the domestic front.

Second, an economic constitution should strive to remove duplication and waste — to "disentangle" where feasible. The views of the former treasurer of Ontario on this subject effectively capture the essence of this point:

> This [the reduction of waste and duplication] is neither a new issue nor a new concern in Canada. In my view, much of the wasteful duplication among governments was the product of political conflict between Ottawa and the provinces in recent years.
>
> Most of the provinces have well-developed programs to support small business and cost-effective initiatives to assist the young unemployed. But too often, Ottawa developed its own set of programs — duplicating provincial efforts. And in the areas where the federal government developed a program . . . to meet a local or regional concern, the province involved would probably launch its own similar initiative. Surely, as a fundamental tenet of our new economic constitution, we can agree that if one level of government is best equipped or situated to deal with a problem, the other level should provide complementary resources and support to make that program work even better — rather than operating a separate program of its own.
>
> That may require both levels of government to "give up turf" on occasion. Canadians now expect us to subordinate narrow partisan interests to the interests of effectiveness and efficiency.[3]

The requirement to "give up turf" is clearly central to effective disentanglement. It may well be that this can be accomplished by mutually agreeable trades within the existing framework, but the parties may also require safeguards of a nature that would call for legislative action or even a formal reallocation of powers. Nonetheless, the politics and economics of fiscal restraint and economic exigency will continue to exert pressure for rationalization and/or disentanglement in some areas.

The third component of an economic constitution would be to ensure that the existing structures and processes of federalism are such as to enable overall policy to reflect the economic needs of the 1990s. From my perspective, the next decade will place a premium on flexibility and adjustment, and the range of socio-economic policies should serve to encourage rather than inhibit this adjustment. Once again, constitutional change may not be the desirable route to follow, particularly in light of the tremendous interdependence that characterizes the policy actions in this area. Moreover, the existing set of arrangements already run the gamut from unilateralism to intrastate federalism. Thus, getting the division of powers "right" is not as important as getting the policy "right": indeed the role of the former should be to facilitate the latter.

A fourth component relates to the optimal instrument assignment. Once there is agreement on the objectives to be pursued by the two levels of government, it is critical to ensure that each level has at its disposal the policy instruments appropriate to achieve the objective.

We could add many more components to this notion of an economic constitution. Moreover, the reader's list would no doubt differ from mine. But, what becomes clear is that any such package will become more in the nature of a design for appropriate policy than a design for appropriate structure. Structure becomes a problem only if it prevents, or makes very costly, the achievement of appropriate policy. In my view, it is difficult to find many cases where our poor economic performance can be blamed on the straitjacket imposed by the constitutional framework (energy policy is probably the exception). The evidence in the above chapters does not lead us in the direction of constitutional change as the key to better economic management. Phrased differently, inadequacies in economic management in our federation are, in the main, a matter of the failure of policy, not structure. This is not intended to rule out formal changes in structure but to suggest that the first priority on the economic management front is to decide on the appropriate policy stance. Once this is clear, the question of structural redesign will become both more obvious and less controversial.

Thus, my overall conclusion is that structure is secondary to policy: the structure and processes should adjust to the economic needs of the federation rather than the situation where the economic policies of the federation come to be determined by structural and constitutional considerations. Constitutional redesign, formulated in the abstract, is not the route to take. As Yogi Berra once proclaimed: "if you don't know where you're going, you may end up somewhere else."

Appendix

TABLE A-1 A Selective Chronology of Personal Income Tax (PIT) Developments

Year	Development	Comments
1851	Ontario municipalities begin collecting PIT.	The collection of PIT by Ontario municipalities continues right through to 1936.
1867	BNA Act	The federal government is assigned power to raise money "by any mode or system of taxation." Provinces are restricted to levying direct taxes.
1876	British Columbia introduces a PIT.	British Columbia is the first province to adopt a PIT.
1894	Prince Edward Island establishes its own PIT.	
1917	Federal government introduces its own PIT.	Challenges prevailing wisdom that the PIT is the exclusive domain of the provinces. The minister of finance, Thomas White, reflects this sentiment even as he introduces the tax: the income tax is peculiarly within the jurisdiction of the province and is a suitable tax for purposes of the province and the municipality. In my opinion, the federal government should not resort to an income tax until it is indispensably necessary in the national interest that it do so.
1922	Privy Council rules in Caron v. R that federal government has the right to levy PIT.	Federal PIT activities challenged by a Quebec cabinet minister. The court confirms that the BNA Act envisaged joint occupancy of the direct taxation field.
1923	Manitoba establishes its own PIT.	
1932	Saskatchewan and Alberta introduce their PITs.	Part of the scramble for revenue in the 1930s that contributes to the field of taxation in Canada becoming a "tax jungle."
1936	Ontario introduces its own PIT. At the same time it concludes an agreement with Ottawa whereby the Department of National	Comment by Premier Hepburn: "This Act [the Income Tax Act] replaced the disgraceful checkerboard system of municipal income tax, full of

Year	Development	Comments
	Revenue would administer and collect the tax. Hence, it is not really an "Ontario-run" PIT.	inequalities, anomalies and hardships."
1938	Manitoba and Prince Edward Island follow the Ontario (1936) model.	
1939	Quebec introduces a PIT on the Ontario model.	
1940	*Report of the Royal Commission on Dominion-Provincial Relations* (Rowell-Sirois Report)	Proposals to restructure federal-provincial financial relations. As part of an overall program, the report recommends that the provinces transfer direct taxation (including PIT) to the federal level.
1941	Conference on the Rowell-Sirois Report.	Provinces reject Rowell-Sirois proposals.
1941	Wartime Tax Agreements (to be in force from 1942–47). This is the first of several agreements that are commonly referred to as "tax rental" arrangements.	Exigencies of wartime finance lead to provinces "renting" personal income taxation to the federal government. Comment by R.M. Burns: "Patriotism accomplished what financial reasoning could not." In return for the rental agreement, the provinces have the choice of: (a) the revenue yield within the province in 1941 from the vacated tax field (selected by Quebec, Ontario, Manitoba, Alberta, and British Columbia); (b) the net cost of servicing the provincial debt, less succession duties (adopted by Saskatchewan and the three Maritime provinces).
1945–47	Conference on Reconstruction (1945). The conference itself is not particularly successful. Those aspects relating to direct taxation eventually result in the 1947–52 Tax Rental Agreements.	The federal government desires to continue the tax rental arrangements for the direct taxes. It buttresses its case by invoking macroeconomic taxation (Keynesian) arguments. Three options are offered: (a) $12.75 per head plus 50 percent of direct taxation revenue for 1940–41 plus statutory subsidies based on 1947 payments; (b) $15 per head plus the statutory subsidies; (c)

Year	Development	Comments
		$2,100,000 (this option was designed for P.E.I.). All options are to be escalated by population increase and GNP growth. Nova Scotia and Saskatchewan choose the second option. Manitoba, British Columbia, Alberta, and New Brunswick choose the first system. Ontario and Quebec do not sign the agreement.
1947	Ontario and Quebec set up their own corporate income taxes.	Represents the beginning of the move away from the centralization of direct taxation that began in wartime.
1950	Ontario announces a 5 percent personal income tax.	The federal government refuses to collect it. Ontario is reluctant to put its own collection machinery in place, and the tax is never brought into effect.
1952	The 1952–57 Tax Rental Agreements. Ontario signs the agreement and abandons its corporate tax. Quebec remains outside the fold.	In addition to the three options of the previous agreement (updated for 1948 levels), the federal government proposes a fourth option: the yield of the personal income tax at 5 percent of 1948 federal rates plus the yield of 8.5 percent on corporate profits earned in the province in 1948 plus average revenue from succession duties plus 1948 statutory subsidies. Payments are escalated as in the previous agreement. In effect, this additional option is designed to bring Ontario back into the agreements. It succeeds.
1954	Quebec establishes a separate PIT. It already has its own corporate income tax.	Establishes a rate of 15 percent of the federal rate. Ottawa responds by establishing a 10 percent federal tax credit for taxes paid to province. Quebecers are still "overtaxed" by 5 percent and face different exemptions under the two systems. Personal income taxation becomes progressively more unwieldy. The search for an alternative solution begins.

TABLE A-1 (cont'd)

Year	Development	Comments
1957	The Tax Sharing Arrangements (1956–62).	If provinces opt to continue to rent the direct taxation field to Ottawa, they will receive shares of these taxes — 10 percent of PIT, 9 percent of corporate profits, and 50 percent of succession duties. Alternatively, they can levy their own taxes on these sources and the federal government will provide an abatement from federal taxes equal to the above percentage. All provinces except Quebec agree for the PIT. Ontario and Quebec do not sign for corporation taxes and succession duties. Equalization program is established in order to equalize the yield of these direct taxes across the various provinces.
1957	Ontario re-establishes its corporate income tax.	
1958	PIT abatement rises from 10 percent to 13 percent.	
1962	The Tax Collection Agreements (1962–67)	Direct taxation is once again returned to the provinces under arrangements called the Tax Collection Agreements. Provinces can levy their own tax rates and have them collected free of charge by Ottawa. They have to accept the federal definitions for such things as taxable income and exemptions. They can levy a tax on "basic federal tax." It has to be a single rate. This regime is still in effect today. Initially, the federal abatement is set at 16 percentage points of the personal income tax.
1962–66	Federal abatement of PIT rises from 16 percentage points to 24 percentage points by 1966.	Part of this abatement relates to the funding provisions for the established programs (medicare, hospital insurance, and post-secondary education).
1967	1967–72 Fiscal Tax Structure Committee, struck in 1964, plays an important role in federal-	Continuation of 1962 agreements. PIT abatement rises to 28 percent, which expressed as a percent of basic federal tax (and

Year	Development	Comments
	provincial financial relations in this area.	taking into account the 1972 tax reforms) equals 30.5 percent. This is the Ontario tax rate until 1977. Marks the end of the abatement process. Ottawa argues that if provinces want more revenue from PIT they can raise their tax rates.
1969	Ontario Treasurer McNaughton notifies Ottawa that Ontario intends to establish its own PIT within two years.	The purpose of this measure is to pressure the federal government to accept some of Ontario's views with respect to the ongoing tax reform. Federal modifications, including the allowing of provincial tax credits (see 1972), eventually satisfy Ontario and the province does not proceed with its own PIT.
1972–77	1972–77 Fiscal Arrangements.	Business as usual.
1972	PIT tax reform and introduction of the revenue guarantee.	Tax reforms include: UIC benefits taxable, increased child-care exemptions, capital gains tax, increase in RRSP levels, increase in personal exemption levels. Later modifications, not part of the original reform, include the $1,000 interest income exemption, the $1,000 pension deduction, the education deduction, and elderly exemptions. In order to encourage the provinces to make parallel changes in PIT, the federal government offers the revenue guarantee (see Chapter 2).
1972	Ontario introduces the first PIT tax credit (for property taxes).	Major initiative in that it is the first of many tax credits covering the spectrum from royalty tax credits to home heating tax credits. The federal government establishes three criteria for tax credits: (1) they must be administratively feasible, (2) they must not erode the essential harmony and uniformity of federal and provincial income tax systems, and (3) they must not jeopardize the functioning of the Canadian economic union.

TABLE A-1 (cont'd)

Year	Development	Comments
1973	Ottawa indexes the PIT (beginning with the 1974 taxation year). Indexation losses are not eligible for compensation under the revenue guarantee.	Provinces go along with indexing, except for Quebec.
1977	1977–82 Fiscal Arrangements. Main PIT impact relates to the block funding of the established programs and the termination of the old revenue guarantee. A temporary and weaker revenue guarantee is introduced.	As a result of refinancing the established programs, the federal government transfers an additional 9,143 personal income tax points (a tax point is 1 percent of basic federal tax) to the provinces. For Ontario, this translates into a provincial personal income tax rate of 44 percent.
1979	Quebec introduces its Stock Savings Plan as part of its PIT.	In computing taxable income for Quebec purposes, a Quebec resident can deduct up to $15,000 for purchases of new shares of Quebec companies.
1979	A British Columbia proposal for a tax credit along the lines of the Quebec program (1979) is rejected by the federal government as not falling within the spirit of the tax collection agreements.	Actually, the proposal covers two tax credits. One is a small business venture capital corporation tax credit (to apply to both personal and corporate taxes) and the other a dividend tax credit. Ottawa refuses to administer these credits because it views them as constituting barriers to the free flow of capital across provincial boundaries.
1979–82	Other provinces propose tax credits that Ottawa refuses to administer.	Basically, these proposals too violate the requirement that the free flow of capital across provincial boundaries be maintained. In several cases Ottawa recommends that the provinces enact these proposals as expenditure programs, i.e., not as part of the tax system. Form appears to matter more than substance.
1981	Ontario raises its personal income tax rate from 44 percent to 48 percent.	This represents the first increase in Ontario personal income tax rates. All previous Ontario tax increases merely took up vacated federal tax room, i.e., they did not represent an overall increase in PIT taxation.

TABLE A-1 (cont'd)

Year	Development	Comments
1981	Alberta adopts its own corporate tax system.	Alberta desires a degree of flexibility in terms of incentives and innovations in its corporate tax system that may not be allowed under the Tax Collection Agreements.
1981	British Columbia serves notice to the federal government that it might withdraw from the Tax Collection Agreements unless the federal government agrees to administer its proposed dividend and venture capital tax credits.	
1982	British Columbia proposes a Housing and Employment Bond Tax Credit. Ottawa agrees to administer it.	This may be a very important precedent. The British Columbia government will issue bonds. The interest income will not be taxable for provincial income tax purposes. (Ottawa refused to exempt this income for federal taxes.) The B.C. government will then lend the proceeds to eligible borrowers – individuals, corporations, and small businesses. This is a remarkable concession by the federal government, since the end result will be to erect barriers to interprovincial flows of enterprises and capital. Since the bulk of these funds was to be targeted to housing, Ottawa probably found it difficult to refuse the proposal in the face of the very high levels of interest rates.
1982	The Ontario government requests the Ontario Economic Council to evaluate the costs and benefits of a separate Ontario PIT.	

Source: Ontario Economic Council, *A Separate Personal Income Tax for Ontario.* (Toronto: The Council, 1983).

Notes

1. Except that, with the patriation of the Constitution, the new amending formula does formally involve the provinces in the process of constitutional amendment.
2. Quebec, 1956. The commission chairman was Thomas Tremblay and the report is frequently referred to as the Tremblay Report.
3. A policy spillover or fiscal externality is defined as a situation in which the benefits or costs of a policy action enacted by one jurisdiction spill over into another jurisdiction. From an efficiency standpoint, if there is a spillover of benefitrs (costs) to another jurisdiction the spending on the policy area in question is likely to be less (more) than optimal.

CHAPTER 2

1. This chapter draws heavily from some of my previously published research, in particular Courchene, 1977, pp. 311–46; Courchene, 1983, chap. 2; Courchene, 1984c, chap. 2.
2. See Courchene, 1984d. This point will also be emphasized in Chapter 9 on the Canadian economic union.
3. Parizeau, 1970, pp. 82–83. The last two paragraphs have been reversed and emphasis has been added.

CHAPTER 3

1. Much of the first half of this chapter is adapted from Courchene, 1973a, pp. 191–206.
2. Were sufficient knowledge and data available so that one could cast Table 3-1 in a linear programming context, the results would be highly interesting. In the objective function we would have the various possible federal policies multiplied by a given set of "prices" — i.e., the contribution of each of the policies to national output. The constraint set would constitute a series of equations that captured the various constraints. The solution to the primal problem would be the appropriate vector of operating levels for the various federal policies. The dual prices would represent the potential increase in national income that could be attained by relaxing the various constraints. In particular, the dual prices associated with constraint (g) of objective function 7 would represent the increase in national output attainable by relaxing the requirement that the minimum income level be "produced" in each province. Assuming for the moment that number 7 was the objective function selected, the dual prices could then be used to calculate the increase in output that would arise from having, say, one Atlantic province rather than four or one Prairie province rather than three. In other words, the thinking of a decade ago that generated discussion of Maritime Union would become a much more important issue when the objective function embodies provincial place prosperity (number 7) than when it embodies only regional place prosperity (number 6). And so on.
3. This diagram has been adapted from a Department of Finance research paper written by Geoffrey Young more than a decade ago. More recently, it has been utilized in a paper by Courchene, 1984a. Much of the analysis in this section is adapted from this paper.
4. This assumes that the federal government is committed to a policy of full employment; and that it takes the existing wage differential as given.

CHAPTER 4

1. For example, Panama does not have its own currency, and Israel has also raised the possibility of substituting the U.S. dollar for its local currency. In terms of subnational

entities, the Scottish chartered banks issue their own notes, but they are tradeable on par with (and indeed backed by) Bank of England notes so that they are not a separate currency. Interestingly enough, however, the Bank of England has recently announced that it will no longer continue issuing £1 notes: they will be replaced by coins. But the Scottish chartered banks apparently intend to continue issuing their £1 notes.

2. Excerpt from Louis Rasminsky's Per Jacobsson Memorial Lecture (Rome, 1966). The phraseology has since been incorporated into the Bank Act.

CHAPTER 5

1. Barber, 1966, cited in Waterman, Hum, and Scarfe, 1982, p. 82.
2. See Ontario Economic Council, 1983b, chap. 11, or Wilson, 1984, various tables.
3. More easy to argue would be the allocative and distributional case for centralizing the CIT. This would follow from the tax assignment principles enunciated in the last section of Chapter 1. Thirsk also makes a strong case for centralizing the corporate tax, based on the fact that it is a "source-based" tax and, hence, its burden can be exported from one province to another. See Thirsk (1980), pp. 118–42.
4. Chapter 7 on equalization will focus on "horizontal" fiscal balance — the allocation of funds across the various provinces.

CHAPTER 6

1. Interprovincial Conference of Ministers Responsible for Social Services, 1980, p. 25, cited in Parliamentary Task Force on Federal-Provincial Fiscal Arrangements, 1981, p. 48. The Task Force report is often referred to as the Breau Report, after its chairman Herb Breau, MP.
2. This section draws from Courchene, 1984b, pp. 16–19.
3. For an excellent overview of these options see Stoddart, 1985.
4. See Graham Scott's comments on the Stoddart paper in Courchene, Conklin and Cook, eds., 1985.
5. Quebec, 1956. The commission was headed by Thomas Tremblay — hence the usual reference to this as the Tremblay Report.
6. Parts of this section are from Courchene, 1985.

CHAPTER 7

1. Much of this section and the following sections on political and economic rationales for equalization are taken verbatim from Courchene, 1984c, chap. 3. This chapter was written jointly with Kevin Dowd.
2. However, it should be recognized that features consistent with the notion of equalization can be traced back to the Constitution Act, 1867, itself (see Table 7-A1).
3. A more thorough discussion of the Australian approach to equalization can be found in Courchene, 1984c, chap. 9.
4. For more details relating to the German model of equalization see ibid., appendix to chap. 8.

CHAPTER 8

1. Anisman and Hogg, 1979, p. 144. The footnotes within quotations have been deleted in all citations in this chapter.
2. *Multiple Access Ltd. v. McCutcheon*, 138 D.L.R. (3rd) 1, 14 N.R. 181, 18 B.L.R. 138.
3. I wish to thank Philip Anisman for bringing this decision to my attention.

4. Much of the analysis in this section is adapted from the Ontario Securities Commission (1983).

5. The suitability rule requires that every broker make such enquiries as are appropriate to determine the suitability of a proposed purchase or sale based on the general investment needs and objectives of each client. This role is part and parcel of "full-service" brokers. Discount brokers, to which the GLIS would be associated, provide only an execution (buy and sell) service and are not in the business of giving advice. The problem here extends beyond GLIS, and the OSC will have a further set of hearings relating to the application of the suitability rule in connection with discount brokers.

6. Ontario Securities Commission, 1983, pp. 16–17. Emphasis has been added.

7. The best source I have been able to find on current moves toward financial integration is that by York University's Seymour Friedland, "The Emerging Financial Service Industry," manuscript (undated). Much of what follows is based on this valuable paper.

8. The OSC has recently held hearings relating to the ownership and cpaital requirements of the securities industry. The "industry position" is that the present restriction should be maintained and even enlarged to cover trading in the current exempt markets. (See Joint Securities Industry Committee, 1984.) Others argue for a removal or at least a dramatic loosening of these ownership and capital restrictions (see Courchene, 1984e). The OSC's ruling on this important issue will be rendered in early 1985 — but too late to incorporate in this monograph.

9. Robert MacIntosh, president of the Canadian Bankers Association, recently focussed on this conflict of interest: "A fiduciary trust company which wants to make commercial loans but which also has the power to act as trustee for a debenture issue of an issuing corporation, and which also acts with discretionary power over the pension fund investments of a client, is in an inherent conflict of interest situation and I don't care how honorable and how honest the people who are doing the function are. They are answering to different masters at the same time and that is a conflict of interest. You can't escape it. If the company is in trouble, is the company going to call the loan first and let the debenture holders go hang? Are they going to sell the stock first and secure their own position, or which? And either way they go they're going to be sued. Either by the shareholder of the company or by the other side. And that inherent conflict you can't escape no matter how high you erect Chinese walls" (Strategic Planning Forum, 1983, p. 35).

10. These thoughts are adapted from Lortie, 1984.

11. This section is based on Ontario Economic Council, 1983a, Part II.

12. See Ontario Economic Council, 1983a, Part II, p. 202. The background piece underlying the council's focus on the federal-provincial overlap in the pensions area is that by Banting, 1984, pp. 189–209.

13. The points in this paragraph are derived from Banting, 1984.

CHAPTER 9

1. Parts of this chapter draw heavily on Courchene, 1984d. I want also to thank the research staff of the Royal Commission on the Economic Union and Development Prospects for Canada, particularly Ivan Bernier, Ken Norrie, Mark Krasnick and John Whalley, for comments on an earlier draft. Valuable comments were also made by Gérald Bélanger and Rodrique Tremblay.

2. This point has been emphasized by Whalley, 1983a.

3. The remainder of this paragraph draws upon some recent work by Melvin, "The Regional Consequences of Tariffs and Domestic Transportation Costs," forthcoming.

4. This paragraph is adapted from some comments by Rodrique Tremblay at a Royal Commission workshop.

5. Bushnell, 1980, p. 135. Internal footnotes in the quotation have been suppressed. Emphasis has been added.

6. The ideas in this section were "stolen" from a conversation with Ivan Bernier, the director of research on the legal side of the Royal Commission.
7. I am indebted to Peter Leslie for suggesting this approach.
8. This is adapted from Courchene, 1985.

CHAPTER 10

1. Cited in Bastien, 1981, p. 48.
2. The summary comments derive from a distillation of some elements of the above chapters as well as from an excellent recent article by Richard Bird, 1985.
3. Larry Grossman, "Remarks at the Primrose Club Luncheon," Toronto, Ontario, September 25, 1984, pp. 5–6.

Bibliography

Acheson, Keith, and John Chant. 1972. "The Choice of Monetary Instruments and the Theory of Bureaucracy." *Public Choice* 12 (Spring): 13–33.

_____. 1973. "Bureaucratic Theory and the Choice of Central Bank Goals: The Case of the Bank of Canada." *Journal of Money, Credit and Banking* 5 (2): 637–55.

_____. 1973b. "Mythology and Central Banking." *Kyklos* 2: 362–79.

Alberta Heritage Savings and Trust Fund. 1982. *Annual Report: 1981–82.*

Anisman, Philip, and Peter W. Hogg. 1979. "Constitutional Aspects of Federal Securities Legislation." In *Proposals For A Securities Market Law For Canada.* Volume 3. *Background Papers,* pp. 135–220. Ottawa: Minister of Supply and Services Canada.

Banting, Keith. 1984. "The Decision Rules: Federalism and Pension Reform." In *Pensions Today and Tomorrow: Background Studies,* edited by David W. Conklin, J. Bennett, and Thomas J. Courchene, pp. 189–209. Toronto: Ontario Economic Council.

_____. 1985. "Federalism and Income Security: Historical Themes and Modern Variations." In *Ottawa and the Provinces: The Distribution of Money and Power,* edited by T.J. Courchene, D.W. Conklin and G.C.A. Cook. Toronto: Ontario Economic Council.

Barber, Clarence. 1966. *The Theory of Fiscal Policy as Applied to Provinces.* Toronto: Queen's Printer.

Bastien, Richard. 1981. *Federalism and Decentralization: Where Do We Stand?* Ottawa: Minister of Supply and Services Canada.

Bernier, Yvan, and Nicholas Roy. 1985. "The Concept of Economic Union in International and Constitutional Law." In *Perspectives on the Canadian Economic Union,* volume 60 of the research studies prepared for the Royal Commission on the Economic Union and Development Prospects for Canada. Toronto: University of Toronto Press.

Bird, Richard. 1985. "Federal Finance in Comparative Perspective." In *Ottawa and the Provinces: The Distribution of Money and Power,* edited by T.J. Courchene, D.W. Conklin and G.C.A. Cook. Toronto: Ontario Economic Council.

Boadway, Robin, and Frank Flatters. 1982. *Equalization in a Federal State: An Economic Analysis.* Study prepared for the Economic Council of Canada. Ottawa: Minister of Supply and Services Canada.

Bouey, Gerald K. 1974. "Would Canadian Monetary Policy Be More Effective If Other Deposit-Taking Financial Institutions Were Subject to Direct Effects of Bank of Canada Operations in the Same Way as the Chartered Banks." *Bank of Canada Review* (September). Ottawa: The Bank.

_____. 1982. "Monetary Policy — Finding a Place to Stand." The Per Jacobsson Memorial Lecture. Toronto, September 5, 1982, reprinted in *Bank of Canada Review.* Ottawa: The Bank.

Breton, Albert, and Anthony Scott. 1978. *The Economic Constitution of Federal States.* Toronto: University of Toronto Press.

Bushnell, S.J. 1980. "The Control of Natural Resources Through the Trade and Commerce Power and Proprietary Rights." *Canadian Public Policy/Analyse de Politiques* 4 (2) (Spring): 313–24.

Canada. 1939. *Report of the Royal Commission on Dominion-Provincial Relations.* Vol. 2. Ottawa: King's Printer.

_____. 1964. Royal Commission on Banking and Finance. *Report.* Ottawa: Queen's Printer.

_____. 1979. Department of Finance. Fiscal Policy Division. "A Review of Constitutional Powers in the Area of Macro-Economic Policy." Mimeo. Ottawa: The Department.

_____. 1981. Parliamentary Task Force on Federal-Provincial Fiscal Arrangements. *Fiscal Federalism in Canada.* Ottawa: Minister of Supply and Services Canada.

_____. 1983. House of Commons. *Report of the Parliamentary Task Force on Pension Reform.* Ottawa: Minister of Supply and Services Canada.

_____. 1984. Royal Commission on the Economic Union and Development Prospects for Canada. *Challenges and Choices.* Ottawa: Minister of Supply and Services Canada.

Chrétien, Jean. 1980. *Securing the Canadian Economic Union in the Constitution*. Ottawa: Minister of Supply and Services Canada.

Conklin, David, ed. 1984. *A Separate Personal Income Tax for Ontario: Background Studies*. Toronto: Ontario Economic Council.

Conklin, David, and Thomas J. Courchene, eds. 1984. *Deficits: How Big and How Bad?* Toronto: Ontario Economic Council.

Courchene, Thomas J. 1973a. "Alternative Regional Development Objectives and Strategies in a Federal State." In *Regional Poverty and Change*, edited by Gunther Schramm, pp. 191–206. Ottawa: Canadian Council on Rural Development.

———. 1973b. "The Poverty Reports, Negative Income Taxation and the Constitution: An Analysis and a Compromise." *Canadian Public Administration* (1973): 349–69.

———. 1976. *Money Inflation and the Bank of Canada: An Analysis of Canadian Monetary Policy From 1970 to Early 1975*. Montreal: C.D. Howe Research Institute.

———. 1977. "The New Fiscal Arrangements and the Economics of Federalism." In *Options: Proceedings of a Conference on the Future of the Canadian Federation*, pp. 311–46. Toronto: University of Toronto Press.

———. 1983. "Analytical Perspectives on the Canadian Economic Union." In *Federalism and the Canadian Economic Union*, edited by Michael J. Trebilcock, Robert S. Prichard, Thomas J. Courchene, and John Whalley, chap. 2. Toronto: University of Toronto Press.

———. 1984a. "Economic Adjustment and Public Policy: A Summing Up." In *Economic Adjustment and Public Policy in Canada*, edited by D.D. Purvis, pp. 237–57. Kingston: John Deutsch Institute.

———. 1984b. "Entitlements vs. Efficiency." *Policy Options* 5 (July/August 1984): 16–19.

———. 1984c. *Equalization Payments: Past, Present and Future*. Toronto: Ontario Economic Council.

———. 1984d. "The Political Economy of Canadian Constitution Making: The Canadian Economic Union Issue." *Public Choice* 44, pp. 201–49.

———. 1984e. "A Really Secure Industry or a Real Securities Industry." Paper presented to the Ontario Securities Industry Commission in respect of its "Securities Industry Review." CANEP Working Paper 84-01. London: University of Western Ontario, Department of Economics.

———. 1985. "The Fiscal Arrangements: An Overview." In *Ottawa and the Provinces: The Distribution of Money and Power*, edited by T.J. Courchene, D.W. Conklin and G.C.A. Cook. Toronto: Ontario Economic Council.

Courchene, T.J., D.W. Conklin and G.C.A. Cook, eds. 1985. *Ottawa and the Provinces: The Distribution of Money and Power*. Toronto: Ontario Economic Council.

Dey, Peter. 1983. "Financial Services Integration: Is It Coming to Canada?" In *Institutions in Transition: The Changing Nature of the Canadian Financial Service Industry*, pp. 47–49. Toronto: Strategic Planning Forum Inc.

Dunn, Sheilagh, and Richard Simeon. 1985. *The Politics of Fiscal Federalism*. Toronto: Ontario Economic Council. Forthcoming.

Economic Council of Canada. 1976. *Efficiency and Regulation: A Study of Deposit Institutions*. Ottawa: Minister of Supply and Services Canada.

———. 1982. *Financing Confederation: Today and Tomorrow*. Ottawa: Minister of Supply and Services Canada.

Forget, Claude. 1984. "Quebec's Experience with the Personal Income Tax." In *A Separate Personal Income Tax for Ontario: Background Studies*, edited by David W. Conklin, pp. 187–212. Toronto: Ontario Economic Council.

———. 1985. "The Harmonization of Social Policies." In *Fiscal Federalism*, volume 65 of the research studies prepared for the Royal Commission on the Economic Union and Development Prospects for Canada. Toronto: University of Toronto Press.

Friedland, Seymour. N.d. "The Emerging Financial Services Industry." Mimeo.

Friedrich, Carl. 1968. *Trends of Federalism in Theory and Practice*. New York: Praeger.

Graham, John. 1980–1981. "Canada versus the Market." *Policy Options* (December 1980/January 1981): 6–10.

Harris, Richard G., with David Cox. 1984. *Trade, Industrial Policy and Canadian Manufacturing*. Toronto: Ontario Economic Council.

Hayes, John. 1982. *Economic Mobility in Canada: A Comparative Study*. Ottawa: Minister of Supply and Services Canada.

Howard, John L. 1979. "Securities Legislation: Structure and Process." In *Proposals for a Securities Market Law for Canada*, pp. 1607–1716. Ottawa: Minister of Supply and Services Canada.

Interprovincial Conference of Ministers Responsible for Social Services. 1980. *The Income Security System in Canada*. Ottawa.

Joint Securities Industry Committee. 1984. *Regulation and Ownership of Market Intermediaries in Canada*. Submission to the Ontario Securities Commission on behalf of Alberta, Montreal, Toronto and Vancouver Stock Exchanges and the Investment Dealers Association of Canada, (September 19).

Kennett, W.A. 1983. "Submission to the 1982 Hearings of the Commission on Diversification and Industrial Ownership of Securities Dealers." In Ontario Securities Commission *Report* (1983), p. 14.

Lemelin, Claude. 1981. "Dimensions of Fiscal Harmonization in Canada." Mimeographed. Ottawa: Department of Finance.

Lortie, Pierre. 1984. "The Re-Regulation of the Canadian Financial Services Sector: Some Prospects." Paper presented to the Financial Times Conference. Toronto, December 6.

MacEachen, Allan J. 1981. *Federal Provincial Fiscal Arrangements in the Eighties*, a submission to the Parliamentary Task Force on Federal-Provincial Fiscal Arrangements. Ottawa: Department of Finance.

Maxwell, Judith, and Caroline Pestiau. 1983. *Economic Realities of Contemporary Federalism*. Montreal: C.D. Howe Research Institute.

McLure, Charles E., Jr., ed. 1983. *Tax Assignment in Federal Countries*. Canberra: Australian National University, Centre for Research on Federal Financial Relations.

Melvin, J.R. 1983. "Political Structure and the Pursuit of Economic Objectives." In *Federalism and the Canadian Economic Union*, edited by Michael J. Trebilcock et al., pp. 111–58. Toronto: University of Toronto Press.

_____. 1985. "The Regional Consequences of Tariffs and Domestic Transportation Costs." In *Canadian Journal of Economics* 18 (2) (May): 237–57.

Mendelson, Michael. 1985. "Rationalization of Income Security in Canada." In *Ottawa and the Provinces: The Distribution of Money and Power*, edited by T.J. Courchene, D.W. Conklin and G.C.A. Cook. Toronto: Ontario Economic Council.

Moore, Milton, J. Harvey Perry, and Donald I. Beach. 1966. *The Financing of Canadian Federation: The First Hundred Years*. Toronto: Canadian Tax Foundation.

Mundell, Robert A. 1968. *International Economics*. New York: Macmillan.

Musgrave, R.A. 1959. *The Theory of Public Finance: A Study in Political Economy*. New York: McGraw-Hill.

_____. 1983. "Who Should Tax, Where, and What?" In *Tax Assignment in Federal Countries*, edited by C.E. McLure, Jr., pp. 2–19. Canberra: Australian National University.

Nowothy, Ewald. 1983. "Tax Assignment and Revenue Sharing in West Germany and Switzerland." In *Tax Assignment in Federal Countries*, edited by C.E. McLure, Jr., pp. 260–86. Canberra: Australian National University.

Oates, Wallace. 1972. *Fiscal Federalism*. New York: Harcourt, Brace, Jovanovich.

_____. 1983. "Tax Effectiveness and Tax Equity in Federal Countries: Commentary." In *Tax Assignment in Federal Countries*, edited by C.E. McLure, Jr., pp. 94–97. Canberra: Australian National University.

Ontario Economic Council. 1976. *Issues and Alternatives 1976*. Toronto: Ontario Economic Council.

_____. 1983a. *Pensions Today and Tomorrow: An Ontario Economic Council Position Paper*. Toronto: Ontario Economic Council.

_____. 1983b. *A Separate Personal Income Tax for Ontario: An Ontario Economic Council Position Paper*. Toronto: Ontario Economic Council.

Ontario Securities Commission. 1983. *Report on the Implications for Canadian Capital Markets of the Provision by Financial Institutions of Access to Discount Brokerage Services*. Toronto: Dataline, Inc.

Ontario. 1983. *Ontario Submission to the Royal Commission on the Economic Union and Development Prospects for Canada* (December 5).

———. Ministry of Consumer and Commercial Relations. 1983. *Proposals for the Revision of the Loan and Trust Corporation Legislation and Administration of Ontario*. Toronto: Government of Ontario.

———. Ministry of Treasury and Economics. 1982. "Ontario Tax Structure Options for Changes." Discussion Paper. Toronto: Queen's Park.

Panabaker, John. 1983. "Financial Services Integration: Is It Coming to Canada?" In *Institutions in Transition: The Changing Nature of the Canadian Financial Service Industry*, pp. 47–49. Toronto: Strategic Planning Forum.

Parizeau, Jacques. 1970. "Federal Provincial Economic Coordination." In *Canadian Economic Problems and Policies*, edited by L.H. Officer and L.B. Smith, pp. 81–92. Toronto: McGraw-Hill.

Parkin, Michael, and Robin Bade. 1978. "Central Bank Laws and Monetary Policies." Research Report 7804. London: University of Western Ontario, Department of Economics.

Pidruchney, William. 1983. "Issues and Dynamics: A Regulations Perspective." In *Institutions in Transition: The Changing Nature of the Canadian Financial Service Industry*. Toronto: Strategic Planning Forum.

Prichard, J.R.S., with Jamie Benedickson. 1983. "Securing the Canadian Economic Union: Federalism and Internal Barriers to Trade." In *Federalism and the Canadian Economic Union*, edited by M.J. Trebilcock et al., pp. 3–50. Toronto: University of Toronto Press.

Quebec. 1956. *Royal Commission of Inquiry on Constitutional Problems. Report*. 4 vols. Quebec City: Government of Quebec.

Rasminsky, Louis. 1966. "The Role of the Central Banker Today." The Per Jacobsson Memorial Lecture, Rome. Washington, D.C.: Per Jacobsson Foundation. Reprinted in *Canadian Bankers Association* 74 (1) (Spring 1967).

Romanow, Roy. 1980. "Economic Union in the Canadian Federation: A Positive Approach." Statement by the attorney general of Saskatchewan before the Continuing Committee of Ministers on the Constitution, July 27, 1980, Document 830-83/005.

Safarian, A.E. 1974. *Canadian Federalism and Economic Integration*. Constitutional study prepared for the Government of Canada. Ottawa: Information Canada.

———. 1980. *Ten Markets or One? Regional Barriers to Economic Activity in Canada*. Toronto: Ontario Economic Council.

Scott, Anthony D. 1964. "The Economic Goals of Federal Finance." *Public Finance* 19 (3): 241–88.

Securities Industry Committee on Takeover Bids. 1983. *The Regulation of Takeover Bids in Canada: Premium Private Agreement Transactions*. A report to the Joint Industry Board of the Alberta, Montreal, Toronto, Vancouver Stock Exchanges, and the Investment Dealers' Association of Canada.

Simeon, Richard. 1972. *Federal-Provincial Diplomacy: The Making of Recent Policy in Canada*. Toronto: University of Toronto Press.

———. 1984. "Some Observations on the 'Powers Over the Economy.' " In *A Separate Personal Income Tax for Ontario: Background Studies*, edited by David J. Conklin, pp. 365–80. Toronto: Ontario Economic Council.

———. 1985. "Federalism in the Eighties." In *Ottawa and the Provinces: The Distribution of Money and Power*, edited by T.J. Courchene, D.W. Conklin and G.C.A. Cook. Toronto: Ontario Economic Council.

Springate, David. 1973. *Regional Incentives and Private Investment*. Montreal: C.D. Howe Research Institute.

Stoddart, Greg L. 1985. "Rationalizing the Health Care System." In *Ottawa and the Provinces: The Distribution of Money and Power*, edited by T.J. Courchene, D.W. Conklin and G.C.A. Cook. Toronto: Ontario Economic Council.

Strategic Planning Forum. 1983. *Institutions in Transition: The Changing Nature of the Canadian Financial Services Industry*. Conference Proceedings. Toronto: The Forum.

Strick, J.C. 1973. *Canadian Public Finance*. Toronto: Holt, Rinehart and Winston.

Thirsk, Wayne. 1980. "Tax Harmonization and Its Importance in the Canadian Federation." In *Fiscal Dimensions of Canadian Federalism*, edited by Richard Bird, pp. 118–42. Toronto: Canadian Tax Foundation.

Todd, John D. 1983. *Price Competition in the Canadian Securities Industry: A Test Case of Deregulation*. Toronto: Ontario Economic Council.

Trebilcock, M.J., J.R.S. Prichard, T.J. Courchene, and J. Whalley, eds. 1983. *Federalism and the Canadian Economic Union*. Toronto: University of Toronto Press.

Trebilcock, Michael J., John Whalley, Carol Rogerson, and Ian Ness. 1983. "Provincially Induced Barriers to Trade in Canada: A Survey." In *Federalism and the Canadian Economic Union*, edited by Michael J. Trebilcock, J.R.S. Prichard, T.J. Courchene, and J. Whalley, chap. 6. Toronto: University of Toronto Press.

Trudeau, Pierre Elliott. 1980. *Transcript of the Opening Remarks to the First Ministers' Conference*. Ottawa, September 8–12.

Tupper, Allan. 1983. "Bill S-31: Is An Ounce of Prevention Really Worth a Pound of Cure." Discussion Paper. Kingston: Queen's University, Institute of Intergovernmental Relations.

Waterman, A.D. Hum, and B. Scarfe, eds. 1982. *The Collected Economic Papers of C.L. Barber*. Winnipeg: University of Manitoba, Institute for Social and Economic Research.

Whalley, John. 1983a. "Induced Distortions of Interprovincial Activity: An Overview of the Issues." In *Federalism and the Canadian Economic Union*, edited by Michael J. Trebilcock, J.R.S. Prichard, T.J. Courchene, and J. Whalley, chap. 4. Toronto: University of Toronto Press.

———. 1983b. "The Impact of Federal Policies on Interprovincial Activity." In *Federalism and the Canadian Economic Union*, edited by Michael J. Trebilcock, J.R.S. Prichard, T.J. Courchene, and J. Whalley.

Wilson, Thomas A. 1984. "Stabilization Policy Issues: Appraisal of Possible Roles of Flexible Fiscal Policies in Ontario." In *A Separate Personal Income Tax for Ontario: Background Studies*, edited by D.W. Conklin, pp. 139–61. Toronto: Ontario Economic Council.

Zysman, John. 1983. *Government Markets and Growth*. Ithaca: Cornell University Press.

THE COLLECTED RESEARCH STUDIES

Royal Commission on the Economic Union and Development Prospects for Canada

ECONOMICS

Income Distribution and Economic Security in Canada (Vol.1), *François Vaillancourt, Research Coordinator*

Vol. 1   Income Distribution and Economic Security in Canada, *F. Vaillancourt* (C)*

Industrial Structure (Vols. 2-8), *Donald G. McFetridge, Research Coordinator*

Vol. 2   Canadian Industry in Transition, *D.G. McFetridge* (C)
Vol. 3   Technological Change in Canadian Industry, *D.G. McFetridge* (C)
Vol. 4   Canadian Industrial Policy in Action, *D.G. McFetridge* (C)
Vol. 5   Economics of Industrial Policy and Strategy, *D.G. McFetridge* (C)
Vol. 6   The Role of Scale in Canada–US Productivity Differences, *J.R. Baldwin and P.K. Gorecki* (M)
Vol. 7   Competition Policy and Vertical Exchange, *F. Mathewson and R. Winter* (M)
Vol. 8   The Political Economy of Economic Adjustment, *M. Trebilcock* (M)

International Trade (Vols. 9-14), *John Whalley, Research Coordinator*

Vol. 9   Canadian Trade Policies and the World Economy, *J. Whalley with C. Hamilton and R. Hill* (M)
Vol. 10 Canada and the Multilateral Trading System, *J. Whalley* (M)
Vol. 11 Canada–United States Free Trade, *J. Whalley* (C)
Vol. 12 Domestic Policies and the International Economic Environment, *J. Whalley* (C)
Vol. 13 Trade, Industrial Policy and International Competition, *R. Harris* (M)
Vol. 14 Canada's Resource Industries and Water Export Policy, *J. Whalley* (C)

Labour Markets and Labour Relations (Vols. 15-18), *Craig Riddell, Research Coordinator*

Vol. 15 Labour-Management Cooperation in Canada, *C. Riddell* (C)
Vol. 16 Canadian Labour Relations, *C. Riddell* (C)
Vol. 17 Work and Pay: The Canadian Labour Market, *C. Riddell* (C)
Vol. 18 Adapting to Change: Labour Market Adjustment in Canada, *C. Riddell* (C)

Macroeconomics (Vols. 19-25), *John Sargent, Research Coordinator*

Vol. 19 Macroeconomic Performance and Policy Issues: Overviews, *J. Sargent* (M)
Vol. 20 Post-War Macroeconomic Developments, *J. Sargent* (C)
Vol. 21 Fiscal and Monetary Policy, *J. Sargent* (C)
Vol. 22 Economic Growth: Prospects and Determinants, *J. Sargent* (C)
Vol. 23 Long-Term Economic Prospects for Canada: A Symposium, *J. Sargent* (C)
Vol. 24 Foreign Macroeconomic Experience: A Symposium, *J. Sargent* (C)
Vol. 25 Dealing with Inflation and Unemployment in Canada, *C. Riddell* (M)

Economic Ideas and Social Issues (Vols. 26 and 27), *David Laidler, Research Coordinator*

Vol. 26 Approaches to Economic Well-Being, *D. Laidler* (C)
Vol. 27 Responses to Economic Change, *D. Laidler* (C)

---

* (C) denotes a Collection of studies by various authors coordinated by the person named.
  (M) denotes a Monograph.

POLITICS AND INSTITUTIONS OF GOVERNMENT

Canada and the International Political Economy (Vols. 28-30), *Denis Stairs and Gilbert R. Winham, Research Coordinators*

Vol. 28 Canada and the International Political/Economic Environment, *D. Stairs and G.R. Winham* (C)
Vol. 29 The Politics of Canada's Economic Relationship with the United States, *D. Stairs and G.R. Winham* (C)
Vol. 30 Selected Problems in Formulating Foreign Economic Policy, *D. Stairs and G.R. Winham* (C)

State and Society in the Modern Era (Vols. 31 and 32), *Keith Banting, Research Coordinator*

Vol. 31 State and Society: Canada in Comparative Perspective, *K. Banting* (C)
Vol. 32 The State and Economic Interests, *K. Banting* (C)

Constitutionalism, Citizenship and Society (Vols. 33-35), *Alan Cairns and Cynthia Williams, Research Coordinators*

Vol. 33 Constitutionalism, Citizenship and Society in Canada, *A. Cairns and C. Williams* (C)
Vol. 34 The Politics of Gender, Ethnicity and Language in Canada, *A. Cairns and C. Williams* (C)
Vol. 35 Public Opinion and Public Policy in Canada, *R. Johnston* (M)

Representative Institutions (Vols. 36-39), *Peter Aucoin, Research Coordinator*

Vol. 36 Party Government and Regional Representation in Canada, *P. Aucoin* (C)
Vol. 37 Regional Responsiveness and the National Administrative State, *P. Aucoin* (C)
Vol. 38 Institutional Reforms for Representative Government, *P. Aucoin* (C)
Vol. 39 Intrastate Federalism in Canada, *D.V. Smiley and R.L. Watts* (M)

The Politics of Economic Policy (Vols. 40-43), *G. Bruce Doern, Research Coordinator*

Vol. 40 The Politics of Economic Policy, *G.B. Doern* (C)
Vol. 41 Federal and Provincial Budgeting, *A.M. Maslove, M.J. Prince and G.B. Doern* (M)
Vol. 42 Economic Regulation and the Federal System, *R. Schultz and A. Alexandroff* (M)
Vol. 43 Bureaucracy in Canada: Control and Reform, *S.L. Sutherland and G.B. Doern* (M)

Industrial Policy (Vols. 44 and 45), *André Blais, Research Coordinator*

Vol. 44 Industrial Policy, *A. Blais* (C)
Vol. 45 The Political Sociology of Industrial Policy, *A. Blais* (M)

LAW AND CONSTITUTIONAL ISSUES

Law, Society and the Economy (Vols. 46-51), *Ivan Bernier and Andrée Lajoie, Research Coordinators*

Vol. 46 Law, Society and the Economy, *I. Bernier and A. Lajoie* (C)
Vol. 47 The Supreme Court of Canada as an Instrument of Political Change, *I. Bernier and A. Lajoie* (C)
Vol. 48 Regulations, Crown Corporations and Administrative Tribunals, *I. Bernier and A. Lajoie* (C)
Vol. 49 Family Law and Social Welfare Legislation in Canada, *I. Bernier and A. Lajoie* (C)
Vol. 50 Consumer Protection, Environmental Law and Corporate Power, *I. Bernier and A. Lajoie* (C)
Vol. 51 Labour Law and Urban Law in Canada, *I. Bernier and A. Lajoie* (C)

The International Legal Environment (Vols. 52-54), *John Quinn, Research Coordinator*

Vol. 52 The International Legal Environment, *J. Quinn* (C)
Vol. 53 Canadian Economic Development and the International Trading System, *M.M. Hart* (M)
Vol. 54 Canada and the New International Law of the Sea, *D.M. Johnston* (M)

Harmonization of Laws in Canada (Vols. 55 and 56), *Ronald C.C. Cuming, Research Coordinator*

Vol. 55 Perspectives on the Harmonization of Law in Canada, *R. Cuming* (C)
Vol. 56 Harmonization of Business Law in Canada, *R. Cuming* (C)

Institutional and Constitutional Arrangements (Vols. 57 and 58), *Clare F. Beckton and A. Wayne MacKay, Research Coordinators*

Vol. 57 Recurring Issues in Canadian Federalism, *C.F. Beckton and A.W. MacKay* (C)
Vol. 58 The Courts and The Charter, *C.F. Beckton and A.W. MacKay* (C)

FEDERALISM AND THE ECONOMIC UNION

Federalism and The Economic Union (Vols. 58-72), *Mark Krasnick, Kenneth Norrie and Richard Simeon, Research Coordinators*

Vol. 59 Federalism and Economic Union in Canada, *K. Norrie, R. Simeon and M. Krasnick* (M)
Vol. 60 Perspectives on the Canadian Economic Union, *M. Krasnick* (C)
Vol. 61 Division of Powers and Public Policy, *R. Simeon* (C)
Vol. 62 Case Studies in the Division of Powers, *M. Krasnick* (C)
Vol. 63 Intergovernmental Relations, *R. Simeon* (C)
Vol. 64 Disparities and Interregional Adjustment, *K. Norrie* (C)
Vol. 65 Fiscal Federalism, *M. Krasnick* (C)
Vol. 66 Mobility of Capital in the Canadian Economic Union, *N. Roy* (M)
Vol. 67 Economic Management and the Division of Powers, *T.J. Courchene* (M)
Vol. 68 Regional Aspects of Confederation, *J. Whalley* (M)
Vol. 69 Interest Groups in the Canadian Federal System, *H.G. Thorburn* (M)
Vol. 70 Canada and Quebec, Past and Future: An Essay, *D. Latouche* (M)
Vol. 71 The Political Economy of Canadian Federalism: 1940-1984, *R. Simeon and I. Robinson* (M)

THE NORTH

Vol. 72 The North, *Michael S. Whittington, Coordinator* (C)

COMMISSION ORGANIZATION

Chairman

Donald S. Macdonald

Commissioners

Clarence L. Barber	William M. Hamilton	Daryl K. Seaman
Albert Breton	John R. Messer	Thomas K. Shoyama
M. Angela Cantwell Peters	Laurent Picard	Jean Casselman-Wadds
E. Gérard Docquier	Michel Robert	Catherine T. Wallace

Senior Officers

Executive Director
J. Gerald Godsoe

Director of Policy	*Senior Advisors*	*Directors of Research*
Alan Nymark	David Ablett	Ivan Bernier
	Victor Clarke	Alan Cairns
Secretary	Carl Goldenberg	David C. Smith
Michel Rochon	Harry Stewart	
Director of Administration	*Director of Publishing*	*Co-Directors of Research*
Sheila-Marie Cook	Ed Matheson	Kenneth Norrie
		John Sargent

Research Program Organization

Economics	Politics and the Institutions of Government	Law and Constitutional Issues
Research Director	*Research Director*	*Research Director*
David C. Smith	Alan Cairns	Ivan Bernier
Executive Assistant & Assistant Director (Research Services)	*Executive Assistant*	*Executive Assistant & Research Program Administrator*
I. Lilla Connidis	Karen Jackson	Jacques J.M. Shore
Coordinators	*Coordinators*	*Coordinators*
David Laidler	Peter Aucoin	Clare F. Beckton
Donald G. McFetridge	Keith Banting	Ronald C.C. Cuming
Kenneth Norrie*	André Blais	Mark Krasnick
Craig Riddell	Bruce Doern	Andrée Lajoie
John Sargent*	Richard Simeon	A. Wayne MacKay
François Vaillancourt	Denis Stairs	John J. Quinn
John Whalley	Cynthia Williams	
	Gilbert R. Winham	
Research Analysts	*Research Analysts*	*Administrative and Research Assistant*
Caroline Digby	Claude Desranleau	Nicolas Roy
Mireille Ethier	Ian Robinson	
Judith Gold		
Douglas S. Green	*Office Administration*	*Research Analyst*
Colleen Hamilton	Donna Stebbing	Nola Silzer
Roderick Hill		
Joyce Martin		

*Kenneth Norrie and John Sargent co-directed the final phase of Economics Research with David Smith